RICHARD BURDON, VISCOUNT HALDANE

RICHARD BURDON HALDANE

AN AUTOBIOGRAPHY

HODDER AND STOUGHTON
LIMITED   LONDON
MCMXXIX

Made and Printed in Great Britain or HODDER AND STOUGHTON LTD.
by T. AND A. CONSTABLE LTD., Printers, Edinburgh

THIS book is perhaps less of an Autobiography than an account of a life-work, a narrative of what was attempted—where there was success, where failure, and what in the writer's view was the meaning of a life which was at least one of constant and strenuous endeavour. It thus no doubt represents its author's view of the events in which he was concerned, and is written with the knowledge that these events are capable of different interpretation by others. The fact that there were times when the whole-hearted esteem of the world was present and times when it was absent makes the story more interesting. To those who looked on with inner knowledge it seemed that the latter were the periods which more certainly revealed the character of the writer.

The origin of the book may be shortly stated. Three years ago, after the death of the mother who played so great a part in our family circle, I was living more constantly with my brother, and he used on Sundays, when he was free, to go over with me certain boxes of letters and papers of interest : of them he wished me to take charge after his death. I pointed out to him that the task would be most difficult were there not a consecutive account written by himself of a life of exceptionally varied interests. After considerable hesitation he agreed, two years ago, to write this account during the comparatively leisured times of the Long and Christmas vacations. As appears, the last chapter was written shortly before the end. The narrative is of course in some respects incomplete, but I feel that it should go to the world as he left it. Had my brother lived, he would, I think, have made certain additions, especially touching the influences of his home life and of the friends who meant so much to him. Of this indeed he spoke.

As to the last weeks of my brother's life there is not much to tell.

iii

40059

He died, as he had lived, in the spirit of the last chapter of this book. He had gone to Cloan before the end of the Session, owing to increasing physical weakness which it was hoped the rest might relieve. Shortly before he left he had addressed at Upham the members of the Workers' Educational Association of Swindon. It was an impressive address. He told his hearers above all to read two books, the Gospel of St. John and Plato's ' Trial and Death of Socrates.' In these they would get the spirit of love and tolerance that would help to guide them through life. It was that spirit certainly that had guided him. This and an address to the Association of Head Mistresses on the Relativity of Knowledge were the last public addresses he gave.

It was a great pleasure to him to know before he left London that he had been unanimously elected Chancellor of the University of St. Andrews—a University he loved, and before which he had delivered his Gifford Lectures.

In spite of every care the hopes of recovery were not realised, and the end came quite suddenly and gently on the afternoon of Sunday, August 19th.

We laid him in the Burial Ground at Gleneagles, which had been the old family home for many centuries, and the little chapel of which had recently been restored in memory of those of the family who had died in the War. Among the numerous mourners there was, as was fitting, a large contingent of soldiers, Regular and Territorial, at the grave. Pipers of the Black Watch led the procession through Auchterarder and up the Glen. And in the midst of the mountains he loved so well we sang the Scottish version of the 121st Psalm:

> *' I to the hills will lift mine eyes,*
> *From whence doth come mine aid.'*

ELIZABETH HALDANE.

CLOAN, PERTHSHIRE,
   October 1928.

CONTENTS

CHAPTER IX

CHAPTER X

CHAPTER XI

LIST OF ILLUSTRATIONS

CHAPTER I

YOUTH

(1856–1885)

To bring back to light one's past so that it shall appear again just as it actually was is far from easy. The point of view has been altering as life has altered, and with it has been changed the perspective. With me that perspective has been changing gradually and almost continuously. In the attempt to record in my story the happenings in my life I have therefore to check my recollections with such letters and documents as I have preserved, and to avoid passing over events even when they may well seem of trifling importance to my readers. But at best no more than a fragment of the whole is attainable.

My career has been an interesting one at least in this respect, that my own mind has been brought into contact with other minds of the most varying types. It has fallen to me to see much of philosophers and of statesmen ; of those engaged in contemplation as well as of those concerned in highly practical affairs. But I think I may say that I have been throughout more absorbed and immersed in the study of the meaning of life taken as a whole than with its particular occurrences. Still, as if by an ironical decree, I have been called on to play a practical part in public business throughout a long period. It has been my duty to try to do the best I could with such light as I had for the public service more often than for my private ends, and this notwithstanding that I have not always felt myself drawn in the direction of public business but have had other attractions. I was once asked to accept a Professorship of Philosophy, and I was for a time a Gifford Lecturer. Circumstances have led to my being a member of many learned Academies and Societies, and to my holding the Doctorate of about a dozen Universities. On the other hand I have been immersed in the toil of a busy leader at the Bar ; and I have sat in Parliament for over forty years, ten of which have been spent in successive Cabinets. I may add, not from any vanity over it, but to complete the narrative of vicissitudes, that I have held the office of Secretary of State for War probably for longer than any one else, and that I have twice been Lord Chancellor. In addition I have sat for many years on the Committee of Imperial Defence, both as its Chairman and as an ordinary but active member, and I have been intermittently but frequently called on to take charge of the affairs of several other departments of Government. Judicial office as a Judge of the Supreme Tribunals, the House of Lords and the Judicial Committee of the Privy Council, has occupied much of my time now for many years, and more recently I have had in addition the superadded duty of leading the Opposition in the Upper Chamber, not as distracting a matter as it might seem. I mention these things only to show that I do not exaggerate when I refer to variety in calling. I cannot say that

I have sought it, and I can add without affectation that about the ups and down in my career I have not cared as much as many people seem to do.

But for the purposes of my story I must turn to how these ups and downs came about. It seems odd to me that the 'ups' should have come at all. For nature did not endow me with the qualities generally required for them. I was gifted with but a poor voice and with only a dubiously attractive personality. What I did indeed possess was inclination to work hard, an inclination which seems to have grown as the years have flown by, and to be at least as strong now as it ever was. I did not possess physical energy in a surpassing degree, at least the kind of energy which gives rise to the impulse to start personal claims and to push them. Such energy is indeed of great use in its own way to him who possesses it, for I have observed that people get things in large measure by insistent demand for them. At this I was rarely good. But at least I did look out for opportunities of work and had some courage in seizing on them if they came within reach. I think that there were few mental or physical undertakings of which I was much afraid. Perhaps I was unduly confident in my own capacities. At least, looking back, I think so now. But that is a matter which has ceased to be important.

I was born in 1856, in Edinburgh, but my father and mother and the rest of us always lived for a good part of the year at Cloan, a small estate which belonged to my father, in Perthshire. It is still my home when I am not kept in London by my duties there. I bought it from his trustees after his death, and added to the house. My father was a Writer to the Signet. It is a profession which resembles that of a solicitor in England, but it has some features of its own. In the middle of last century the Scottish law relating to land was more complicated than even that south of the Border. The Writers to the Signet had a special relationship to the Court of Session. They were, what the Conveyancing Counsel in England also were, the depositaries of the technical tradition relating to conveyancing, and their position in the legal hierarchy was important. They transacted, too, a good deal of the financial as well as of the legal business of their clients, whose near relations, as well as confidential advisers, they often were. My father had numerous relatives among the Scottish landowners, and, in accordance with the then custom, he was much employed by them. As a boy I was often brought into contact with our relations and came to know a good many other people through them.

My mother belonged to a well-known Northumbrian family, the Burdons of that county. Her father, who was a nephew of Lord Eldon and Lord Stowell, had a good deal of property in Northumberland, and I used often to stay as a boy at Jesmond, one of his houses.

At home we were an affectionate family. My father had been twice married, and I had half-brothers and sisters of his first marriage. But difference in years resulted in most of the elder ones marrying and having families of their own, and in us younger ones being mainly those at home. Affectionate as were their relations to each other, the two sets of children did not come into constant contact. I had three full

brothers and a sister of my own. We sometimes lived
in Edinburgh, where my father had a house in Char-
lotte Square, and his office. But we were always
drawn to Cloan, in those days called Cloanden.
During the autumn we used to have a tutor, with
whom we carried on our education. In the winter we
went to Edinburgh. There I was sent first to a preparatory school carried on by one of my former tutors.
It was a rough and somewhat democratic school, and
only moderately well organised. After being there
for a year or two I went to the Edinburgh Academy,
a well-known day school, which again, although of a
superior type, was not from a modern educational
point of view very highly administered in those days.
School was indeed never an interesting period to me.
But I had as my principal master at the Academy
Dr. Clyde, a remarkable personality, the father of the
present Lord President of the Court of Session. In
him I found a real influence. I learnt much from him,
above all, the character of a stoicism which never fell
into oblivion with him. He was in his outlook on life
an old Roman, and he was also in classical learning a
fine scholar, though he did not inspire us with much
of the higher meaning of classical literature. But he
taught us always to seek for truth in the first place.
It was his duty to read the Old Testament with us.
While setting himself to avoid disturbing our faith
in the Old Testament narratives, he could not help
letting us feel that he himself did not accept what they
recorded. One result was that I soon became detached in my attitude towards the earlier Bible teaching. My experience then and later on has made me

doubt whether it is ever wise to let religious teaching be given by any one who is not in real sympathy with it.

During the autumns I was at Cloan, where my education was carried on by Duncan Macdonald, the younger brother of an earlier master. He was a most conscientious companion and teacher, though he did not inspire us with the deeper understanding of the meaning of learning. I was also prepared in Latin and Greek, towards the end of my time at the Academy, by Hugh Wilson, the Assistant to the University Professor of Latin, Sellar, with whom later I was to become well acquainted.

When I was sixteen I was sent to the University of Edinburgh, where I entered on the Arts Course. I studied Latin under Sellar, Greek under Blackie, and English Literature in the lecture-room of Masson. Sellar and Masson were what Professors ought to be, real inspirers ; but Blackie, though always interesting, was too erratic in his methods to be an adequate teacher. I had not been put through the mill at school sufficiently to enable me to draw all the benefit I might have done from Sellar, but he was a great scholar and he made me realise what Lucretius ought to be to those who knew his poem. Masson, too, was a fine guide and also a real personal influence.

I used to attend closely the deliberations of the Students' Philosophical Society, where I took an active part, and became the intimate friend of Andrew Seth, afterwards Professor Seth Pringle-Pattison, as well as of Robert Barbour, W. R. Sorley, and William A. Haswell—a remarkable student, afterwards to become a Biological Professor in New South Wales. These were all young men of unusual quality. With Seth I was afterwards to co-operate in producing in 1883 a volume called *Essays in Philosophical Criticism,* dedicated to the memory of T. H. Green, the articles in which, written by ourselves and others, made some mark. In my first year I also matriculated at the University of London, and the sustained and systematic discipline required to prepare for its external examination, which I just scraped through, did me much good. It was then that I first became concentrated mentally.

Besides all this I did a good deal of miscellaneous reading. I came, too, to know intimately Hutchison Stirling, the author of *The Secret of Hegel.* T. H. Green and Edward Caird by their writings impelled me in the direction of 'Idealism.' I worked also at Physics, under Professor P. G. Tait, a man with a very powerful mind. But it was Sellar who influenced me most. He was kind to me, and used to ask me to his house when he had men like Jowett and Matthew Arnold with him there. I learned so something of the wider outlook on life which literature could give, and his own influence was always strongly in that direction.

It was the *De Rerum Natura* of Lucretius that fascinated me most, when I heard Sellar lecturing on it. It is more than fifty years since I listened while he declaimed to us his favourite passages. The lines at the beginning of the Second Book still remain in my memory, and I often repeat them to myself when alone :—

'Sed nil dulcius est, bene quam munita tenere
Edita doctrinâ sapientum templa serena,

Despicere unde queas alios passimque videre
Errare atque viam palantis quaerere vitae,
Certare ingenio, contendere nobilitate,
Noctes atque dies niti praestante labore
Ad summas emergere opes rerumque potiri.' [1]

That was his creed, and it has ever since I heard him
been mine also. I think that I have in the main
followed Leonardo da Vinci in the faith that it is even
better to know than to be.

At Cloan, to go back, we children read much, and we
were also fond of outdoor life. I was in those days a
keen sportsman. I rejoiced in the possession of a gun,
and I used to rise before daybreak to stalk the grouse
and black-game which visited the stubble fields. We
were fond of swimming too. There was a deep and
rather forbidding pool near the house, and there we
used to go with a large black Newfoundland dog which
was deeply attached to us. But he was highly in-
telligent, and he did not approve of our running risks
by leaping into the deep water. He would jump in
after us and claw our backs to make us come out. He
was devoted to us, and nothing seemed to give him
more pleasure, while we were children still small
enough, than when we four got into his kennel. Then
he got in also and sat in front guarding the entrance.

To my father all animals were intimate friends.
The pigeons lit on his shoulders when he went out to

---

[1] Lucretius, ii. 7.   Munro's Translation (adapted):—

 ' But sweeter far to dwell remote, aloof
  In some high mansion, built on Wisdom's hill:
  Thence watch the errant crowd go to and fro,
  Matching their wits, striving for precedence,
  Toiling and moiling, hurrying night and day,
  To rise to fortune and possess the world.'

feed them after breakfast, and the horses and ponies nosed his pockets for the bread which he carried there for them. He was a man of an old-fashioned type, and he loved a simple country life. He was very devout, and had fitted up a barn where he used once a fortnight to preach to a considerable audience of old-fashioned Scottish country folk who came to hear the Word of God in all its strictness. On alternate Sundays he used to ride miles to various villages and preach there, and I used to ride with him on a pony named ' King Cole ' which one of our many relatives had given me.

My mother was also deeply religious, though less dogmatically so. She taught us children the Bible, the contents of which she had under great command, and she watched closely over our welfare. Altogether it was a happy though simple home. Not much pocket-money was allowed to us, but for that we were none the worse, even when we were at school or college in Edinburgh. Our mother was gentle in her relations to us. She was always trying to bring about what she believed to be best for us, and we were devoted to her.

As we grew up we developed considerable capacities for physical exertion. We became energetic walkers. I have more than once started from Cloan on foot to walk to the top of Ben Lawers, a mountain four thousand feet high in the Grampians, opposite to our home in the Ochils. I recall once starting at two in the morning with my younger brothers, and walking to the top of the Ben and back, seventy-three miles, within twenty-three hours. When we got to the foot of the great hill we found a rival party, who had slept the night in an inn, aspiring to do the climb in record time, but our wind was better than theirs, owing to our having been walking over hill and dale all night, and we easily left them behind. These same younger brothers a little later walked from Ballater to Cloan, again over intervening Grampians, doing a walk of one hundred and one miles in thirty hours and fifty minutes, without over-fatigue. In after life, when I was at the Bar, I was able, without being in training, to walk from Brighton to London easily in between thirteen and fourteen hours. Later on in life, when I was War Minister, I remember going down to Lewes, there to inspect the troops commanded by the General of the Division. The motor which was to have taken us to our destination after the inspection did not turn up, and the General asked me rather timidly if I felt equal to walking a little of the way along the Brighton to London road. I smiled and proceeded to set the pace.

In the glens around Cloan we had some experience in stiff climbing. Afterwards, when I went to the University of Göttingen, I accompanied the Professor of Geology and a party of the students on an expedition through the Hartz Mountains to search for fossils. We came opposite to a steep and high cliff, and the Professor said that if we could only do what was impracticable, get at some rock which appeared on the face near the top, we should probably find some striking specimens. I said nothing, but put my hammer in my pocket and suddenly proceeded to scale the cliff. The Germans were not in these days as athletic as they afterwards became. There was an agonized adjuration to me to come down. But I got to near the top, and with my hammer extracted from the surface of the rock a likely looking lump. When I got down again, after a not really difficult climb, this was examined, and from it was extracted a rather valuable specimen of fossil. I was reproached for the supposed risk to which I had subjected the party as well as myself. But the fossil was extracted and cleaned, and placed in the University Museum under the title ' Petrefactum Nomine Haldane.'

My reading in my sixteenth and seventeenth years had begun to disturb my faith in what I then took to be the essential foundations of Christianity. I was at this time much under the influence of religion. It was religion of a somewhat emotional type, stimulated by a wave of feeling which at that time was pervading Scotland. But presently questions forced themselves upon me. Was the basic foundation of such feeling reliable ? I began to read copiously. Such books as the *Old Faith and the New* of Strauss, and the criticism and analysis in Renan's *Life of Jesus*, compelled me to put new questions to myself. The divines to whom I turned for personal guidance in those days could not help me much, for they had not themselves gone deeply enough down. I was driven to look to the philosophers, and I then began the study of metaphysics. The idea of my parents was to send me to Balliol College. But they dreaded the supposed influence of the Anglican Church atmosphere of Oxford. However, the Professor of Greek at Edinburgh, Blackie, a man of imagination, who took a great interest in me, had an alternative plan.   I had talked with him and asked him for guidance, as indeed I had asked guidance of other men whom I knew.   Of these some were distinguished in the theological field, but they could do little more than advise me to read Sir William Hamilton and the other survivors of the Scottish School who had written on the Philosophy of the Infinite.

Blackie, with all his erratic methods, was a man of wide views, and he said, ' There is one who can do you good and help you, and though he is far from here you must go to him, and I will make it my business to see that you are well received.'   He persuaded my parents to let me go to Göttingen, at which University Lotze, one of the greatest and most spiritual of modern German thinkers, was then in the height of his fame. I was seventeen and imperfectly acquainted with German, but I set off in a steam-boat from Leith harbour for Hamburg on a Saturday afternoon in April of 1874.   My mother and my old nurse came down to see me off.   The steamer was heavily laden with iron and was not luxurious, and as I sailed away in these new surroundings my heart sank.   However, I found on board a Scottish student of Chemistry called Rogers, who had been at Göttingen before, and who was going back after his holidays.   He befriended me, and when we got to Hamburg we spent the day in that city and started at night in a train which was due to reach Göttingen about four in the morning.   We got there, and he very kindly took me to his rooms, in the Groner Strasse, where I slept for two hours on the sofa.   But I did not go to sleep without first looking out of the window, and there, in that strange University town, everything that I saw seemed to be so unfamiliar that I longed for my home. In the grey of the dawn what particularly distressed me was to see a woman and a dog drawing along the street a cart containing a man and a calf. I felt that these were odd and unfamiliar people among whom I had come to live. In the morning I found rooms, settled in, and began slowly to make acquaintances. I took lessons in German from a lady with whom I became great friends and whom I visited most years at Göttingen in the period before I became Lord Chancellor, after which I could not go abroad while holding office. Fräulein Schlote, to whom I shall refer again later, has now passed away. The grief of the War—for to her it was a great grief—combined with old age to end her life. But she was a good friend to me and gave me much help in my studies. After I was out of office I used to visit her, and we kept up a constant correspondence till her death.

Lotze, to whom I bore a letter of introduction from Blackie, was very kind. A quiet, reserved old man, he saw the nature of the crisis my mind was passing through, and he set me to read Fichte's popular works, and particularly the *Vocation of Man*. With the aid of these and of Berkeley I began to work myself out of my mood and, under the stimulus of Lotze's teaching, to acquire a wider point of view.

The students were a very miscellaneous set, and although I came across some good ones among them, I am not sure that I saw the best of them. They took an interest in the English stranger and made me a

member of a ' Verbindung '—the Hildesia Verbindung,
a sort of second-rate students' corps, the members of
which used to meet weekly at ' Kneipen,' and some of
whom, including myself, used to dine together.   I
began to learn German rapidly and to fall into the
ways of the University.   Göttingen was then a primi-
tive place, with about half the population it has now,
and it had not become the admirable University
centre, so far as the permeation of the social life of the
town by the University was concerned, that it became
in the years before the Great War of 1914.   But I saw
something of its distinguished men, and the University
life was a very interesting one.   I took up, as a by-
study, Geology, under Professor von Seebach, who
lectured on that subject.

I made tours round Göttingen, and walked a great
deal, and was present at duels fought by members of
my ' Verbindung.'   These seemed to me no light
matters ; the wounds were sometimes formidable, and
I have seen blood spurting an inch high from a vein.
At the ' Verbindung ' the students had rather riotous
meetings.   I recall, too, that we owned as a society a
large poodle dog, whom I remember well, the only
confirmed drunkard I have seen among the canine
species.   He used eagerly to lap up the beer that
had been spilled into a bowl placed to catch the
overflow from the spigot of our beer cask, and to
become so tipsy that despite all efforts he could not
get on his legs to come to us when summoned.   At
our meetings, which took place weekly, there was
naturally much talk, and I picked up colloquial
German quickly.

The life of the students at Göttingen in 1874 was somewhat rough. It seemed to me to be odd, when I was matriculated at the University, that I should have to bind myself not to walk out in the streets in a dressing-gown and slippers, but I soon found that this University law, which was enforced by the University police, was not an unnecessary one. The ways of the students were eccentric. I lived in rooms opening off a staircase ending in the street, the ground floor of the house being occupied by a furrier called Nöhden, in the Zindel Strasse, close to the Rathskeller. To enter the house, and indeed all the students' lodgings consisted of rooms opening similarly off staircases entered from the street, we were each provided with an enormous key, called a ' Hausbar,' which we carried slung to the bands of our waistcoats and detached when we wanted it. These keys often opened many street doors, so that there was not much privacy in one's rooms, into which brother students were in the habit of penetrating very freely. I remember one night when I awoke in my room, which, although it belonged to me alone, had two beds, I became conscious that something else was stirring close to me. I leant over the edge of the bed and saw two red eyes glaring at me from underneath it, and was much concerned. I then heard something which was unmistakably a snore from the other bed, which ought to have been unoccupied, and striking a light, I found that a drunken student who had missed his way had let himself in with his great key and had come up the stairs and got into my room and gone to sleep in the other bed, leaving his poodle to sleep under mine. I extended hospitality by resuming my couch and falling peacefully asleep.

The rooms were very dirty and the washing facilities but scanty ; therefore we used to go in the morning to bathe in the Leine, the stream which Bismarck is said to have made famous as one into which he jumped to avoid his creditors in his student days. To bathe was really the only effective mode of getting a bath which we possessed, and the Leine was not a particularly clean river. The town in those days reeked of tanning, as it was a great place for the manufacture of a rough kind of leather, but the main feature was then, as always, the University, the Professors of which were a very brilliant set. Although I remained a matriculated student at Göttingen for some time, I did not return as a student there ; my next period, in the following year, being spent at Dresden, where I went because I wanted to read Philosophy in peace, and where I had no friend except the Professor of Philosophy in the Dresden Polytechnic. Later on I began to visit Göttingen pretty frequently, and established an intimate relation with a good many of the Professors. The theologians wanted, years later, when I had become well known in Germany and had written books, to confer on me the Honorary Doctorate in Theology, but the Arts Faculty insisted that it should be a Doctorate in Philosophy, coupled with the honorary degree of Master of Arts. This they did confer on me, bestowing it at the same time upon another person whom they held in esteem—Admiral Tirpitz. The elaborate address which they presented to me, commemorative of my honorary degree, I have kept, and even during the War my name was never expunged from the list of their graduates. In this respect they set one example which some over here would have done well to follow.

Notwithstanding the distractions of student life at the University I was not really deflected from the purpose with which I had gone there. My main occupation was the study of Philosophy, with a certain amount of Theology. Through the effort this required my mind became further awakened. I had broken away from the creeds of the churches at home, and I now seemed to be coming back to a larger outlook, which made that breaking away taken by itself seem less important than I had formerly thought it to be. When I returned to Scotland it was in much better spirits, and with the first steps taken towards the attainment of something like a settled outlook, which was as time went on to mean much to me.

Despite the exuberances of German student life, many of my fellow-students worked hard and systematically. Some of them were good company, companions who were trying to seek after truth. There was certainly no tendency in the University circles to any form of ecclesiasticism. Indeed, religion of any definite kind was little talked of. Great teaching was given to us, however, by some of the Professors about the ultimate nature of things. I was instructed to read not only Fichte and Bishop Berkeley when I was there but also Kant, and was taught to reflect. When my time at Göttingen was over, I brought back with me a stock of new ideas, Berkeley's teaching in particular having laid hold of me. I had now become

B

emancipated from religious depression, and my attention had become concentrated on a search for light about the meaning of God, Freedom, and Immortality. Lotze's influence had set me to pursue the search in a new spirit, and with a fuller consciousness of the vast theoretical obscurity in which these subjects were buried.

There was real reverence for the personalities of the great teachers who abounded, and who drew disciples from distant parts of Germany. It was felt that in the University, if anywhere, progress might be looked for in solving the problems of existence. Despite appearances, the community was a seriously minded one, and it was not easy to live there without being moved by the sense of this. Even so, one felt that the war with France, concluded in favour of Germany three years earlier, had not failed somewhat to let down the old spiritual level. Money had come to count for more than was the case in the days of Herbart and Gauss and Ewald.

I used to learn about the past of the University from my old teacher in German literature, Fräulein Schlote, to whom I have already referred. She had for many years presided over a school for girls, of high standing. She was also one of the most accomplished women I ever came across. She knew her Goethe as only a scholar could, and she had a wide acquaintance with English literature. In after years, when I went to revisit Göttingen, as I often did, I saw her regularly. During the War she had lost her savings and had much hardship to endure, and I was able to be of some little use in helping her to face these difficulties until she died in 1925. In her letters she kept me informed of new movements in German opinion and literature and theology. She was as devout as she was instructed, and the consciousness of what she taught me fills me with affectionate gratitude.

I had returned to Cloan in August 1874, after being at Göttingen, but so altered in appearance that my family hardly recognised me when I got out of the train. I had let my hair grow long and had cultivated a moustache, and had become very thin. Göttingen at that period was not a very salubrious place. It is now an expanded and admirably organised town. But what I lost temporarily in physique was made up by gains in other directions. I had been taught to study systematically, and a passion for philosophy had been awakened in me. I had learned that if a book is really worth reading it must be read carefully through, and its standpoint mastered. That cuts indeed both ways, for it tends to reduce the number of books one can read. But the desire for sport and amusement, once so strong, had been much lessened by even the short period spent in the atmosphere of the German University. There was now more time and inclination for the study of literature, and a second language was open to me. I became immersed in Kant, and I kept up the study of Fichte. Presently Hutchison Stirling and Green were to impel me towards Hegel.

But, of course, there was a change in my general outlook. I went to Göttingen in deep depression, uncertain in which direction to look. I left it with a conviction that the way to the truth lay in the direction of idealism. Berkeley and Fichte had pointed me to regions which lay beyond even their teaching. I began to feel that there was possible an even larger outlook for me, and that in the great thinkers of ancient as well as modern times, including artists of the level of Shakespeare and Wordsworth and Goethe, I might find the impulses which would enable me to advance on a difficult but sure way. Oxford might indeed have given me something similar, though of a different kind, but I do not think that she would have given me more of what I then required.

When I got back to Scotland I pursued this path. I went on at the University of Edinburgh, mainly under the old Professor of Philosophy, Fraser, a stimulating personality. I took up work again with my old friends and fellow-students, Pringle-Pattison, Barbour, Sorley, Haswell, and others. We were all encountering similar difficulties, and I had come back from Germany freshened up. I had learned how to study closely. I did not find it difficult to get first-class honours in the Arts degree, or to win the Bruce of Grangehill Medal in Philosophy, or the Gray Scholarship, or the Ferguson Scholarship in Philosophy of the four Scottish Universities. But I met with one check. I thought I ought to take the degree of Doctor of Science in Philosophy. I sent in the requisite thesis. The subject I chose was Immortality. The thesis was approved by the Professors of Philosophy. But technically it had to be approved also by the Professor of Botany, as Dean of the Faculty of Science. He was a very orthodox believer of the old school, and he firmly refused to sanction a thesis which contained what he considered to be dangerous doctrine.

So I never became D.Sc., and my friend and fellow-student Pringle - Pattison was so moved by my experience that he refused to send in a thesis of his own for this degree. However, it did not matter. All that we thought clear was that those who were not themselves philosophers were not suitable persons to decide questions of qualifications in such a candidature.

As I have said, when I matriculated at the University of Göttingen it was to enter as a student under Lotze. I do not describe him here, or the impression his lectures made on me, because I have already done so, fairly fully, in another book.[1] I used at times to hear other great teachers. Ritschl was there, and von Jhering, whose books on Jurisprudence I was to study later. Wöhler, the discoverer of synthetic urea, although he no longer lectured, was also a familiar figure in the streets. Gauss and Riemann were dead, but Göttingen remained a great home for mathematicians, and the statue of Gauss bending over the stooping figure of Weber, the physicist, and explaining to him the way out of certain obscurities in the results of his experiments, had been erected on the walk along the wall which surrounded the town as it then was.

There were, however, troubles of a new sort at this juncture. My father and mother were devoted to me and left me every liberty. But my father particularly was of the old school in theology. He was a convinced Baptist, and consequently none of us children had been baptized in infancy. Although he professed to

[1] *Universities and National Life* (Murray), 1912, at pp. 22 *et seq.*

believe, and I have no doubt did believe, that baptism was not essential to salvation, still he was very uneasy that his son should grow up unbaptized. He and my mother entreated me to consent to end this. I took the view that the mere ceremony, though I would rather have avoided it, mattered little among people whose custom as citizens was to be baptized, provided one assented to no formula and gave no undertaking. My parents' anxiety was more to me than my own reluctance, and if, but only if, this anxiety could be relieved on terms that did not compromise me, I was willing to undergo the ceremony. My father did not, I think, realise in the least how far away from each other our minds were on foundational questions. He proposed that the ceremony should be gone through quite privately at the church to which the family went when in Edinburgh, and that no one should be present excepting those immediately concerned. I do not think that he had taken in the importance which I attached to this undertaking. Anyhow, he seemed to have let the appointment be known, for, when I got to the church, there were present not only the minister, but a crowd of deacons and other on-lookers. My mind was at once made up. To begin with, I told them all openly that I would not refuse to go through the ceremony, but that I should make a definite explanation the moment it was over. I rose dripping from the font, and, facing the congrega-tion, announced to them that I had consented to go through what had taken place only to allay the anxiety of my parents, but that now, as those present might have misunderstood, I must say something to them.

It was that I could not accept their doctrines ; that I regarded what had taken place as the merest external ceremony ; and that for the future I had no connection with the church, or its teaching, or with any other church. I then changed my clothes and walked away from the building. There was much consternation, but nothing was said, probably because there was nothing to say. My cousin, the late Bishop of Argyll, who was present, walked after me and was very kind and sympathetic. But the incident was a closed one. It was never alluded to afterwards, and silence was preserved in our household on the subject. But it brought me a new friendship. The brother of my father's first wife was George Makgill of Kemback. He was a man of striking appearance and of a wide outlook. He was an old-fashioned Tory, the friend of Christopher North and the old Blackwood set who had survived from the time of Sir Walter Scott. He was also a man of considerable reading in German philosophy and literature. A rich man of leisure, he had accumulated a fairly large library of German philosophical books. He entered into the difficulties which he knew I was going through at home, and I have preserved wise letters from him on the subject. Soon afterwards he died, bequeathing to me his library. I hold his memory in high regard.

Only once afterwards had I an approach to a difference with my father about theology. I had been out at a meeting of the Philosophical Society, and when I returned I went into the dining-room to find three books which I had left there. They were Neander's *Life of Christ*, Renan's *Life of Jesus*, and George

Eliot's translation of Strauss's *Life of Jesus.* Neander's was a treatise of high orthodoxy. But I found my father about to consign this particular book to the flames on account of some minor heresy which he had detected on glancing at it. I was only able to rescue the book on the plea that it was a library book which had to be returned. Renan and Strauss he passed over indifferently. The names meant nothing to him, nor did he ask whether the authors questioned the doctrine of verbal inspiration, a doctrine in which he had been brought up to believe firmly.

But my father was a kind and affectionate man, devoted to his children and concerned deeply for their spiritual welfare. He now left me free and did not try to interfere. I chose my own career, and he let me do so, and helped in every way he could. My mother was at least equally devoted. She watched over and lived for us. Her tenderness I can never forget. Later on she was to develop in spiritual stature and to add increasingly in every year to the remarkable personality which came in her later days.

Perhaps the most attractive among us children was my younger brother, George, who died of diphtheria when he was sixteen. He was deeply religious, untroubled by doubts. He had a passion for music, for which he was developing a great gift when he passed away. His touch on the piano, and his power of expressing the deep feeling of the best music, were remarkable. His was a beautiful nature, and I doubt whether it was not a nature too sensitive to have been able to encounter later on without unhappiness the rough side of life. His death was a terrible blow to his parents, and to the others of us it was a deep and lasting grief. I remember well, just when his end was approaching, being sent by the doctor to summon my father from his room. He received the summons with profound sorrow but without moving a muscle, and then, in a tone of deep solemnity, said, ' Before the foundations of the world were laid it was so ordained.' When my father's own death approached, two years later, his attitude was the same. It was the Will of God that he should pass away ; in that Will he found peace ; and to that Will he commended his wife and his children.

My mother was broken with grief at George's death, and unknown to us contracted the disease her boy had died of. We went to Lowwood, on the banks of Windermere, and there, in the peaceful neighbourhood of Wordsworthian surroundings, she slowly recovered herself, and we all felt better. We then returned to Edinburgh (this was in the summer of 1875) before going out to Cloan. Great care was taken of my mother and of us all by Betsy Ferguson, my old nurse, who had watched over us since my childhood. She was an ideal nurse for us all, single-minded and devoted. In me she took a special interest. It was the tradition, derived from a sort of family agreement on the subject, that I should ultimately go to the English Bar. One of my great grand-uncles, John Scott, Lord Eldon, had been Lord Chancellor, and another, his brother, William Scott, Lord Stowell, had been a great jurist and judge. When I was about six years old and my nurse had taken me on a visit to Montague Grove at Hampstead, the London house of Richard Burdon Sanderson, my maternal grandfather, she conducted me to see the House of Lords, then in recess. She persuaded the attendants there to let her place me seated on the Woolsack, and then exclaimed : ' The bairn will sit there some day as of right.' ' Perhaps so,' our Highland butler observed, ' but by that time, Mistress Ferguson, your head will be weel happit.' At all events, for the English Bar I was destined by general family acclamation, and into the spirit of the decision I entered early.

When we got back to Edinburgh from Windermere I went on with a strenuous course of reading in philosophy, and this began to extend itself so as to include the philosophical foundations of jurisprudence. The atmosphere of the Edinburgh of those days was a stimulating one. The University was distinguished by groups of famous professors, and their influence penetrated through the society of the city. Great judges, like Inglis, were sitting on the Bench. The Church was equally distinguished by the stature and eminence of the preachers. The medical profession had at its head Joseph Lister and other men of world-wide reputation. The Bar and the Writers to the Signet had among the members of their orders men of high distinction, not only in their professions but in learning. There were, too, younger men, like Robert Louis Stevenson, whom one encountered often. I was encouraged on all sides after my return from Göttingen. The influence on me of Lotze and Göttingen was accepted as worth attention. My parents lived mainly in a religious circle, but I was allowed to go wherever I could, and was encouraged to make my own friends. I began to study Law and to go to London to eat dinners at Lincoln's Inn. I read in Edinburgh in the offices of two well-known Edinburgh firms of Writers to the Signet, Tods, Murray & Jamieson, and Drummond & Reid ; with the first for conveyancing and feudal law, with the second for the mercantile side of legal business. The partners were sympathetic and helpful to me, and I learned a good deal which I could not otherwise have assimilated.

In 1877 my father died, at the age of 72. He passed away as he had lived, full of faith in what for him were eternal verities. He had been throughout too far away from the subjects that were interesting us who were his younger children ever to enter much into our inner lives. But he was full of affection, and when we succeeded in anything he took pride in our success. He lived a simple domestic life, whether in Edinburgh or at Cloan, travelling abroad with my mother a little at times, but not often. His dominant interest was in the Calvinism which he had inherited from his father and uncle, who had sacrificed much in order to be able to testify to and preach the faith that was in them. They had founded a school of religious thought on the Continent, which continued for long, especially at Geneva. When I went to the south of Germany later on, people would still ask me ' Are you a Haldanite ? ' Prominent members of this school existed in the 'seventies and used to come to see us.

When my father passed away, a good deal devolved

on me at first, as the oldest of his second family.
The first family had for the most part married and
set up for themselves. My brother George had
died two years previously. My next brother, John,
had already begun to develop the passion for biological
investigation which has engrossed him through his
career at Oxford and elsewhere. He was working at
Physiology, with ideas of his own. He was interested
also in Philosophy, and he and I wrote together the
essay on the Relation of Philosophy to Science which
appeared in 1883 in the volume to which I have
already referred, *Essays in Philosophical Criticism*.
In that essay we sought to demonstrate, from our
respective points of view, that the phenomena of life
were unintelligible unless there entered into the constitution of biological experience relations of a wholly
different order from those of mechanism. He has
pursued this theme undeviatingly since then from the
standpoint of experimental science, while I have been
occupied with it from that of the theory of knowledge.
My sister, Elizabeth, came next in order of age.
She too betook herself to the study of Philosophy
and published books concerning it. She has since
written on a variety of subjects, ranging from the Life
of Descartes and the History of Nursing to the Life
of George Eliot, and has done much public work in
education. My brother, William, the youngest of us,
threw his energies into business. He became a
successful Writer to the Signet, and was Crown Agent
for Scotland during many years. I owe him much
for the affectionate care he has bestowed on my private
affairs, and for relief from the burden of attending to

Photo: James Ross

GEORGE, JOHN, AND RICHARD, AS CHILDREN

them. He has become a considerable landowner, and has devoted much time to the management of land and to the study of the methods that are required if farming is to be successful. He and my brother John are married and are the fathers of families. My sister and I have never been so. She lives with me at Cloan, and in London at Queen Anne's Gate.

What I have thus jotted down is in outline an account of the period of my youth. It ended after my going to London, and my early days at the Bar. It was to me an interesting phase of life, although I am not sure that it was in one respect wholly satisfactory. I had indeed got a very real University training, but it was not a training of the kind that those who were to be my rivals at the Bar and in Parliament had been given. Moreover, I had lived unduly much in the society of men much older than myself. I had a few intimate friends; one of the last of them was John Kemp. Along with him I translated Schopenhauer, and with him I kept up an intimacy that lasted till the close of his life a few years since. We conversed much together, but the topics were almost exclusively supra-mundane. My other friends were also rather serious young men. Of sport and of general society I saw almost nothing in my early days in London. The outcome of this was a certain awkwardness. Moreover, I had no attractive presence to make up for other deficiencies, and I had a bad voice. These were serious deficiencies for a career at the Bar. On the other hand, I could sit down and think systematically, and I had an accurate memory which let slip little of what I had read.

Besides this I was active and tenacious in a high degree, and was confident, probably to an undue extent, of my power to succeed in whatever I undertook.

Then I had what is unusual, a really definite point of view. The materialistic outlook had been superseded. There was no longer for me any conflict between science and the religious standpoint at which I had arrived. That standpoint was indeed not the orthodox one. The churches had little attraction for me, although among my friends were such men as Henry Drummond and George Adam Smith. But my religious outlook was a genuine one. Its origin was a deep conviction that the more experience is spiritual the more it is real. My old master, Lotze, had influenced me towards this conviction, and so had Hegel, whom I had been studying as closely as the state of my then knowledge permitted. With all this had come the further conviction that not only in philosophy but in science it was true that no systematic knowledge is sufficient in itself unless it leads up and points to first principles. This doctrine later became valuable to me even as a guide in work at the Bar. It did not help in the business of cross-examination. I was never good at that, nor in the conduct of *nisi prius* cases. But it was invaluable in preparation for the presentation of great questions to the Supreme Tribunals, where the judges were keen about first principles and were looking out for help from the advocate.

In this state of training I went to live in London soon after my father's death in 1877, and from that time my home has been in London and at Cloan. I had rooms at first in St. Petersburg Place, off the Bayswater Road. Of money I had not a great deal, but taking the view that to maintain a good appearance was important, I borrowed, on the credit of what would come to me after my mother's time, enough for all my purposes. It was not a great deal, and I easily repaid it later out of my earnings at the Bar.

I began by reading in Equity drafting and conveyancing in the chambers of William Barber. He was a Junior of high standing on the Chancery side, and I got on very well with him personally. In the year spent in his chambers in Old Square, Lincoln's Inn, I worked closely in answering cases for opinion and drawing drafts of pleadings and deeds. Nothing in this region seemed difficult in comparison with sifting the books of the German metaphysicians. Not only did I work all day, excepting when in Court watching cases and the way in which the great leaders opened them before great judges like James and Jessel, but I read law almost continuously. Philosophy receded and I began to feel something like a passion for law.

Barber had a very large business, and there was an unending stream of cases for opinion and instructions for drafts, which poured in from solicitors in the country, as well as in London. He had a very able 'devil,' Ingham, a man of powerful mind and large experience, who helped him to dispose of his work. Ingham's was a rather grim and unapproachable figure, but we pupils regarded him with immense respect. I was later on to be able to exercise some influence in getting for both him and Barber appoint-

ments as County Court judges. At night, in my
rooms, and often in my bed, I used to read law books.
The original editions, uncorrupted by the comment-
ators who had half obliterated the substance by
bringing it up to date in new editions, especially
fascinated me. I read John William Smith's first
edition as other people read general literature. I
also studied much in the library at Lincoln's Inn.
An exceptionally good memory enabled me to recall
the cases I had studied, and even the volumes in
which I had found them, better than most other
people. The result was that Barber used to turn me
on to the really difficult cases that came to him for
opinion, and my duty was to write a draft for him
to consider. This was an excellent way of being
trained. To this hour I can recall many of the
authorities with which I became familiar in his
chambers.

Most of my fellow-pupils in Barber's chambers
were fond of sport and not very industrious, and I
had the pick of the work in consequence at my disposal. Barber used to invite us to his house at
Pinner, and there I met with society that was mainly
legal. This was all to the good, and I got to know a
good many members of the Chancery Bar. For the
rest, the other people whom I then met in London
were mainly the scientific friends of my uncle, Professor, afterwards Sir, John Burdon Sanderson. He
and his wife were indeed kind and hospitable to me.
But some desire for social life of a different kind
began to be awakened in me, and I even took lessons
in dancing, in the company of a grave and distin-

guished member of the medical profession, Mrs. Elizabeth Garrett Anderson, who had become eminent in public affairs, and who, like myself, was desirous of making up for the deficiencies of a somewhat restricted upbringing. At her house I began to go to dances, and to dances I was invited out, an experience which was rather new to me. However, this inclination was of brief duration.

The passion for reading law continued. I moved into rooms in Bruton Street, and there pursued it. Philosophy still continued to interest me much, but law became predominant, and I was also taken up with Political Economy. I came into contact with Chapman, who was then still editor of the *Westminster Review*, and he used to send me books for short reviews in his magazine, which was then, however, losing its glory and was approaching the end of a famous history.

When my year with Barber was over I wished to study the Common Law, and on the introduction of Farrer Herschell, Mrs. Burdon Sanderson's brother, and later on Lord Chancellor, I entered as a pupil with Lumley Smith, a busy Junior in the Temple, at his chambers in King's Bench Walk. There I began to learn a good deal of common law. Lumley Smith had heard about me from Barber, and my knowledge of equity was useful to him. He used, like Barber, to give me his more difficult cases to look into, and was helpful in every way. I remained with him until I was called to the Bar in the end of 1879.

I then took chambers in the form of a garret at 5 New Square, Lincoln's Inn. As I had little work to do, I spent my time in reading up authorities and text-books. But Barber had not forgotten me. He had been editor of the last edition of a famous book, Dart's *Vendors and Purchasers*, and with the assent of Dart he entrusted me with the preparation of a new edition which had been called for. This work took some time. I had begun to get a little business before it was over, and with Barber's assent I associated Sheldon, who had been my pupil, with me in the work. We finally produced the new edition. I do not think that it was accounted for more than a careful performance, but we certainly put a great deal of work into it, and introduced some new statements of the law about the disabilities of purchasers standing in various fiduciary relations to their vendors.

Looking at my old fee-books, I see that in my first year I made only £31, 10s. I knew almost no London solicitors, and what I got came from Scottish sources. The next year, 1881, was only a little better. I received £109 in fees. Nor was the third year a great improvement. It yielded only about £160. But in the fourth year after my call to the Bar (1883-4) the amounts began to shoot up. I received about £1100. I began to be known as an energetic and pretty ingenious Junior, and, as I stayed in London through part of the Long Vacation, solicitors who heard of me began to come to 5 New Square. I used often to remain there until midnight, and I read the authorities copiously when I was not employed. A chop at the old ' Cock Tavern ' in Fleet Street served for dinner. I moved to Down Street, Piccadilly, where I had rooms next door to the Junior Athenæum Club, of which I had got myself made a member. Although I knew a good deal of equity and law, I do not think that I was really a very good Junior in those days. My training had been too abstract, and I had not been sufficiently in contact with the world of men and affairs to be a good judge of it. But I was full of knowledge and industry, and I fought hard in Court. A leading Chancery Queen's Counsel of these days told me that he suffered greater strain from encountering me in argument than from encountering any one else at the Bar.

But before I go further I must speak of a new influence which had come into my legal life. Horace Davey was then in the early stages of the great career at the Bar which was his as a ' Special.' Barber, knowing that he was over-pressed with cases and needed some young Junior who would read his briefs and ' devil ' up his authorities for him, recommended me. I was only too glad to get the chance, for at the time I had too little to do, and had to try to gain legal experience in such ways as acting as honorary legal adviser to a charitable Ladies' Aid Society. I now became immersed in Davey's cases. I used to read them carefully, make out what I thought to be his real points, and hunt out the authorities. Davey was, I think, the finest advocate on pure points of law that I have ever seen. In legal matters he had a mind like a razor, and he was accurate to the last degree. It was difficult indeed to put him in a corner, for he knew, almost instinctively, what was a bad point, and avoided all such. He could not cross-examine well, nor could he address a jury. But these were not the things for which he was wanted by the public. It was in the House of Lords and the Judicial Committee of the Privy Council that his power became apparent. Even a great advocate like Charles Russell, although Russell was a fine lawyer, was at a disadvantage against him. Herschell perhaps came nearest, but then Davey knew more than Herschell. I suited him when I had taken enough trouble, for I devoted myself, as he did, to unravelling first principles of law. I used often to go to his private house, in Queen's Gate Gardens, early on the Saturday morning, stay all day, and return to him on the Sunday. We thus could clear out the preparation of arguments and deal with the cases for opinion, of which he had an almost overwhelming number. I used in the summer to go down to his country house near Haslemere to do the same sort of work in the week-ends. His wife and daughters were very agreeable women, and he lived in a good deal of luxury, for his professional income had reached the, for those days, astounding figure of over £25,000 a year. He was a keen Liberal, but as bad as a politician and parliamentarian as he was good as a lawyer. He sat for Christchurch latterly, and I used sometimes to go down to speak for him there.

It was while I was with Davey that I first came into prominence at the Bar, through two cases. He had been given a brief on an application for special leave to appeal by the Government of Quebec. The sum at stake was very trifling, and it seemed doubtful whether the Privy Council would grant leave to appeal against the judgment of the Canadian Courts

But the matter was of high importance, involving as it did the validity of a statute embodying the Quebec Government policy. In order if possible to get rid of the judgment, the Solicitor-General of Quebec had been sent over to get leave to appeal to the Privy Council. However, he was not to argue himself, but to leave this to Davey.

Late in the evening before the case was to be heard Davey was summoned to continue an argument in a part-heard appeal to the House of Lords, a summons imposing on him a duty which took precedence of that to the Privy Council. No other leader of eminence could be got to take a brief at very short notice in a case involving a complicated question of Canadian constitutional law and, besides, a great responsibility. In despair Davey sent his head clerk to find me at my rooms about eight o'clock at night, and to summon me to a consultation at the Privy Council at 10 A.M. next morning. I was not used to shrinking from responsibility in things that had to be faced, so I told the clerk that it would be all right. I sat up through much of the night and mastered the real point. Next morning Davey broke it to the agitated Solicitor-General and to Freshfields, the well-known solicitors, that he must leave at once for the House of Lords. He proposed that the Solicitor-General for Quebec should open the petition. The latter firmly replied that he was precluded by his orders from doing so. If he did, and the application was refused, the responsibility would be such that the Government of Quebec might fall. Davey then said that fortunately he had brought to the consultation his learned friend,

Mr. Haldane, who knew the case thoroughly, and would conduct it, and he then seized his hat and disappeared. This did not comfort the unhappy clients. Old Mr. Wiseman, the well-known Privy Council Clerk of Freshfields, rose from his seat and said, 'The House of Freshfield has briefed Sir Richard Bethel, Sir Hugh Cairns, Sir Roundell Palmer, and other great men, and none of them ever treated the firm as Mr. Davey has to-day.' It was now only five minutes till the case would be called. I said that we had better apply our minds to what was useful and not to idle lamentation, and I proceeded to put on a wig and gown. The case was called, and the Judicial Committee seemed surprised to see it about to be opened by a youth who had never appeared before them on any other occasion. I opened my argument as shortly and moderately as possible, and stated the point on the constitution of Canada concisely. It might lead to real injustice, I suggested, if we were not allowed to bring a question that was of far-reaching public importance before the Supreme Tribunal of the Empire. True, the amount directly at stake was very small, and they might think it right to order us to pay the costs, even if they were in our favour. The Judicial Committee hesitated much ; they then deliberated. They did not know my name, but they said that what had been stated had satisfied them that we ought to have leave to appeal. Our triumph was so far complete.

Neither the Solicitor-General nor Freshfields said a word of thanks to me. They went away as persons aggrieved. But a few days later who should climb up the narrow stairs to my garret at Lincoln's Inn but old Mr. Wiseman himself, the venerable representative of the great firm of Freshfields. He said that the partners had read the shorthand note of the brief argument at the Privy Council, and now sent me a brief for the Province of Ontario in a great case. There might, he said, be more to follow, and indeed it so turned out. This particular brief was marked 150 guineas, and it introduced me to many Canadian cases over here.

The other case to which reference has been made was of a different type. It was the Scottish Petroleum case, which is fully reported in the Chancery Law Reports for 1883. The question was whether the appellant was entitled to have his name removed from the register of a Company on the ground of misrepresentation, he having repudiated informally without taking proceedings in Court before the date of a petition upon which an order had been made to wind the Company up. Mr. Justice Kay, before whom the application of the appellant originally came, had dismissed it rather contemptuously. We appealed to the Court of Appeal. Davey was to lead me. He took the most hopeless view of our case, and said that it was concluded by authority. In the end he proved to be right, but not till a long interval had elapsed. Owing to the congestion of business in the Court of Appeal our case was delayed for some weeks. As I had no other brief of my own I studied it closely. Every Monday morning I suggested a fresh result of meditation on the authorities to Davey. He brushed all my suggestions aside, and said that when the case was reached he should discover an engagement in another Court and leave me to open our appeal, of which he was sure he could make nothing. The case at last came on, before the great Sir George Jessel and two Lords Justices of Appeal. They did not know me by sight, for I had never argued there before.

Jessel, when he had caught the point, began to play with me as a cat does with a mouse. But I had the authorities even more at my fingers' ends than he had, the consequence of portentous study. He could not break me down, for I would not yield an inch. He began to get excited and to throw the power of his personality into the struggle with me, while his colleagues remained silent. Four o'clock came and he looked very ill. He was suffering from Bright's disease, but such was his courage that he had gone on with his work. Next day the Court was empty, for the Master of the Rolls was, as we were informed, ill. Next day we were told that he was dead. The appeal was adjourned, and we were informed that it must be opened afresh on a subsequent date. My brother barristers affected to reproach me for having killed Jessel. If I had, it was indeed unwillingly, for I had the highest admiration and deepest regard for that great judge.

A few weeks later the appeal was opened again, before Baggallay, Lindley, and Fry, Lords Justices. Davey again left it for me to conduct. This time I had worked up in the light of the first hearing even more masses of the law bearing on the question. I succeeded in destroying most of the points on which Mr. Justice Kay had relied in deciding against us.

SIR GEORGE JESSEL
Master of the Rolls

PROFESSOR LOTZE OF
GÖTTINGEN

MR. HORACE DAVEY
Afterwards Lord Davey

Then came the main question, whether the appellant could get rid of his status as a shareholder by a mere repudiation before the date of the winding-up petition. For the affirmative view of this proposition I contended tooth and nail, relying, as the official report shows, on what I contended was the preponderance of authority. The Lords Justices were much more impressed than Jessel had been with the argument. They called on the other side, who had a difficult time. Then I replied, expressing my regret that Davey could not be there to make the reply. But, as the report itself records, the Court of Appeal answered me that they considered that my clients had not suffered by the absence of Davey. Judgment was reserved for many days, and at the end, as he had predicted, the decision was against me. But three firms of solicitors who had been waiting for their own cases to come on in the Court, and had been witnesses of the prolonged fight, sent me briefs in other cases which they had coming forward.

My business now began to grow, and I was keen about it. In the next year it grew to about £2000, and after that, before I took silk, to nearly £2500. And it might have reached a higher figure had it not begun to be somewhat interfered with by politics.

It is here that the first period in my story closes, and that public duties began for the first time to absorb me. To this new period I must presently turn. But before this is done, the story of the Bar must be brought to an end.

CHAPTER II

LIFE AT THE BAR

(1885-1905)

At the end of 1905 I quitted work at the Bar finally. During the twenty years before this I was also in the House of Commons. I propose, in the pages which immediately follow, to confine myself almost exclusively to the story of legal work, reserving the political developments which accompanied it for separate narration in a subsequent section. This is done only for the sake of clearness, for of course the two phases of life were during these twenty years closely intermixed.

During this second period of life at the Bar my business grew very largely. My career there became a successful one, and the number of my briefs became very great, especially in the House of Lords and Privy Council. I had probably more business before these particular Tribunals in my final years than almost any other of my contemporaries, for I was not only taken in to argue many English and Irish appeals, but I had a large share of the Scotch appeals, and in the Privy Council I was in an enormous number of causes from every part of the Empire, including India. The task before that Tribunal was to master and marshal the facts, to bring them under principle,

42

and to exhibit them in the light of the varying systems of law and jurisprudence in the different dependencies of the Crown which applied to them. For this I was well trained. It was easy for me to pass from one system to another wholly different, and to bring out what was really distinctive of the varying systems with which we were dealing. This became progressively easier as experience grew. I remember, for instance, one fortnight within which, towards the end of my time, beginning with a case of Buddhist law from Burmah, I went on to argue successively appeals concerned with the Maori law of New Zealand, the old French law of Quebec, the Roman-Dutch system of South Africa, the Mohammedan law and then the Hindu law from India, the custom of Normandy in a Jersey appeal, and Scottish law in a case from the North. It was this kind of work that was easiest to me. Long practice had taught me to be accurate in presentation of the facts, and a retentive memory kept me supplied with stores of precedents and authorities. The result was that in my final days as an advocate I was not very easy to catch out or to drive into a corner ; and solicitors, finding out that I had the confidence of the Supreme Tribunals, heaped retainers and briefs upon me in cases from every quarter of the British dominions.

Notwithstanding this kind of success I was conscious of certain natural deficiencies, and I envied the great advocates of the past their power of form in presentation. One thing experience impressed on me was that the essence of advocacy in such appeals is candour and frankness about the difficulties of one's own case. To get the sympathy of the Tribunal for himself ought always to be one of the first objects of the advocate. He must remember, too, the idiosyncrasies of the judges before whom he practises and follow the movements of their minds and be sympathetic to them. One of the developments that comes in the later stages is that of an artificial memory. In my early days I have toiled long over the complicated facts of a brief which in my later days I could dissect and get through in a very short time, and be nevertheless so accurately informed that I should have considered it a disgrace to be caught out not knowing any material fact. And yet my memory for verbal quotations and for verse was always below par, while this other kind of memory became and has since remained exceptional. To this hour I can recall without difficulty many cases reported in the various reports—those that are old as well as those that are modern—which I have not read for years; and this is a source of comfort and enjoyment in judicial work.

I have said so much for the purpose of referring to the way in which a one-sided set of faculties was trained and harnessed to the labours of the Bar. I do not think my training was of the best kind for the work. On the whole I am inclined to the belief that a really first-class humanistic education at Oxford or Cambridge is the best preparation for that profession. Mine was of a very different kind; the classical side of it was altogether subordinated to the study of philosophy. The only advantage which this line of study brought for the purpose of the Bar was the habit it developed of seeking for the underlying principles in dealing with facts, however apparently confused and complicated.

However, I was from the beginning a keen student of how the work at the Bar was handled by some of those who were then my seniors, and I learned the importance of inspiring confidence. Success in the profession was essential if it were to be possible for me to devote myself later to public life, and this I always had in view. I realised that it was necessary to understand and pay attention to other people, and to try to make myself as far as I could a man of the world. It is curious to look back at this distance of time on how this desire grew. I am not trying to write any full narrative of my life at the Bar as I passed towards middle age, but one or two anecdotes may be useful as illustrating what I had to learn.

One of my first briefs came in a curious way. It happened in my earlier days in the law, but I narrate it because it shows how phases may be profitable that are more human than legal. I was shooting in the north of Scotland with a friend of mine whose wife had a considerable fortune. Among the party, which was large, there was a distinguished-looking old gentleman with gold spectacles who, observing that I looked sympathetic, confided to me how he was suffering from the absence of the kind of champagne to which he was accustomed at dinner. On my responding encouragingly he asked me whether I was soon to be in London, and on my saying that I was, he invited me to dine and see the quality not only of his champagne but of a cellar of claret of which he was very proud. I learned on inquiry that he was

one of the heads of a great firm of City solicitors who
were watching over the affairs of my hostess. When
I got to London I received the invitation he had
promised, and I went to dine. There was a party
of personages eminent in the law whom I was glad
to meet. After dinner we drank, after his champagne,
some famous Château Margaux of 1864, and then
came the ' pièce de résistance '—a bottle of still more
famous Château-Laffitte of 1858, then in its perfection. To the dismay of my host the old gentlemen
who were present, and who were in various stages of
gout and rheumatism, intimated that it was as much
as their lives were worth to drink further, and my
host himself by his doctor's orders had been per-
emptorily cut off. I saw that there was nothing else
for it if I wished to save him from real mental pain,
so I proceeded to drink out the bottle, paying a well-
deserved tribute to the merits of each glass. Presently the others were all stimulated to taste, and
the great wine had a well-deserved success, and I was
able to walk home none the worse, and with the feeling
that I had done a kindly deed.

Three days later the clerk of whom I had a share
at my garret in Lincoln's Inn opened my door and
unexpectedly showed in a young gentleman, whom I
did not know, carrying a bag. He introduced himself
as the son of my recent host, who, he said, had not
ceased to speak of the tact and appreciation of the
duties of a guest of the young barrister who had
dined with him. ' With such a one,' he said, ' our
firm ought to associate itself, for I am certain that
his gifts will raise him to high eminence in his pro-

fession.' My friend's son then produced from the bag a substantial-looking brief. But my host did more; for not only did he send other briefs, but he advised well-known solicitors in London to come to me, and still more briefs began to drop in.

But I must pass on. I remained a Junior for ten years, after which I took silk. At the end of my first five years as a Junior I felt justified in thinking of Parliament. I was pressed to become Liberal candidate for West Perthshire, where my home was, it being thought that Sir Donald Currie, the sitting Liberal member for the entire county, which had just been divided, would choose the eastern and more Liberal division of Perthshire in view of the approaching election. However, he selected the western division. I was then invited to contest East Lothian, which for many years past had always been represented by a member of the family of Lord Wemyss. I threw myself with all the energy I had into a prolonged contest, and in December 1885 ejected the sitting member, Lord Elcho, by a large majority. Having turned him out from a seat which by tradition had long been a Conservative one, I had of course to fight hard afterwards to keep the constituency. But it became a splendid Liberal seat. By working in it as constantly as I was able, I got to know the new electors whom the recent extension of the franchise had brought in, and through subjects in which the older electors were interested irrespective of politics I got to know them also. I had the devoted help, as my Chairman, of Mr. Lawrie of Monkrigg, an able man of business and of high character, and at his house I had always a home during my frequent visits to the county. For East Lothian I sat unbrokenly for a quarter of a century, having to fight no fewer than eight contested elections during the time. It was very difficult to combine the business of a Junior who had a good deal of drafting to do with the work of a Member of Parliament. When I got a night off from the House of Commons I used to go to Lincoln's Inn and work till midnight, dining on a chop at the old 'Cock Tavern' in Fleet Street. At first I went on 'devilling' at times for Davey, from whom I continued to learn a great deal. I did not have the volume of cases or the vast practice of some of the fashionable Juniors, but I came to have in the end probably not less important and intricate cases than any of my contemporaries at the Junior Bar. For example, I appeared throughout as Junior in the great Peruvian Guano case, and in such litigations as that between the London, Chatham and Dover and South Eastern Railway Companies. In 1890 Lord Halsbury who was then Lord Chancellor and before whom I had often appeared, gave me a silk gown, when I had been just ten years at the Bar, whispering to me as he handed me my patent, ' I think this will be a great success.'

According to custom I attached myself to a particular Court in the Chancery Division, first to Mr. Justice Kay, and then, after he went to the Court of Appeal, to Mr. Justice Romer. In the Court of the latter I had a large business. But the cases were many of them small and uninteresting questions of mere fact, and the work did not really suit me. Romer and I had minds of quite different types, and although our personal relations were very friendly, we never really understood each other. He was very quick and decided, and fond of jumping somewhat to conclusions, and I was not as good at catching his mind as Neville, Q.C., my chief rival in the Court. But when we appealed to the Court of Appeal, for which my faculties were much better adapted, I used to have the best of it, and often reversed his judgments, somewhat, I think, to Romer's annoyance, for he used to say to me, ' You did not make these points before me '; and I used to reply, ' You would not listen to them when I did make them.' But Romer was a strong judge and taught me a good deal.

About 1897 I took my life in my hands and went ' Special.' Indeed it was almost necessary, for I had had to do a great deal of work of a political kind for the Liberal Government over the Home Rule Bill in the House of Commons and in connection with the new Death Duties Bill. At all events I felt the time had come to take the risk of going ' Special,' which meant that I would not appear in any Court of First Instance without a special fee of fifty guineas in addition to that marked on my brief. I was largely influenced in deciding to do this by the advice of a solicitor who is now dead, but whom I looked upon —I think justly—as one of the ablest men in the profession, Mr. Hill of Collyer-Bristow & Co. When I went ' Special,' following his advice, he began to employ me greatly. He took me into the appeal to the House of Lords in the great real property case Foxwell v. Van Grutten, where I won a complete

D

victory for him. And I began to be employed, not
only very largely in Canadian cases in the Privy
Council, but in Indian and other appeals. I had also
an increasing number of Scotch appeals to the House
of Lords from an early stage.

My mind, which had not been really well suited
to work in the Courts of First Instance, went along
much more smoothly with those of the judges of the
Supreme Tribunals, and notably with those of Lord
Halsbury, Lord Watson, Lord Lindley, and Lord
Macnaghten. I got many judgments from them as
the result of arguments on which I had spared no
pains. It is not possible in these Supreme Tribunals
alone to make the biggest kind of income, and I never
did. But I had also an increasing amount of special
work in great cases in the Courts of First Instance
and in the Court of Appeal. Although I do not think
I ever in any one complete year earned more than
15,000 guineas, it is plain from what my fee-book or
my last year at the Bar shows, that if I had gone on
and had not left the Bar I should have been making
a good deal more. My final year was broken by my
becoming Secretary of State, but for the part of that
year which was completed my book showed earnings
at the rate of at least £20,000, and the amount was
only limited by the impossibility of doing more with
the heavy political and other work I had on hand.
For not only was I doing much work in the House of
Commons, but I was sitting on the Explosives Committee and presiding over various other Committees
and organisations, as well as composing and delivering
Gifford Lectures. Indeed, it was about this time

that I was informally offered the Chair of Moral Philosophy in St. Andrews University, a prospect which attracted me, although I felt bound to reject it. Philosophy is as jealous a mistress as is the Law.

I may observe here on the difficulty of comparing the volume of practice of leaders in one period with that of leaders in a later period. Sir Roundell Palmer had an enormous number of briefs. But fees were then much smaller than a generation later, when Davey led the Bar in purely legal cases. The custom in Palmer's time was to give briefs in a single case to several leaders, one of whom always attended. I remember Lord Selborne (Sir R. Palmer) himself telling me that he made a point of managing to take part in every case in which he was briefed for *some* part of the day. But in Davey's day clients had begun to ask for more time from the advocate, and consequently fees had risen much. Later on the clients began to stipulate for exclusive time, and as the result of this the fees of fashionable leaders have become enormous compared with those that were paid even to an advocate of the position of Davey. My information leads me to think that in the cases at least of the heads of the Bar the fees on the briefs are more than double what they were in Davey's time, and that his were probably on the average double those paid to Palmer. In the old days the volume of actual work required to yield a great income for a fashionable leader was consequently much greater than it is to-day.

I never had, nor had time to have, one of these colossal practices. But towards the end of my life as a 'Special' my chambers were a spectacle. The floor of the clerk's room was strewn with briefs. It was a question only of which one should take and how many had to be rejected. I received a not inconsiderable income in the shape of general retainers and special retainers, in respect of which, by initialling a slip of paper, I received five guineas or one guinea as the case might be, and held myself retained if the cases matured. I also had a large business in cases for opinion. It is a common delusion that when the opinion of counsel is taken he encourages litigation. There may be some truth in this with a Junior or somebody in a small practice who is anxious for work. But with me it was just the other way, for any disposition to set agoing new cases which I should be called on to argue was tempered by a desire not to be encumbered with suits about which I did not feel any degree of certainty ; and about comparatively few law cases is it really possible to say with certainty in the early stages how they will turn out.

I knew the judges in the House of Lords and Privy Council so well that I could follow the working of their individual minds. If, for example, Lord Watson, who was by no means a silent judge but who was a man of immense power, started off by being against me, I would turn round to some colleague of his on whose opinion I knew he did not set much weight, and who would be sure merely to echo what Lord Watson had just said. By devoting myself to the judge who had merely repeated Lord Watson's point I well knew that I should speedily detach Lord Watson from it and bring him out of his entrenchments. The psychology of advocacy is always an important phase

in it, and not least with the Supreme Tribunals.
Latterly I came to find that when I was opening an
appeal in the House of Lords or Privy Council much
depended upon great candour of statement and on
the impression made in the first twenty minutes or
half-hour. I have sometimes stated the point as it
had been decided against my side in the Court below
before the Tribunal could realise on which side I was
arguing. I have done this when I saw that they
were in an obstinate mood, with fairness, but with
the result that they jumped from sheer combativeness
against the proposition of law which I intended in
the end to overthrow, and it was then that I gradually
disclosed how it was that I was really there to argue
the other way. The results were sometimes good.

Before I pass from this kind of experience there
are two or three cases which I was in and which may
be worth while referring to.

One I remember in particular, for it was among the
last that I argued before leaving the Bar. A distinguished Crimean General, who had retired from
the Army and was old, would not refrain from the
pleasure of directing Companies, notwithstanding that
he already had a considerable fortune. Whittaker
Wright, the well-known promoter, was at this time
in the height of his glory, and the General was made
a director of one of Whittaker Wright's Companies.
The Company, although speculative in its business,
was very honestly managed by Whittaker Wright,
who was at this stage showing himself not only a
great man of business but, as far as I could discover
from my experience of suits which I conducted for

him, for the time a thoroughly honest one.   Latterly, under pressure, he departed from this meritorious attitude under circumstances which are still well remembered.

The General of whom I speak had become a director and taken part in issuing a prospectus in Whittaker Wright's best days. In order to be scrupulously accurate in disclosing all the contracts to which the prospectus related, and so comply with the Companies Acts, he and the other directors had specially employed a firm in the City at a large fee to advise them if they had done everything that was proper. The solicitors, however, had been careless, and one contract—a quite unimportant one, but enough to make the directors possibly liable under a highly technical section of the Companies Act of these days—had been overlooked. The result was that when the new Company came to grief and went into liquidation, in the general crash which brought Whittaker Wright down the directors were attacked. A somewhat speculative firm of solicitors sent round circulars to the shareholders intimating that, if they would subscribe a small sum, the solicitors were of opinion that they could recover the amount of their shares from the directors personally by reason of the non-disclosure of the particular minor contract to which I have referred.

I was retained for the General, who was confronted by claims which would have made him bankrupt, by an eminent firm of solicitors in the City. I told them that before the judge of First Instance they were bound to be beaten. Certain decisions of the Court of Appeal which had been given in other cases were too strongly against them. I said that my one chance of success was to fight the case up to the House of Lords, which alone could disregard the previous decisions of the Court of Appeal on the particular section of the Companies Act. They took my advice. I led in the Court of First Instance before a shrewd and kindly Chancery judge. I opened my case in a way which made him sympathise with the position of a director who, however foolish in becoming a director at all, had done his best to be honest, and had taken the trouble, which I detailed, to see that the contracts were all specified in the prospectus. I saw that my only chance was to put my client in a good moral light, and I purposely put him into the box, knowing that he would disclose a lamentable incapacity for business. He could not tell even on which continent were some of the mines with which his Company was concerned. At the end of a three days' trial the judge said to me that he must decide against me. 'You can go to the Court of Appeal,' he said, 'and I will find all the facts in your favour, because I am satisfied that your client, while thoroughly incompetent as a director, is a very honest gentleman who did his best.' We went to the Court of Appeal, where the comments were not so sympathetic. Much criticism was however made on the negligence of the solicitors who had been specially consulted, and I remember being amused by receiving from the firm in the course of the argument a general retainer to defend them should the appeal fail and a case for negligence be brought against them. Our appeal did fail, being dismissed with costs. We then went, as had been our plan from the beginning, to the House of Lords. I opened my case delicately, brought out the honourable character of my client, was candid about his stupidity, and pointed out that the whole question was whether he was to be made liable on purely technical grounds because of these decisions of the Court of Appeal, which bound that Court but which were not binding in the House of Lords. These authorities I examined critically.

As I had anticipated, the Lord Chancellor and the Law Lords poised themselves, hesitated, and slowly descended on my side of the fence. I went on for a couple of hours, simply clinching the points, and then, whispering to my Junior that he might be wise not to try to add anything, left the Lords to call up the other side. The other side had a very bad time, largely owing to the fact that the litigation had been inspired by the firm of speculative solicitors of whom I have spoken, who had succeeded in starting one hundred and forty-four actions. I replied with full effect, and felt at the end that the Lords were about to deliver a judgment taking a truer and less technical view of the section than the Court of Appeal had—a view which would result in delivering the old General. Judgment was reserved, and before it could be delivered I had become Secretary of State for War.

One day there came into my room at the War Office the General himself to inform me that the deferred judgment had just been delivered, and that it had been entirely satisfactory both there and as regarded the Court of Appeal, and he had come to thank me for his deliverance. I congratulated him, and said good-bye. A few days later I had, as the new Minister for War, to see the Sovereign on the subject of the K.C.B.'s which were to be awarded at New Year time to retired Generals as well as to those on the active list. King Edward said to me, ' Now, you do not know the Army yet, and although it is for you to make recommendations to me, I am not sure that I cannot be helpful to you. There is General ——, a retired Crimean veteran, a man of great eminence and ability in his profession, whom you know nothing of.' I recognised my client at once, and I said to the King I was not quite in such ignorance as His Majesty supposed. I told him about the law case and said, ' The General has emerged without the smallest reflection upon his character, and any reflection upon his abilities as a Company director has nothing to do with his military career, which was sufficiently distinguished.' The King was much amused. We decided that the name should be included in the list of K.C.B.'s for retired Generals.

About the same time as the above I had a curious case to conduct for a German bank, the Deutsche Bank, in which I was instructed by Freshfields to lead. The German bank had rashly entangled itself with a syndicate in the City, and a serious dispute had arisen about their liability under an agreement. The syndicate instituted a Chancery suit, and Dr. Siemens, the head of the bank, and some of its chief officials, were compelled to come to London and bring the books (for taking which out of Berlin they were subject to a daily fine) in order to defend the action. The delay in England seemed interminable, and the

Germans were much disheartened. It was a very curious case, for in my brief were copies of letters from the Kaiser to the Sultan of Turkey about concessions to the bank in Anatolia. Who was right and who was wrong of the litigating parties was a very doubtful question.

The Germans were examined on commission and their documents were kept in Court, and they could not understand the English practice, according to which it is not usual to fix a definite day for the trial but to leave the case to take its chance in the list. When they were cross-examined on commission they thought the English counsel laughed at them, and being touchy persons they wanted to throw up their case and go home. I told them not to be so foolish ; that they and the English never understood each other, because their ways were different. I expressed my surprise that the Deutsche Bank should have gone into such a transaction when it might have had its business done by some great firm like Rothschilds, but Dr. Siemens told me that, although the Deutsche Bank was an enormous bank, it was a bank of quite a different kind from any we were accustomed to in England, and it made its money by dividends from investments which an English bank would not deal in.

At last I persuaded them to be calm and to await the result, and I opened the defence on their behalf. Instead of, as they thought, the judge showing prejudice against them because they were Germans, he treated them, as I knew he would, with the utmost fairness ; and after a three days' trial I managed on a narrow point to save the case and to procure the dismissal of the action against them with costs. They were immensely delighted, and Dr. Siemens, who was a clever man, said to me that he thought it was hopeless for English men of business and German men of business ever to understand each other unless they were brought into close personal relation, as I had been able to bring them with Mr. Justice Byrne.

Another great case in which I was engaged a little earlier than this was the constitutional appeal of the Island of Jersey. The question was that of the constitutionality of an Order in Council made by Queen Victoria on the advice of the Home Office, and it was brought to the Channel Islands Committee of the Privy Council. The Channel Islands Committee of the Privy Council was a semi-judicial body established for the guidance of the Crown in determining constitutional justice in affairs connected with the Channel Islands.

The origin of the dispute was a curious one. A French lady residing in Jersey was convicted of an offence against public morals, and in accordance with the antiquated law of the Islanders was sentenced to death. Not unnaturally the French Government addressed a communication to the Foreign Office. ' Our subject,' they said, ' has committed an offence which would have been an affair of police and a fine with us, and your island has condemned her to die.' The Foreign Office through the Home Office remonstrated with the Jersey Authorities, but the Jersey Authorities were very stiff. The Queen then issued a reprieve, but the reprieve, according to the custom which the Island claimed to be part of their constitution, could not, as the Authorities there alleged, become operative until it had been registered with the States or Jersey Parliament. The States had adjourned until after the date fixed for the execution, so that the reprieve could not be made operative. The British Navy was, however, equal to the occasion. The lady was imprisoned in the Jersey prison, the Castle of Mont St. Orgueil. A gunboat party landed and took possession of the prisoner and conveyed her away out of danger.

The Home Office, not content with this, got an Order in Council passed giving themselves a majority on the Prison Board, by which in future the Jersey Prison Board might be directed to give effect to a reprieve or other Royal Command. Thereupon the Island made representation against the authority of the Order in Council, and this representation came before the Channel Islands Committee for consideration. It was based on the allegation that the Island had by course of tradition a history which had resulted in a constitutional system—the result of charters from time to time granted for assistance rendered by the Island in English wars. It was said that in the result no Order in Council could be passed operatively without the concurrence of the States or Parliament of the Island. Needless to say, on the establishment of this proposition and on its denial vast labour was expended by the Island Authorities and by the Law Officers of the Crown respectively. The case for the Island amounted to several thick volumes of charters

and other documents, and that for the Crown was
almost as large. Originally Sir Henry James had
been retained to lead for the Island, and he was
succeeded by Sir Horace Davey. I, who was Junior
at the beginning, found myself, by their translation
to the Bench, the leading counsel. The Privy Council
Tribunal sitting on its Channel Islands Committee
was a very impressive one. My recollection is that
the Prime Minister—and President of the Council—
Lord Rosebery, presided, and several Law Lords sat
also, along with distinguished lay Privy Councillors,
making in all a Tribunal of about eight to hear the
case. I opened it and was prepared to go into the
whole constitutional history. But after I had spoken
for a couple of days, the Tribunal, somewhat dismayed
at the length of the opening, took the point that I
need not establish more than that what had been
done was a breach of an agreement come to by Lord
John Russell, acting when Home Secretary, soon after
the Reform Bill, with the Island Authorities. On
the ground of breach of this agreement the Privy
Council was disposed to recommend a disallowance
of the Order of the Queen in Council, intimating that
they hoped the great constitutional point would never
have to be decided. The Law Officers of the Crown,
Sir Charles Russell and Sir Robert Reid, were called
upon. They fought hard, but had a very difficult
time and could not remove the impression of the
Tribunal. The result was that the Island was victorious. I had prepared a full précis of what was
to have been the argument on the constitutional
point, and I presented this, together with a complete

set of the books, to the Library at All Souls', where it now remains a theme for some future constitutional historian, who will find an immense mass of valuable historical material put in order for him.

After the case was over the Parliament of the Island formally voted a resolution of thanks for my help, and I was invited to proceed to Jersey as a State guest, and there I was entertained, and finally conducted in a somewhat triumphal procession round the Island.

Another remarkable case in which I was engaged I refer to because of the illustration it afforded of the tremendous powers of cross-examination of Sir Charles Russell. The late Mr. Samuel Morley had left a large fortune to one of his sons, a young man of a religious disposition but not of a powerful mind. He had a tutor who was a Close Plymouth Brother and a man of attractive but dominant personality. Under the influence of his tutor young Morley embraced Plymouthism, and was persuaded by the tutor to migrate with him to a place in Cornwall, a few miles from Launceston, where a section of the Close Brethren had set up a little community under the guidance of this man as their leader. After a time young Morley's mind appears to have given way, and he fled from the community to Launceston, only to put an end to his life in a hotel there.

The family naturally inquired into the transaction and found that a large part of the fortune of about £140,000 which their brother had possessed had been transferred by him to his spiritual leader. There was evidence that the community near Launceston had been established and run on a scale of reckless personal extravagance. An action was brought by the family to set aside the transfers to the leader and to recover the money on the ground of undue influence exercised in what was claimed to be in equity a confidential relationship.

The case was tried before Mr. Justice Wright. Sir Charles Russell led for the family, and I, who was at that time an equity Queen's Counsel, was retained as his Junior for the sake of the equity questions which were likely to arise. The whole case at the trial turned on whether the defendant had suggested to young Morley that he should make the transfers to him, and had exercised his spiritual influence to induce him to do so ; or whether the gifts were spontaneous and free, and made without the intervention of the defendant. It was clear that the latter had become to all appearance the absolute owner of the money, and his case was that the sums of money had been freely 'laid on the altar' by Morley and entrusted to the representative of the community in which Morley worshipped, to lay out in the service of God. The defendant was obviously a very clever man. In manner and appearance he reminded me not a little of the late Mr. Parnell. For a whole day he baffled Sir Charles Russell in the witness-box. I, who was sitting by him, saw that Russell was getting depressed ; the more fiercely he cross-examined, the more quietly the defendant replied. 'You may call it a gift to me,' he said, 'but in our language the gift was laid on the altar through myself as the humble means.' Russell could make nothing of him, although he was

at his best that day. But during the adjournment
a curious little old lady came up to me just before
the Court re-assembled after luncheon. She said to
me, ' I was a member of the community, and I
know that the defendant is a bad man. He got the
money out of Morley and lived luxuriously with it,
and I have come here to see if I can help justice to
defeat him.' I asked her whether she knew his handwriting, and she said she knew it intimately. When
the Court resumed, I took up a letter which had been
disclosed in the discovery of documents, and in which
Morley, apparently quite spontaneously, had instructed a firm of brokers to prepare the transfer of
some stock to the defendant. On the mere chance
of a result coming, I asked the counsel on the other
side to let me have the draft from which this letter
had been written. I had no notion whether he had
such a draft or not, but I was sure the language was
not Morley's own. Somewhat to my surprise, on
looking through his papers the Junior on the other
side produced a draft and handed it to me. It was
a draft of the very letter, but not in Morley's handwriting. I beckoned to the old lady, and I said,
' Whose writing is this ? ' ' That is the defendant's
writing,' she said. ' Are you quite sure ? ' ' Yes.'
I then touched Sir Charles Russell's elbow while he
was cross-examining, and apparently getting to the
end of his material, and it was only necessary for me
to say to him five words, ' Draft in his own handwriting.' His hand came down firmly and silently
on my own and on the paper. He went on cross-
examining as though he were bringing his questions

to an end and, apparently concluding, asked whether this particular letter was one which it was quite clear was Morley's own idea. The defendant said it was, and repudiated the suggestion that he had either seen it before it was written or had prepared the draft of it. In a moment, Sir Charles, his eyes flashing and his voice like thunder, and his whole personality thrown into the question, asked him, ' Is that, sir, your handwriting ? ' tendering the draft. The witness saw that the game was up. It was a few minutes before four, when the Court adjourned, but these few minutes saw a terrible cross-examination. Next morning, when we re-assembled, the defendant should again have gone into the box, but a doctor stepped in in his absence, and said that he could not go on, that he was very ill, and had been vomiting blood through the night. The judge found that under the cloak of religion he had used undue influence to obtain these gifts, and he set aside the whole of the transactions. The final cross-examination was one of the most effective things I have ever witnessed.

I was engaged in many other great cases, such as the cordite case about the Nobel patent for the combination of nitro-glycerine and nitro-cellulose into a low-burning propellant—a case in which I first appeared for Nobel against the Crown, and later for the Crown against Maxim—a case, too, in which I learned a good deal of the chemistry of explosives, which was of use to me when I sat as a member of the Explosives Committee after the South African War, and later still when I was Secretary of State. Into the details of these numerous cases I will not

E

wander much further. Some of them were interesting,
and among them were those which involved a class
of learning which appears as if it were now becoming
of little use. I mean the learning connected with
English Real Property Law. I used to have a good
many of such cases, from the days when as a Junior
I practised conveyancing down to nearly the end of
my time at the Bar. But they became progressively
less frequent, and indeed the old class of Real Property
lawyers is nearly extinct. I remember an Irish appeal
which was the subject of great interest to me. It
came to the House of Lords, and there we took the
point that the appellants were entitled to succeed
on the ground that a novel but legitimate kind of
Conditional Fee Simple had been created. The
case was surrounded with the quintessence of the old
Real Property learning, and turned on decisions
some of them given prior to the time of Lord Coke.
I worked hard at it with the late Mr. Challis, then
one of the most learned Real Property lawyers of
Lincoln's Inn. We argued it, and there was
counter-argument by Sir Horace Davey. The result
was that the House of Lords was much puzzled, and
Lord Selborne presiding, reserved judgment. Un-
luckily the next day was Derby Day, and the law
clients met on the racecourse, and were said to have
settled the case there, so judgment was never delivered. The only place where the nature of the case
is reported and explained is in an appendix to Mr.
Challis's book on Real Property.

I find myself now among the few remaining who
have really read Fearne on Contingent Remainders

Hargrave's Tracts, and the old conveyancing books of an earlier date. It is an obsolete learning—fortunately for the public. Yet it was very interesting, and at one time I was very familiar with it. As a token of regard when I became Lord Chancellor, the Institute of Conveyancers, a body the standards in old law of which are held to be very high, gave me a dinner. Later on I introduced a great Bill into the House of Lords for the recasting and codification of much of the law relating to Real Property and Conveyancing. To the prospects of this Bill the War put an end. It was somewhat revolutionary. But after the War it was unearthed by Lord Birkenhead, and passed by him in a rather improved form. When I was Chancellor for a second time, in 1924, I expanded the scope of this form largely. My successor, Lord Cave, expanded it still more, and in the shape which he gave them the Bills became part of the law of the land. That is how great reforms come about, through the co-operation of successive Chancellors. I put much work and thought into this reform of our law of property, and later on, when out of office, presided over the Joint Committee of the two Houses of Parliament which revised the draft measures. We had much assistance from some of the best and most learned conveyancers of the day in the revolution we effected.

Among the many cases which were laid before me for opinion at this time I remember one which consisted of a blank sheet with a substantial fee and the names of three other well-known counsel,

junior to myself, who were to advise with me. The
questions were two :—

(1) Could a Roman Catholic be Lord Lieutenant
of Ireland, and
(2) Could a Roman Catholic be Lord Chancellor
of Great Britain ?

The case purported to have been submitted on
behalf of a gentleman with a name associated with
Protestantism, but I doubted at the time whether
he was the real client. I gave an opinion, in which
my fellow-counsel concurred, that a Roman Catholic
could, on the true construction of the statutes, hold
the offices. I afterwards discovered that the real
client who had taken my opinion was Lord Russell
of Killowen, then Lord Chief Justice of England,
and I rather think the fact of his having taken the
opinion is mentioned in his *Life* or elsewhere.

Looking back upon these days at the Bar, now
that I have sat for years on the Bench as Lord
Chancellor and as a Law Lord, I feel that they were
days of work so heavy that I should not care to face
them again. An advocate ought to be well under
sixty. Talking over our experience among ourselves one day at luncheon, I found that the whole
of my brother judges agreed with me that they
would not like to face the racket of the Bar over
again. The strain and labour require not only the
energy of youth, but interest and keenness of a kind
which one wishes at a later period of life to devote
to problems of a different class. I do not know that
I should care to face again even the work of the

six and a half years I spent at the War Office. These things are intensely interesting, but one cannot go on striving in the same groove for an indefinite period. Even as regards the Lord Chancellorship, which is to an extraordinary degree a traditional office depending upon surroundings and customs which have come down from antiquity, I could not undertake it again with anything like the interest which it possessed for me when I first entered on it. A friend of the late Lord Herschell told me that when he congratulated Lord Herschell on the probable coming once more to power of the Liberal Party, and of himself again to the Chancellorship, Lord Herschell replied, ' No, I have been three years Chancellor, and that is as much as any one ought to care to have of the Office.' I agree with Lord Herschell. The judicial work of the Office is intensely interesting, but it is pleasanter to have that as a Law Lord free from the incessant worry caused by political interruption of judicial business. But I wish to record my strong conviction that, at all events for a judge who is to sit in the Supreme Tribunals of the Empire, and particularly in the Privy Council, a House of Commons training is a real advantage. One learns there the nuances of the Constitution, and phases of individual and social political life which are invaluable in checking the danger of abstractness in mental outlook. I myself was peculiarly in need of such training, and I am thankful to have had twenty-five years of the great university of public life.

The Bar has its uses as a training for the House

of Commons, but it is not really a good school. The outlook in the House is very different from the outlook in the Courts. If less scientific about details, the House of Commons' mind is wider. I am not sure that a first-rate Minister, although untrained as a lawyer, does not bring in a great legal Bill better and more effectively than the best trained legal mind, unless that mind has, what is rare, the political gift by nature in a high degree. The atmosphere is quite different. I remember once arguing a case in the Court of Appeal before Lord Esher and Lord Justice Rigby. Lord Justice Rigby, an old and valued friend of mine, had entered the House of Commons late in life. He never quite understood its ways, and was not appreciated to the extent which his sterling qualities of a non-political kind warranted. I was opening an appeal on the construction of an Act of Parliament, and I was arguing that the statute must be read as a whole in order to collect from within its four corners what I called the ' mind ' of the legislature in the controlling purpose which the sections indicated. ' Mind of the legislature,' cried out Lord Esher to me from the Bench, ' and you, Mr. Haldane, have been twenty years in the House of Commons and yet speak of it.' ' Yes,' thundered out Lord Justice Rigby, ' and the House of Commons is a place where if a man talks sense they call him a lawyer.' Notwithstanding this, Law and Politics may go better together than some people think.

It may be interesting if I add to my recollections of my Bar days a few details about the great Free

Church of Scotland case. It is hardly exaggeration
to describe this as probably the greatest litigation
of its particular kind which ever occurred in our
history. More than two millions of money was
claimed against those who had in the main subscribed it along with their predecessors by a small
minority of the Free Church of Scotland, who had
declined to concur in the Union of the Free Church
and the United Presbyterian Church in 1900 under
the name of the United Free Church of Scotland.
The case of the claimants was that the Union was
incompetent, because it involved a sacrifice of principles which formed a fundamental and essential
part of the constitution of the Free Church, and
particularly a departure from the doctrine of Predestination as embodied in the Confession of that
Church. It was also contended that the Trust
Deeds which were executed at the time of the Disruption in 1843, and which constituted a trust for
the Free Church, meant a trust, not for such persons
as held the doctrine and submitted in ecclesiastical
matters to the government and discipline of the
Free Church as prescribed by its founders, with
such modifications as might be made from time to
time by the General Assembly, but for the support
of certain unalterable and distinctive doctrines. Had
there been a breach of trust which entitled the
claimants to say that they were the only persons
remaining of the old Free Church who remained
within the trust and were therefore entitled to the
property ? One question was whether the affirmation of both the doctrine of predestination and of

free will contained in the new statement of principle
was in harmony with the doctrine of the old Church
and could be accepted. On this there was a vast
theological and semi-metaphysical discussion. Lord
Halsbury and Lord James of Hereford were of
opinion that the doctrine of predestination as occur-
ring in the old Confession of the Church could not
stand along with its new affirmation of free will.
In the end, however, on this point the Law Lords
by five to two took a contrary view, and were against
the claimants. I argued for this view strenuously,
showing that the same statement of the two doctrines
side by side occurred in the New Testament. I
had got my mother, whose knowledge of the Scripture
was very great, to make me out a list of the texts
containing both doctrines from the various gospels
and epistles, and I read these out with effect in
the course of the argument. One of the Law Lords
fought hard against me on this, declaring that it
was impossible that if he, sitting where he did,
predestined my will I could be free. Gently raising
my hands to the top of my full-bottomed wig I
replied, ' But your Lordship is so anthropomorphic.'
To which his reply was that he wished I would use
words he could understand. We cited masses of
theological authority, and we went through the proceedings and the creed of the Synod of Dort, and of
the Commission which framed the Westminster Confession. In the end the majority held that the
doctrine was a mystery, and that they could not see
their way to dissent from our claim, however little
intelligible, that there was no contradiction from a

proper speculative point of view. Had the case been heard by Scotsmen, I do not think it would have taken us so long to get rid of this point. But it was very unfortunate that for some reason Lord Kinnear and Lord Moncreiff, who were judges of the Court of Session and as Peers were qualified to sit in the House of Lords, were not summoned instead of two English Law Lords who were without knowledge of the spirit of theology in Scotland.

On the second ground, that of the Trust Deed, the House of Lords decided against us, reversing the unanimous decision of the Court of Session, and holding that we had departed from the terms of the Trust Deed. We strenuously argued that this was wrong, and we said that a trust for a Church was not a trust to promulgate a body of rigid doctrine, but might be a trust for an organisation with powers of self-government wielded by its General Assembly, and which, so long as it did nothing to destroy its identity, was free to mould its own doctrine and its own constitution. Lord Macnaghten and Lord Lindley took this view strongly, but the majority decided the other way, and held that the Dissentient claimants had become the sole beneficiaries entitled to the Trust Funds. We of course maintained that the real beneficiary was the Church, which was an organisation like a club or the State, with autonomy such that it could make changes that did not destroy its own identity. It seemed to me at the time that even if the House of Lords were right—as we strenuously contended they were not—in taking a different view, what they ought to have done was to refer the matter to the Court of Session to settle the further terms of a proper charitable trust, ' cy-près,' and so make the funds available in accordance with what must have been the general as distinct from the particular intention of the founders of the trust in 1843. But of course it was not open to us, consistently with the view we were putting forward, to propose that this should be done. It was the business of the House of Lords to say that it should be done, and because they failed to do this, Parliament promptly reversed the decision by means of a statute, and set up the Elgin Commission to make a proper distribution ' cy-près ' of the property.

The irritation in the public mind caused by the case was intense. I feel now, as I felt then, that the decision was a wrong one, and that the popular instinct was right. That it should have been decided that the Church could be controlled by a Court of Law, was tied to a rigid doctrine, and had not power to manage its own affairs, was enough to bring Dr. Chalmers and the founders of the Disruption of 1843 out of their graves. But such was the decision, and it was a very cruel one, for it not only stripped the United Free Church of the whole of its property, including what had been contributed by the very men who were defenders at the Bar, but it condemned them to pay the costs of the litigation personally.

I well remember how at the close of the case Principal Rainy, the leader of the United Free Church, was for the moment almost stunned with grief. He took my arm after the judgment was

over, and we walked to my rooms in Whitehall
Court. I then said to him that I had an instinct
that this defeat would be put right by public opinion,
and that the United Free Church would emerge
stronger than before. He said, ' I feel force in what
you say, but I am now an old man of eighty without
the strength to begin the world again.' I said to
him, ' Let us begin the effort on the spot. It is
worth the sacrifice even of your life.' He assented,
and I proposed to him that a subscription should be
started at once. I said, ' I am not a member of
the Church, but I feel this so strongly that I will
begin the list with £1000, which I can well do, considering the fees I have received.' This encouraged
him, and before many hours were past, over £150,000
had been subscribed. We set to work, he in the
North and I in London, and I saw Mr. Balfour—
at that time Prime Minister; he was most sympathetic and helpful. Lord Dunedin, who was then
Scottish Secretary, Lord Balfour of Burleigh, and
the Archbishop of Canterbury were equally keen,
and I went down to Hatfield and spent the week-
end with Mr. Balfour there to explain to him the
facts. Parliament came to a practically unanimous
decision to pass the Bill which put the matter right.
Dr. Rainy was splendid in his courage, and he lived
to see a great transformation take place, and the
United Free Church stronger than before, and its
relations to the Established Church put on a new and
better footing, the benefit of which is in course of
being reaped, and which is operating to the profit
of Scotland.

About the case I had always entertained a strong opinion. I had advised along with Mr. J. B. Balfour, afterwards Lord President of the Court of Session, who was the most eminent Scottish advocate of the day, that the United Free Church ought to succeed in the litigation, as they did before the Court of Session, and I put all the energy I possessed into the argument of the case. The theologians who attended in consultation to support us did not seem to me to be as fully possessed of their subject as were their predecessors in the great days of theology in Scotland, but with their aid, and with that of the philosophers, we produced a tremendous body of authority at the Bar on the subject of Predestina tion. Never before had the House of Lords had to listen to citations from great works such as Vatke's *Menschliche Freiheit* and the Metaphysical Treatise of Mr. F. H. Bradley. I am bound to add that the only book which appealed to Lord Chancellor Halsbury was Mosely on ' Predestination,' but even to this he was unwilling to yield. Lord Halsbury himself quoted Greek from the Woolsack, and suggested that the antinomies of Kant had something to do with the antinomian heresy. The discussion wandered to the introduction of St. Augustine's doctrine by Thomas Aquinas, and to a stiff controversy between the Bench and the Bar over ' effectual calling.' Even Origen, and Clement, and Justin Martyr were brought in. Looking back, I cannot say that the controversy as recorded was a very edifying one. I find this in the report of the case :—

LORD JAMES OF HEREFORD : ' How can He enter into a covenant with those who are predestined ? '

MR. HALDANE : ' Because the doctrine of predestination is not to be understood as the power of one man over another. It is not anthropomorphic. It is to be understood as something that occurs irrespective of the forms of space and time, and the freedom of the individual as a free and finite spirit is to be reconciled in relation to its identity with God from whom proceed all things.'

LORD JAMES OF H. : ' I never knew how incapable I was of understanding these things until I heard your argument. I know it is my fault entirely, but I cannot follow you.'

MR. HALDANE : ' The whole system of the philosophy of Plato and Aristotle, of Kant and other great thinkers, cannot be put into half an hour's address.'

LORD JAMES OF H. : ' You cannot put them into my head in half an hour.'

MR. HALDANE : ' Nor can what the Church has insisted upon as being a mystery be taken in half an hour.'

LORD CHANCELLOR : ' Everybody who has taken that test is not supposed to have gone through a whole course of Greek philosophy; the words themselves are very plain.'

The case is over, and has passed into history. It left on me the impression that Dr. Rainy was a very remarkable man, who if he had chosen the field of politics would probably have been regarded as a great leader.

All this was in the summer of 1904. Twenty years later I was to have much to do with the development which arose from the case in Scotland and subsequently in Parliament.

I was so often engaged in these days at the Bar
of the House of Lords that I had frequent occasion
to search for authorities in the library of the House.
There I found a friend, whom I had indeed known
for some years, but whose friendship was from this
time onwards to ripen into a very intimate one.
The Librarian in those days was Mr. (afterwards
Sir) Edmund Gosse. A born man of letters, he
attracted to him those who cared for books as he
did, and he had long since made a great impression
on the public as an author. I saw him constantly.
I went often to his house and he came often to
mine. The intimacy did not diminish when his
time as Librarian was over several years subsequently. I shall have occasion in later pages to
refer to one who had and continues to hold a high
place with me among my most valued intimates.

CHAPTER III

ENTRY INTO PUBLIC LIFE

(1880–1895)

I BEGAN to be active in politics about 1880, but this activity took five years to develop into full effect. It was after this that the foundation of the so-called Liberal Imperialist Party, with which I became closely connected, was really laid. Earlier than that time, in 1880, it had become evident that Mr. Gladstone was returning to his old position of power, and many of us young Liberals threw our energies on his side. One of the most prominent among us then was Albert Grey, afterwards Earl Grey. He was a man of enthusiasm and charm, somewhat vague in his political ideas, but a genuine believer in progress, and particularly in the future of the Empire. He got some of us younger Liberals together in what was then called Albert Grey's Committee. But divergences of opinion about the ideals of Liberalism after a time arose, and we founded, independently of him, the 'Eighty' Club, as it was named, after the year of Mr. Gladstone's triumph.

The Albert Grey Committee then split up, and it may be worth while to refer to the emergence of the 'Eighty' Club, for this became and remained a very active organisation. The Albert Grey Com-

and we assembled from time to time in the houses of prominent members of the Liberal Party of those days, such as Lord Northbrook, who had been Viceroy of India. Albert Grey was at first our leader. By degrees, however, he became regarded by us as erratic in his political outlook, and in 1880 the Committee had decayed in vitality and was practically defunct. I was, however, myself very keen about the work it was doing in keeping us together, and one wintry January day in that year I trudged on foot in deep snow from house to house of the prominent members of the old Committee, insisting that we should not abandon our effort. In the end we established in its place, but on a small scale, the ' Eighty ' Club. I was the first Honorary Secretary, and as we had no paid secretary there was a good deal to do. I lived in those days in Bruton Street, Berkeley Square, in the Berkeley Chambers, and that was at the beginning practically its headquarters. By degrees Mr. Bickersteth and Mr. Snagge, afterwards a County Court judge, associated themselves with me as honorary secretaries, and we used to organise meetings. Among other people with whom we had a good deal to do was the late Lord Dalhousie, then a Commoner and a very keen Liberal, who later on stood for Liverpool unsuccessfully. Slowly the Club took shape and grew, until at last it was necessary to take an office and appoint a paid secretary. Mr. J. A. B. Bruce was nominated to that position and held it for many years. I was an energetic member of the Club for a long time, and

RICHARD BURDON HALDANE IN HIS FORTIETH YEAR

was its Chairman during several years. I presided
at various dinners, and among them at the dinner
given later on to Mr. Parnell. He was one of my
two guests, the other being George Meredith.

The 'Eighty' Club gave another dinner subsequently at which Mr. Parnell was present. This
was at the time when the Report of the Commission
had acquitted him of being the author of the letters
forged by Pigott. I remember the incidents of
that dinner. It took place in Willis's rooms. It
was a dinner really given in honour of Lord Spencer,
and Lord Rosebery was in the Chair. But, although
this was the occasion, the great feature of the evening
was that Mr. Parnell had accepted an invitation to
come as the guest of Sir Charles Russell. Sir Charles
Russell asked me to sit next Mr. Parnell, and I
recall his conversation. He arrived half an hour
late, but the company stood in such awe of him that
it would not begin dinner until he came. He did
not take much notice of anybody, but informed me
during dinner that he was late because he had thought
Willis's rooms were in Oxford Street, which was near
his residence. I guessed that he meant the Euston
Hotel. I said to him that I was sure he would
be called on to speak, and that however much he
might dislike doing so, speaking would be difficult
to avoid. He replied that if so he supposed that
he ought to say something about Lord Spencer,
and he asked me to make sure that Spencer had
been twice Lord Lieutenant, and had been there
when the Irish Church Bill was passed. But when
he was called on with overwhelming enthusiasm, not

F

a word did he say, so far as my recollection guides me, about Lord Spencer. Nor did he even remotely refer to the deliverance in his favour of the Report of the Parnell Commission on the Pigott letters. This seemed to him as though it were an incident not worth alluding to, although the pronouncement of the forgery had only just been made. What he did say was that there were two ways, and two ways only, in which Ireland could be governed. One was by full Home Rule. The other was through a Dictator. But for such Dictatorship there was one man unfit, and he was Mr. Arthur Balfour. I was the more impressed by this because he had said to me only a few minutes before that he had been reading a most remarkable book, which threw more light on the Irish question than any book he had seen. I had eagerly asked what this new source of knowledge was, and he replied, ' It is a book called *The English in Ireland* by a Mr. Froude.'

Parnell was indeed as extraordinarily gifted as he was eccentric. He was no orator, and yet he was one of the most effective speakers in Parliament I have ever heard. One night in the House of Commons Sir George Trevelyan had tried in a speech to be civil to Chamberlain, from whom, although originally a Liberal Unionist, he had split at last, and Chamberlain had replied to him somewhat brutally. When Chamberlain sat down it was twelve minutes to midnight, when under the rules of those days the House adjourned. Parnell rose immediately after Chamberlain, and the expectant silence was such that it seemed as though one might have heard

pin drop. He paid no attention to Trevelyan, but
he made a speech in slow deliberate tones about
Chamberlain which made me feel as if he were
dropping vitriol down Chamberlain's neck. The
House was pained and yet overcome by the power
and incisiveness of Parnell's words. There was a
general sense of relief when twelve struck, the speech
was automatically interrupted, and the House melted
away.

It was several years before this that to me personally something even more interesting had happened.
I met Herbert Henry Asquith, with whom I was afterwards to be so closely associated, about 1882 for the
first time. He was a young barrister like myself, but
about four years older. We sat by each other at
dinner at Lincoln's Inn, and after that a great friendship arose between us. I had been ill, and I went to
stay at his house in Hampstead to recover strength,
and then and afterwards I saw him and his first
wife constantly. He and I used to dine together
once or twice a week, and we saw each other almost
every day. We had both a passion for law, and
liked to discuss the few cases each of us had. He
was a very fine lawyer of the Common Law type,
while I was Equity trained. We used to go abroad
together at Easter. We went on one occasion to
Paris, our companion so far being Alfred, afterwards Lord, Milner. Asquith and I then proceeded
alone to Monte Carlo, Pisa, and Florence. On
another occasion we two made a tour in Ireland,
where he produced a great impression by the searching way in which he cross-questioned the Nationalists

about matters of fact. In 1885 I came into Parliament, and in 1886 I was able to arrange that he should follow as Member for East Fife. Our friendship continued, and subsequently I was his best man on the occasion of his second marriage, in 1894 I think, at St. George's, Hanover Square.

When Asquith and I were in the House of Commons, although young members, we knew a great many people, and we used to give a dinner annually of a special character. We chose a public house in Cork Street called 'The Blue Posts,' and there each year we used to entertain eight guests—four were distinguished men of letters or artists, and four were always distinguished politicians. I remember that at one of these dinners we had Burne-Jones, Lord Dufferin, Alfred Lyall, Russell Lowell; and, among the politicians, Randolph Churchill, Chamberlain, and Rosebery. I recall a slight scene on that occasion between these last three. I was sitting at the end of the table between Rosebery and Randolph Churchill who were interchanging rapid and brilliant words. Chamberlain, a powerful personality but not so quick at that kind of thing, endeavoured to join in, but without much success. Finally, on his making some rather belated remark, Randolph Churchill beckoned the waiter and said, ' Waiter, put a flower pot there,' indicating a spot between himself and Chamberlain. But the incident passed without an explosion. These dinners at ' The Blue Posts ' went on for several years, and we only gave them up just before the Liberal Government came in in 1892.

To Asquith I will return, but here it seems appro

priate to interrupt the political narrative in order to indicate the kind of ideals that were from an early stage influencing my public action. Indeed, one reason why I never became a really well-equipped politician was because of the dominance over me of these ideals. One of them was based on the mould-ing influence on education of the German literature of the beginning of the nineteenth century.

The personality of Goethe had begun to draw me closely to the study of his creed about life. I had an intimate friend, very different in his ways from myself and my political intimates, who was equally fascinated by the figure of Goethe. P. Hume Brown, afterwards Professor of History in the University of Edinburgh, had become a very close friend at Cloan. Originally he came to us in the autumns as tutor to the younger children. But we all grew so fond of him that afterwards, when he had given up such work and had become a Professor at the University of Edinburgh, he used to visit us constantly and to spend the autumns with us as one of ourselves. This lasted until his death in 1918. He was a born student of literature as well as of history, and he did much to develop among us at Cloan a taste for both. I was very intimate with him, just as the rest of us were, and as time went on we began to spend each Easter recess in Germany, to enable ourselves to assemble materials for a book he felt ought to be written about Goethe, a book which he was then projecting. It was published some years later on as his *Life of Goethe*. He died before he had time wholly to complete it, and by his desire it fell to me and to my sister to finish and publish the two volumes. I wrote the account in the book of the second part of *Faust*. Hume Brown's was a very interesting personality, concentrated and refined rather than powerful. His spirit and devotion were those of the finished scholar.

He and I began our systematic journeys abroad later on, in about 1898. We used at first to make our headquarters at Weimar. Afterwards we chose Ilmenau as our centre for inquiry. But we visited Jena, Eisenach, Wetzlar, and Göttingen for the purposes of our search for materials. I have always regretted that Hume Brown's reticent disposition prevented him from using the notes we made about places in which Goethe delighted but of which there is little record even in the voluminous Lives of him which have been written. There was, for instance, Schloss Dornburg on the Saale, a place described at page 646 of Hume Brown's book, where Goethe used to take Frau von Stein and her children to stay. We found there a very old custodian, not indeed old enough to have known Goethe, but who had learned from his father, who had been custodian before him, in Goethe's time, something of the way in which Goethe lived when there. He remained, so our informant told us, shut up daily with his work in his room, and was not accessible until four in the afternoon excepting to Frau von Stein, who went in and out as she pleased to talk to the great man. The latter used to come into the garden in the afternoon and to cut out profiles in black paper of her and the children. Examples of these, some of which had been preserved, the old custodian showed us. Then at Ilmenau there was not only the Kickelhahn, which Goethe, when at Ilmenau, used to ascend regularly, but the old seat by the summer-house on the top, on which he sat while composing the famous lyric, transcribed by him in pencil on its wall, ' Ueber allen Gipfeln ist Ruh.' I have sat with my companion scores of times on that old seat, and with him have watched the summits fading in the oncoming evening as the poem describes them. We tracked out, too, the walks Goethe took with the Grand Duke, and rested by the favourite waterfall described in his poems.

Weimar itself, although now modernised, remained the same so far as the park which Goethe laid out and the banks of the Ilm were concerned. The old librarian of the Schloss showed us the small room which Goethe selected for his work in preference to the larger one. Why ? ' Because,' said the old man, ' from its window he could look at the windows of the Frau von Stein.'

I have referred to these expeditions because they had much effect on Hume Brown and myself. Me it turned more and more to the study of what is best in the literary story of modern Germany, and especially to what was unique work in the world of that time, the organisation of higher education. With this subject, as will be seen later on, I was to have a good deal to do over here, and I learned much by reading about the work of Humboldt and Stein and other founders of the German system of education.

As telling what these expeditions meant to us both, I quote here a letter which Hume Brown wrote to me on our return to work from one of the typical fortnights at Ilmenau. 'Before taking up my burden I must write a line to say how greatly I have enjoyed this our last visit to cherished Ilmenau. It seems as if each successive visit were pleasanter than the last. I cannot but feel that it is to you that I owe this annual refreshment for mind and body, for though Ilmenau has many attractions, it is seeing it with you that makes it what it is in my memory and imagination. I never have such talks as we have at the Tanne (the Inn) and in the glades of the Thüringer Wald, and it is to these I look forward rather than to the beauties of the Kickelhahn. What I feel is that these our annual pilgrimages have given a zest to these last years which nothing else has given. To-day I feel somewhat indisposed to take up my wonted tasks, but I pull myself together when I remember that Ilmenau is in vain if it does not enable me to go more briskly through the rest of the year. Still it is not in human nature not to feel the contrast *here* and *there*.'

In none of these German expeditions did my political associates of these days interest themselves particularly, though they were not averse to my adding to the variety of our ideas by making them myself. The House of Commons from 1885 to 1892, as known to Asquith and myself, was of the old-fashioned sort and did not care much about education, especially of Continental types.

Professor Hume Brown and I continued our annual visits steadily, even during the time that I was War Minister. We travelled incognito and lived very simply, and the Germans did not try to interfere with us. But I remember that on the last occasion when we were at Göttingen I had given the name at the hotel of ' Mr. Brown ' to avoid attention, as by that time I was well known in Germany. However, within twenty-four hours from our arrival ' Mr. Brown ' cigars were being sold throughout the town by an enterprising tobacconist, and a box was sent to us with this title inscribed. Probably they thought afterwards that we came to look at their defences !

Philosophy had passed out of fashion, in Berlin at any rate, and indeed throughout the most of Germany, in this period. When I went later on to make the formal visit to the Emperor in 1906 to which I shall refer subsequently, I had a State carriage at my disposal, and I told the coachman to drive me to the old churchyard of the Dorotheen Kirche, where Fichte, Solger, and Hegel lie buried together. I found the tombs sadly neglected, and indeed had great difficulty in finding any one who knew the way to them. When I returned to the Palace I told the Emperor and the Empress of my sadness at this, but the Emperor said that these names were no longer of importance for Germany. I observed to him that in the ' Helden Allee ' with its long row of statues which he had put up to the distinguished men at different periods in German history I missed some of the figures best known in

literature. ' I know,' he said. I went on to observe
that I would like to add at my own expense at least
two statues. ' I know,' he said, ' you want to put
in the statue of Körner, my great war poet.' But
I said it was not of Körner that I was thinking.

By this time I had come to see that what we needed
badly in our own country was more Universities, and
Universities of the civic type, in different parts of
these Islands. Turning to these matters, one of the
first of the new University movements on which I set
to work was that in Liverpool, where my public-
spirited friend, A. F. Warr, M.P. for one of the
divisions, now passed away, prepared the ground
for me. I addressed the men of business of the
city in a speech, which is printed at the beginning
of the little volume subsequently published under
the title of *Education and Empire*, warning them of
their peril from German rivalry if they continued
to neglect Science and Education. Liverpool presently made a splendid response. I also worked
hard in London and at Bristol, where the University
was ultimately founded of which I am now Chancellor. During this period the affairs of London
University were approaching a crisis, and in the end
I undertook the Chairmanship of the Royal Commission, which sat for four years and finally reported.
I managed to carry this on through the later period
of my tenure of the War Office and during the earlier
part of my Lord Chancellorship until the Report
was signed. That Commission was a very interesting
one. Among my colleagues were Lord Milner, Sir
Robert Morant, Sir William M'Cormick, my old

friend the ex-judge Sir Robert Romer, and Mrs. Creighton. We were unanimous in our recommendations. I have since been Chairman of the Royal Commission on the University of Wales, which after sitting for two years finally completed its work, and in the Report of its labours laid the foundations of the present University of Wales.

The Gifford Lectures at St. Andrews University, which I undertook about the same time, were difficult to prepare for under the intense pressure of work to which I was subjected in different forms in the years 1902-4. But I used to go on with the fruits of research made at odd times, and of the meditations in periods spent every autumn at Guisachan, the Highland home of my great friends, Lord and Lady Tweedmouth. There I occupied during the day, while the others were stalking and fishing, a ruined cottage, and composed elaborate notes for the Gifford Lectures. They were delivered extempore from the results of these notes and taken down in shorthand, and so fashioned into the two volumes which were published under the title, *The Pathway to Reality*.

I ought to say that my investigations in Germany had at an early stage impressed me unfavourably with the separation which had been made there between the Universities and the great Technical Colleges, and when subsequently, after studying the organisation of Charlottenburg on the spot with the aid of my friend, Geheimrat Witt, the Professor of Chemistry there and Head of the School, I set to work in London, along with Mr. Sidney Webb and

Sir Francis Mowatt, to found the new Imperial
College of Science and Technology, I decided to press
for the application of a different principle. The new
College was to be fashioned so as to be brought as
quickly as possible into a reconstructed University
of London. I presided over the Departmental Committee which prepared the Charter, or rather presided
over it during the second and final year of the inquiry
During the first year the duty was carried out by
Sir Francis Mowatt, whose health compelled him to
resign the task before it was complete. I hoped
that in the end any semblance of separation which
still existed might be got over, for I was convinced
that it is only in the larger atmosphere of a University
that technical education of the finest kind can be
attained.

To return to politics. I had not been many
weeks in the House of Commons in 1886 before
Mr. Gladstone was defeated over Home Rule and
we went into Opposition. It was not long before
Asquith, who was now elected and had brought a
great reputation with him from Oxford, made a
remarkable maiden speech. After that half a dozen
of us younger Liberal M.P.'s began to draw together
under his leadership. Mr. Gladstone was magnificent
over Home Rule. But he was not, old as he had
become, really interested in the new ideas of social
reform which were beginning to stir us younger ones
Nor did any of the other Liberal leaders excepting
Morley understand why we were discontented. The
result was, as I have said, the formation of a small
group. I had begun in 1886 a friendship that was

to become a very intimate one with Sir Edward Grey. A. H. D. Acland, who became a real reformer in elementary and secondary education and to whom I was attracted on this account, was another of our members. Mr. Gladstone never cared for him much because, having once been a clergyman, he had renounced his clerical orders so as the better to be able to enter public life effectively. But, partly I think in response to the strong appeals some of us made to him, Mr. Gladstone, when he next came in in 1892, made Acland Minister of Education, a position in which he did splendid work. Sydney Buxton was also among the adherents of the new group. He had a seat for a London constituency, Poplar, and was naturally keenly interested in urban social questions.

Of this group I was in some ways the most active member in arranging the programme. I was intimate even then with members of the Fabian Society and used to study stimulating ideas with Sidney Webb, Bernard Shaw, and other Socialists. But I was not less attracted by a subject which did not appeal much to them—the Constitution of the Empire. I was opposed to the rigid bonds of Imperial Federation and Imperial Preference. I believed that if we only gave the free rein to the Colonies they would rally to the Empire. If the principles laid down and established in the Report of the Imperial Conference of 1926 had been put forward then, I think that they would have made some of us thoroughly content. For I had already begun to see a good deal of the Colonial statesmen and jurists who

brought large questions to the Judicial Committee
of the Privy Council. The outlook of the Liberalism
of our group extended to all that the ideals of general
Liberalism reached to. But it extended further, for
it sought to appeal beyond the shores of these Islands.
We were strong Home Rulers because we held that
it was only by giving Ireland freedom to govern
herself that we could hope to satisfy her. But we
felt not less the necessity of studying how the sense
of liberty might be made to reach Canada, Austral-
asia, and even India.

These reflections brought Asquith, Grey, and myself
especially into contact with the Irish politicians and
Morley, who was the guardian of these interests,
on the one hand, and with Rosebery on the other.
It will be convenient at this stage to look at these
two distinguished men as they presented themselves to the gaze of our group from 1887 onwards.
It is the less difficult for me to do this because I
was the member of the group who was probably
seeing most of them.

Morley was then as afterwards a complicated and
very interesting personality. I first came into contact with him through a letter which I wrote to the
Times in criticism of Chamberlain in 1886. The
latter had proposed, somewhat rashly, to offer to
Ireland a Constitution resembling that of a Canadian
Province. I had an easy task in demonstrating
that such a Constitution could not satisfy Irish
aspirations. The powers that alone fell within it
under the terms of the Act of 1867 which established
the Constitution of Canada were limited and specific

powers which a Provincial legislature could not
seek to go beyond without infringing the principle
of *ultra vires*. There was little in the proposal
which could appeal to the sense that was at the
root of the Irish demand, the sense of nationality.
I think that my letter helped to prevent the idea
from being persisted in, for it was known that I
was familiar with the interpretation which had been
put, by a series of judicial decisions of the Privy
Council, on the Imperial Statute of 1867 which had
set up the Provinces. Anyhow, the letter to the
Times brought me a letter of warm congratulation
from Morley. He asked me to come to his house,
and the incident started a friendship that became
intimate, and that lasted, through occasional divergences, until his death. I have in my repositories
many letters from him dealing with every kind of
political question.

Morley was a Radical, but he was a Radical politician with a highly critical spirit. There was a
good deal of the Conservative element in him. He
was devoted to Mr. Gladstone, whom I think he
influenced much over Home Rule. His Life of his
leader shows how intimately Morley had entered
into the understanding of his nature, not on one side,
but on all its sides, including that of religion. The
book is a book to study, not merely on grounds of
personal and historical interest, but as the picture
of a very great if one-sided individuality, a picture
which is the work of a great literary artist. Probably, from the point of view of quality, Morley
would have done best for himself if he had devoted

his life to literature instead of to politics. But
that was not his wish. He was not ambitious in
any commonplace sense, but I think that he was in
reality very ambitious. I have always believed that
his real desire was to be Prime Minister. But for
such a position he was wholly unsuited by his nature,
physical as well as mental. I am not sure that he
did not know this. He had courage in drawing
conclusions, but he had not much physical courage.
I have seen him shrink from an encounter with a
strong personality when he need not. As a speaker,
when he had time to prepare closely and polish his
phrases, he was very effective. His speeches on the
platform were among the best of the time. But
for the House of Commons he was lacking in individual force. He was not good at the lightning-
like decisions which debate there often requires.
Nor was he a great man of business or a born administrator. He was prone, in these regions, to pay
undue attention to the conventional view, and as
a result to misjudge. Consequently, although when
he came to be the head of a great administrative
department he was always a distinguished personality
with views that were original, he did not judge men
well enough to be a Chief of the most effective
order.

But notwithstanding these defects he was a most
interesting figure, with a wide outlook, and we
young Liberals looked up to him with deep respect.
Had he been less under the dominion of views which
he had derived from those with whom he had worked
in older days, he might have shown us the way

out of difficulties into which the Liberalism of the 1886 Opposition was tending even then to fall. As it was, he was a wise, if not always a courageous, critic, and we turned to him for counsel gladly.

Morley was determined to be a political figure of a high order, and could not be diverted from this purpose. Joseph Chamberlain told me that he himself had urged him to elect for literature and to remain detached from public life, but in vain. Later on, when in 1905 Campbell-Bannerman formed his Government, I think that Morley desired to be his Chancellor of the Exchequer, with the second place in the Cabinet and the House. But Campbell-Bannerman, who was pretty shrewd and was under few illusions about his friends, saw that this would not do, and gave the place to Asquith. Although Morley had been a stimulating Irish Secretary he was not by nature a man of affairs. On the other hand, he was admirable in conversation, even if hardly what is called a really brilliant talker.

He came under the dominion of a much more powerful personality, that of Mr. Gladstone, and in some respects this was damaging to his originality. Nevertheless it helped him to write, not one but two brilliant books. His *Life of Cromwell* is only second in the fruits of his study of great statesmen to his *Life of Gladstone*. Much the same may be said of his *Walpole*.

Morley had in him, as I have already observed, a strong vein of Conservatism. He admired men of action like Disraeli and Bismarck. He had few illusions. I do not think that he was ever a Believer

G

with a big ' B,' but he was always inspiring. His rich store of reading and of results of reflection was always productive of freshness in conversation. I think that this quality had to do with the very real intimacy between him and Lord Rosebery.

At one time he was very great friends with Meredith. Later on they had differences which estranged them for some years. But they got over this divergence, and in the end of Meredith's life they came again to see a good deal of each other. It was an intimacy rooted in early life. Meredith used to write to me in his later years to come down to Boxhill to dine with him, and to bring any one I liked—' But don't bring Morley, for he and I have evenings together which we must have alone, because we have a past, which is outside the time of you young men ! '

Anyhow I saw Morley very regularly, more often probably than any other of those with whom he was then in political contact. As age began to tell on him he gave up his house in Elm Park Gardens and moved on to Southfields, near Wimbledon. There I used to go to him and spend Sunday afternoon and dine in the evenings. The talk always ranged over literature as well as public affairs. Sometime I brought down to him people he did not come across, such as the Sidney Webbs. He was always interested and sometimes very critical.

Looking back on Morley, I think his was the most interesting personality I ever knew. That I always suited him I do not believe. But that was my fault and not his. His range was so wide that he always saw beyond what one was saying to him

On the other hand, to see where he fell short as a judge of men you have only to turn to the two volumes of his *Recollections*. There you find how he wished to rule and how he had not it in him to rule, at least to the extent he desired. I doubt whether his permanent officials found him very agreeable to deal with. On the other hand, a great business man like Lord Inchcape, who had sat on his Council, and whom he esteemed highly, but not more highly than Lord Inchcape esteemed him, made a deep impression on him. It was the man of affairs, the soldier, the diplomatist, or the ruler, who moved Morley most. I remember on one occasion at his request asking Field-Marshal Lord Nicholson, the Chief of the Imperial General Staff and a fine exponent of his own views, to lunch alone with us two. The Field-Marshal, who was a most vigorous person and had served for long in India, summed up his view of India to Morley by saying, It is only with the sword that India can be governed.' Morley had become impressed and did not even murmur dissent. I myself had lived too much with soldiers to take their political views very seriously. But Morley for the moment yielded. Later, of course, he saw round and over the opinion of the Chief of the Staff.

My correspondence with Morley lasted from 1886 to the end of his life. In the last six months of his life I saw less of him, and I think that this was partly due to the feeling that he had no longer the energy to contend and controvert, and found to be easiest those who accepted what he said for gospel.

But we remained on affectionate terms to the last.

The other personality looked up to by our group in these days and afterwards was that of Lord Rosebery. His was a very different nature from that of Morley. He was one of the most formidable and impressive men in England, with a power of personal dominance which the other did not possess. His influence on Asquith, Grey, and myself was not the less great because he seemed to appreciate fully that Liberalism must, if it were to have a future, be lifted out of the rut into which it was tending to fall. The future programme could not be fashioned by the officials of the National Liberal Federation, but only by a statesman with an outlook which was fresh and appreciative of this country as the centre of an Empire. We saw much of him and began to be constantly at his houses in town and in the country. He was genuinely interested in our effort.

But I do not think that in its essence it ever fully appealed to him. What moved us greatly was the social problem. With this he had had little to do excepting in an interval when he was Chairman of the London County Council. Education and the land question signified much less to him than they did to us. Consequently, although we saw him much and found in him a pillar of political strength, he was not really as helpful in consultations over these subjects as was Morley. We had to plough our furrow mainly by ourselves. But such was his position and power that even so the prestige of his name and leadership was a great asset to us.

The little group worked steadily away on its own lines in the House of Commons, as the Hansard of the time shows. Asquith's splendid gift of speech recommended him to Sir William Harcourt and the other official leaders. Moreover, he had fewer views of his own than most of us. But his judgment was wise and his gifts in debate made him popular with the older men. Distinctly he would have office before very long.

Grey they found more difficult. He had a most attractive personality and embodied the best tradition of the Whigs. But he was advanced in his views and of a very independent mind. The Whips could not count on him as they could on Asquith. With Grey and his wife I was in constant and intimate communication. We were much together and were of the same views on most subjects. I used to go to Fallodon frequently, and they, like Asquith, used to come to Cloan. They were not learned people, but they cared for books, and this taste they combined with a passion for country life. About Parliament they were not really keen. They were a very attractive couple, and although they did not like going into Society they attracted much notice. All of us spoke frequently in our constituencies and elsewhere.

I myself was not so popular with the leaders or the Whips. I was not only independent but I was rather impulsive, and had the reputation of persuading my friends to take courses which they might not have taken apart from me. I was looked on by the official group as an intriguer. I was not a first-rate speaker moreover. But I had energy and some knowledge and imagination about the political future, and I was always launching new ideas. Indeed we three in the group worked admirably together. For instance, when the Liberal Front Opposition Bench somewhat hastily took up leasehold enfranchisement in a form which would have led to the creation of a multitude of small freeholders under no adequate public control, we opposed the Bill, and succeeded in defeating it. Sidney Webb, who, though outside Parliament, had been earnestly on our side in this, wrote me a letter of affectionate enthusiasm over this effort of the group. But when we brought in our alternative Bill, which sought to empower urban authorities to purchase compulsorily land within their areas, and to exclude after a future date any element of price due to unearned increment in value caused by congestion of population, we did not succeed. The Conservatives who had helped us over the other Bill would have nothing to do with this one, and the old Liberals denounced it as Socialism.

But we did other things. We introduced into the House of Commons new ideas about payment of members, free education, and free trade. And I myself wrote and published in 1887 a *Life of Adam Smith* in which the Free Trade doctrine was restated in a form qualified by recognition of the necessity of paying attention to considerations of defence.

Grey used to express himself in public admirably, and he had a first-rate judgment with the caution characteristic of an older man. He was less formidable in his speeches than Asquith, and he was lacking in the range of knowledge that came to the latter from an intellectual curiosity that was absent in Grey. But Grey was even then a first-rate statesman. To his Whig instincts he added democratic views, and he had no prejudices, class or otherwise. What he did love too well for his political work was the attractions of country life. Anyhow he and I were very intimate, and I helped to keep Asquith in close contact with him. Arthur Acland was also a stimulating personality, full of knowledge, particularly about primary and secondary education.

Asquith lived in these days at Hampstead with his first wife and their children. Hers was a beautiful and simple spirit. Among my letters is one which he wrote to me on her death, a letter which shows how fully he was aware of the fineness of her quality. London Society came, however, to have a great attraction for him, and he grew by degrees diverted from the sterner outlook on life which he and I for long shared. We were both rising at the Bar. But to Asquith a career in the Law, however great it might be made, at no time presented any attraction. From the beginning he meant to be Prime Minister, sooner or later. For this position nature had endowed him to a great extent, but not completely. He had as fine an intellectual apparatus, in the way of grasp and understanding, as I ever saw in any man. In his earlier political days he was a very serious person. I remember once passing along the Horse Guards with him. He touched my arm and pointed to the figure of John Bright walking in front of us. ' There,' he said, ' is the only man in public life who has risen to eminence without being corrupted by London Society.'

It was in 1885 that, as I have already said, I fought East Lothian and got into the House of Commons. I had taken the risk, a considerable one for a barrister without private fortune, of entering Parliament while still a Junior at the Bar. Next year Asquith followed my example. I introduced him to the adjacent constituency of East Fife, where he won a victory and had a secure seat for many years. He had not been long in the House of Commons before his great Oxford reputation and a brilliant maiden speech turned towards him the attention of the public as well as the Liberal leaders in the House. His diction was even then faultless, and his voice was a powerful one. He rarely made a bad point, and it was a surprise to nobody when, on returning to office in 1892, Mr. Gladstone made him Home Secretary. He was one of the best Home Secretaries of recent years. He was just, he was thorough, and he was interested in the new bearing which science was beginning to have on industrial life. The miners and the factory hands began to realise that with the Liberal Government a watchful eye was surveying the whole field of their lives. While still at the Bar he had distinguished himself before the Parnell Commission by an admirably analytic cross-examination of the business manager of the *Times*. He was the Junior of Sir Charles Russell in the conduct of the Nationalist case before the Commission.

About 1888 the little group of young members began to expand. Dinners were held, sometimes at the National Liberal Club and sometimes at the Savoy Restaurant, to which politicians outside the group were invited. Rosebery and Morley were frequently present at these dinners, which included those who had been invited to join what we called the 'Articles Club.' Among them were men like Frank Lockwood, who afterwards became Solicitor-General. In the House of Commons Mr. Gladstone was the figure to which we continued to look up. But the daily work of leadership was in the hands of Sir William Harcourt. He was a great Parliamentarian, though hardly a great statesman. He had ideas, but they were not of a far-reaching order. Still, he was a powerful figure in the House.

The Parnell divorce case and the inquiry into the Pigott letters now began to absorb public attention. On the question of the letters Parnell won conclusively. But the divorce was a very serious matter. The Nonconformists, who were a power in the National Liberal Federation, resolved to have nothing to do with him, and a split over Home Rule became inevitable, Mr. Gladstone's tremendous exertions notwithstanding. As the official Liberal Party of the time had no other great cause with which it could move public opinion, the prospects of defeating the Unionists at the coming General Election became overclouded, notwithstanding that the Liberal Party had so long been excluded from office. We remained of course strong Home Rulers. Nothing that had happened could shake the foundations on which our convictions rested. But Home Rule was no longer a clear issue after the Irish Party had become divided over its leadership, nor had Parnell himself done much to make things easier for us. Our group had much to say on topics in addition to that of Ireland, but it had not yet won a position from which it could command public confidence.

We fought on in this fashion until the General Election came in 1892. Rosebery, while a Home Ruler, was not wholly an enthusiast about the cause. He was more taken up with Foreign Affairs, over which he was the main authority on the Liberal side. But he fought along with us in his own way against the Unionist Government. At last the election came. The Liberal Opposition had been out of office for six years, and but for the split over Parnell would probably have come into power with a considerable majority. But as, apart from Ireland, it had no programme which struck the public imagination, it did not get an independent majority at the election. It came back with a majority indeed, but this was small and made up only by counting in the Irish members. Parnell was now dead, and the Irish Party were not easy to deal with. Only one thing was evident, having regard not only to our convictions but to the composition of our majority. It was that we must introduce a Home Rule Bill. About this Mr. Gladstone was clear, and it was to do this that he accepted office. The elections had been rather disastrous. Notwithstanding the natural swing in favour of an alternative Government drawn from the party that had been so long out of office, Mr. Gladstone's own colossal majority in Midlothian shrank to a small figure. My own majority in the adjacent county of East Lothian likewise fell down to very little. It was plain that we were a paralysed party with little prospect.

Still there was much work that we could do. Harcourt was now Chancellor of the Exchequer. Asquith was made Home Secretary, and Grey became Under-Secretary for Foreign Affairs, with Rosebery as his Chief. Acland went to the Board of Education. I remained outside. I did not want to take office, for I had, in 1890, taken silk and had an uncertain future before me at the Bar. But I resolved to work hard in the interests of the new Government and so to gain experience. The new Home Rule Bill was in some respects different from that of 1886. When it got into Committee there was raised by the Opposition a multitude of points on its clauses. My training in the learning of the Canadian Constitution gave me an almost unique opportunity in the House of expounding and defending the Bill, and of this opportunity I made, as a reference to Hansard shows, full use, with the general assent and good will of the Commons.

A little later Harcourt introduced a Bill for the establishment of death duties in an extended form. He put me on the Committee to which the preparation of the Bill was entrusted. I knew the subject, and learned still more in the course of the work, and I took a good deal of part in the discussions of its clauses in the House of Commons, besides spending much time with the Treasury Officials who were engaged in shaping them. This made my work at the Bar very difficult, for it took up my time and

I lost ground for a period in the Courts. But I had got the reputation of knowing the Death Duties Act well, and after it had been passed into law, a process over which Harcourt showed much skill, I began to be employed extensively by the public in answering the conundrums which arose under it, and in arguing cases about its provisions.

The Liberal Government held out for three years. In the end the Home Rule Bill and others of our Bills were thrown out in the House of Lords. Our majority in the Commons dwindled and the inevitable moment arrived when we were defeated in the Commons over a vote about the supply of cordite for the Army. Mr. Gladstone had retired and had been succeeded by Lord Rosebery as Prime Minister. But the relations between the members of the new Cabinet were not happy. Harcourt thought that he ought to have been sent for, and, although Morley was on the side of us younger Liberals in preferring Rosebery, there was a substantial section of Liberal opinion which held that Harcourt had the better title.

I saw Rosebery constantly while he was at the head of affairs. He often sent for me to Downing Street to see what suggestions I could make to him. I believe that through these days I knew as much of his mind as any of his colleagues. He proposed to me, when the office became vacant, that I should be put forward as the nominee of the Liberal Party for the Speakership of the House of Commons. But I considered that I had neither the voice nor other requisite gifts for the work. Asquith agreed with me in thinking that there was quite different work for me to do in the future, and that it was wisest not to avail myself of this chance but to work on in the way I was doing.

This brings me towards the end of a period. I had much strengthened my position in my own constituency by the work I was known to have done, and by my independent views, and when the election came, notwithstanding the set-back of Liberalism throughout the country, I was returned by an increased majority as Member for East Lothian.

Before closing what I write about this time there are one or two minor incidents which I may record. I entered the House of Commons in the end of 1885. Mr. Gladstone was our undisputed Chief. His personality and his genius for certain phases of public administration put him into a different class from anybody else. Of course I never knew him well. But I heard many of his speeches and was his enthusiastic supporter in his Irish Policy, destined to grow into something much bigger and to be carried into effect by some of the very Conservatives who were opposing him then. I saw a little of him personally. He was a man of extraordinary courtesy as well as of individuality. I may add one or two personal reminiscences. I went, as quite a young Scottish member, to dine with Mr. and Mrs. Gladstone at Dollis Hill, which Lord Aberdeen had lent to him. There was among other new Scottish members Mr. M'Ewan, a remarkable man and a great brewer in Edinburgh. After dinner, we young and reverent people were astonished to see Mr.

M'Ewan, who was standing in a corner of the room with Mr. Gladstone, put his arms round Mr. Gladstone's head. We thought this an unusual act of reverence on the part of Mr. M'Ewan. As we walked to the station we asked him what he had been doing, and he told us that he had said to Mr. Gladstone that he (Mr. Gladstone) had improved very much in personal appearance, and looked a much greater man than when he (M'Ewan) had first listened to him in Leith Walk, Edinburgh, in the year 1846. Mr. Gladstone replied, ' Yes, I have developed physically in a curious way. My head is now so much bigger that the hat which I took with me to Balmoral on my first visit there, and which I still have, will not now go on my head.' ' I observed,' said Mr. M'Ewan, ' that that was very remarkable.' ' Yes,' said Mr. Gladstone, ' and if you like you may feel my bumps.' M'Ewan, who was a pawky person, accepted the invitation and extended his arms round Mr. Gladstone's head. ' What did you say to him ? ' we asked. ' I said,' replied M'Ewan : ' " Mr. Gladstone, sir, if the bumps on your head had developed as much on both sides as they have on one, you would be a very remarkable man indeed ! " '

A second incident which I remember was at a dinner which was given in 1887 by Lady Rendel in Carlton Gardens while her husband was away. Mr. Gladstone was staying there, and she got up a little dinner for him of eight persons, to which I, a young member, was invited. She started, not very wisely, a game of six-handed chess. Mr. Gladstone did not wish to play chess, and sat by himself in an inner drawing-room. I was also left out and sat opposite him, looking reverently at my great Chief, who was on a sofa with his eyes closed. After a little he opened them, fixed them on mine and beckoned me to come across the room to him. I came with due humility and sat myself by his side. 'Have you observed,' he asked me, 'anything in the House of Commons which you have entered now for the first time that disappoints you?' I replied that I was struck with a greater absence than I expected of that tradition which had made the House of Commons so famous in the world—the tradition of Parliamentary manners. 'And do you,' he asked, 'put that down to any cause?' I then, I am afraid, played up, and I replied, 'Well, sir, it is hardly for me to say, but after reading the accounts of Mr. Disraeli's treatment of Sir Robert Peel in the 'forties, and observing the tone of the violent speeches he made, I cannot but think that deterioration set in about that time.' 'I would not myself have said it,' replied Mr. Gladstone, 'but that is not because I do not agree with you. I think you are right. But in justice to that remarkable man let me say to you that no one who has not had to lead the House of Commons against him can realise how tremendous a figure he was and how extraordinary were his Parliamentary gifts.'

Mr. Gladstone was not always quite consistent in his policy. In the autumn session of 1888 he had apparently thrown over the plan he had put forward in 1886 for buying out the Irish landlords. He decided to oppose the Unionist Government's proposal to extend the Ashbourne Acts for this purpose. Grey and I were strongly convinced that this was a mistake, and we voted against Mr. Gladstone's motion. I felt that we ought to resign, and I wrote to Mr. Gladstone expressing our sense on the subject. But he replied as follows :—

DEAR MR. HALDANE,—Let me thank you and with your Sir E. Grey for your kind note. Incidents of this kind do not in any way shock or shake me. I have comfort in referring them very much to the nature of the Liberal Party, and the laws under which it exists, laws on the whole so healthful and beneficial and free. I am much pleased to know there is no alteration as to confidence on your part, and I can assure you there is none on mine. Believe me, Very faithfully yours,

W. E. GLADSTONE.

Nov. 21.88.

Law but not politics I had learned at the feet of Davey, who despite his deficiencies in the House of Commons was a consummate advocate. I remember à propos of his politics that Mr. Gladstone wished him to make a great speech against the Irish Crimes Bill in the House of Commons. Mr. Gladstone thought the speech would be important, and that Davey was so great a lawyer that it would be decisive. Davey put aside all his work, and applied himself with the greatest excitement to his speech. I was doubtful of the choice, but I could not get down in time to hear the speech. I went, however, to the House of Commons late that afternoon and met Morley. 'How did Davey's speech go off?' 'Go off,' replied Morley; 'it went off exactly like a magnum of soda water that has stood for two days with the cork out.'

Among my intimate friends in these early days were Mr. and Mrs. Sidney Webb, two most remarkable people. She was the daughter of a rich man, who had been Chairman of the Great Western Railway and lived near Stroud. He was in the Colonial Office, and through unremitting energy and acuteness had become one of the leaders of the Fabian Society. The two attracted each other, but Sidney Webb was so determined a Socialist that it was plain that if an engagement were announced her father might object. They were secretly engaged, but it was known only to one or two. By their desire I went more than once to stay at her father's house. He was then an invalid, bedridden and dying. I went, and by arrangement asked that my friend, Mr. Sidney Webb, who happened to be lecturing near there on the Saturday night, at Stroud, might also come for the week-end. The governess, who was in charge, thought this was all right, because she put me down as the fortunate young man. She was old, and when she found us in the schoolroom late at night she thought it was all as it should be, and retired, leaving us to put out the lights. I then said, ' I must have a walk on the common alone, otherwise I shall not be able to sleep, and I can't be away for less than an hour.' This I did, and came back, and found the happy couple had had a conversation which they could not otherwise have had. Soon after that Mr. Potter, her father, died, and they were married and have done together very remarkable work. It is the custom to

H

criticise it as abstract, and no doubt it is so. But none
the less they have written a remarkable succession
of books on economic history, which has made them
rank among the most prominent people of the Labour
movement throughout the world. I never belonged
to the Fabian Society, but was always very much in
contact with Sidney Webb, and I brought some of
his ideas into the consultations which Asquith and
Grey and I used to hold about the future of Liberalism. If these ideas had been more studied in the
days of Campbell-Bannerman and before that, the
fading away of the Liberal Party might, I think, have
been averted, and a party still more progressive in
spirit might have grown up, not of extreme views,
but as a body of thinkers among whom Labour and
Liberalism might have come to dwell under a common
roof, a roof sheltering them as the real and united
alternative to the Conservative Party. I still keep
up the most warm friendship with the Sidney Webbs.

I shall conclude this chapter by quoting from a
letter in which I wrote in 1894 to a friend some words
which define what was my attitude towards public
affairs, both during this period and, I think, through
my subsequent political life. ' Do you remember me
once saying to you that I had a strain of insanity in
me and your replying " Yes, but you ought not to
tell it to any one." It is the best strain in me really
that insanity. The struggle over what was good and
decent in the Liberal revolt brought out and has
lifted me away from much that had become or was
becoming familiar. I will tell you in a few words
what I mean. Some one sent me a portrait of myself

in a Scotch newspaper on Saturday which I believe to be a partly true one, and I enclose it to you to save repetition. It represents, so far as political work is concerned, what I wish to do and be thought to do. Political success is not to be an admired Minister surrounded by a devoted group of adherents. It is to have a belief that is true and leads others to follow it. I do not propose to leave the Bar. I must live by it. Besides I like it, and have never before done my work there so efficiently as I am now doing it. But I cannot allow it to swallow me up. If I were to become like Lord Herschell or Lord Selborne I should look back on chances wasted of doing really good work in the world. Just at present I am exercising what I believe to be a useful influence in the direction indicated in the Scotch article. I mean to follow it out, going to meetings in the large centres of industrial life where I can do most. Later I shall try to exercise the influence so gained in office —not legal office, but one like the Local Government Board or the Scottish Office—if I can persuade them to appoint me. If they won't, the outside process must continue. That is the life which seems to me best, and it is no breach, so far as externals go, of the life I have been pursuing. I would rather be like Arthur Acland, with all his fanaticisms, than any one I know just now. This is, I think, a plain statement. As for the Sidney Webbs, whatever be their failings socially, they are splendid workers, and should be proud to feel that I had given up so much for a cause as they have. . . . I think that Lord Rosebery could not, with the existing friction, re-

construct his Cabinet just now. No doubt if there
had been no visions and some other qualities had
taken their place long since, things would have been
easier. But my visions are better, by their leave.
The most ridiculous weakness is to be afraid of
seeming ridiculous when you know you are in the
main right.'

CHAPTER IV

PERSONS AND PROBLEMS

(1895–1898)

COME now to further phases in my life. These periods cover the years which followed on the defeat of the Liberal Government in 1895. For me throughout them the absorbing political subject was higher education.

But it would be contrary to the plan on which I am telling the tale of my life to omit altogether matters which were private and personal, for these have at times had a moulding influence on one's outlook on life. It was so in my own case.

I will for the moment revert to the year 1890. I had fallen deeply in love with a remarkable girl of distinguished quality and of good position. The response to me on her side came slowly, but when it did come it seemed to have come very surely. We had many tastes in common and much the same outlook on life and affairs. We became engaged in March 1890, and there followed some weeks of unbroken happiness. Towards the end of April I had left her, in order to return to my duties, after a visit we made together in Devonshire. Suddenly, without previous warning, and as a bolt from an unclouded sky, there came to me in London a note saying that

all was over. She felt that she had misunderstood
herself, and her decision to break the engagement
must be taken as final. I could not realise what had
happened. Our friends urged on her that the original
decision, working out admirably as it appeared to
be doing, was right and this second and sudden
decision a mistake. Her family, who were intimate
friends of mine, and some of her friends asked whether
she was sure of her new declaration. The attempt
to shake her resolution proved to be useless. The
decision was as irrevocable as it was rapid, and she
would not go back by a hair's breadth on what she
had intimated to me in writing. Only once or twice
again in the course of my life did I see her, and then
only momentarily and casually. After five weeks
of uninterrupted happiness, happiness, to the best
of my judgment then and now, for her as well as for
me, all was changed and at an end.

My grief was overwhelming, for I had a strong
sense of the irrevocableness of the decision. The
shock upset me. I could find relief only in constant
work, and for long not much even in that. Sleep
when it came, was the only deliverance from black
depression. But there was no moment in which I
either blamed her or pitied myself. My feeling was
that somehow I had failed. I had read and thought
so much that I knew this might well have been so
notwithstanding that I was unconscious of it.

To this hour I treasure the memory of these five
happy weeks, and bless her name for the return she
made in them to my devotion to her, and for the
feeling inspired apparently in both of us. I came

to realise afterwards, when the pain was past, that my love for her, though it failed, had brought to me not loss but great gain. For it enlarged the meaning and content of life for me. All is now over. She died in 1897, but the memory of her is a precious possession.

In 1893 I gained a great friendship which helped to broaden my outlook. I came to see much of Sir John Horner, of Mells, in Somersetshire, and of his wife. He was one of the most perfect gentlemen I ever knew, and also a considerable scholar. He had studied under Freeman the historian, with whom he was intimate, and he was himself an accomplished student of history. His wife was one of the cleverest women I have seen, and as full of insight as she was clever. They moved a good deal in society, and she had been educated under the guidance of Ruskin, Rossetti, and Burne-Jones, all of whom were attracted to her. She had read much and possessed a great sense of the beautiful. She had many accomplished friends who found in her mind the response to this sense in themselves. Philosophy she did not care for, but her range was so wide that she took in what it could mean.

With these two I became great friends, and the friendship was one that grew more and more as time went on. I was very often at Mells, and I saw much of them in London. Lady Horner did much to enlarge my outlook on my fellow human beings, and to diminish the angularity of my views of life and society. Sir John has now passed away, but she remains my great friend, from whom I have learned much that has been of value to me in life. When later on I was attacked and misrepresented over my Army reforms and my efforts after peace with Germany, and finally was driven out of office, they both stood staunchly by me through thick and thin, and refused to be moved by clamour of such volume that it at last amounted to a blast such as the majority found irresistible. What I learned from her was that all sections of society have good as well as bad qualities. These one has to learn to understand and to appreciate for what they really are. In this lesson women are among our best instructors. Goethe discovered that, and he often speaks of it.

I began in 1893 to move a good deal in what is called ' London Society.' There was a group of well-known people nicknamed the ' Souls.' They sometimes took themselves much too seriously, and on the whole it is doubtful whether their influence was on balance good. But they cared for literature and art, and their social gifts were so high that people sought much to be admitted into their circle. Among the men were Arthur Balfour, the late Lord Pembroke, George Curzon, Harry Cust, George Wyndham, and Alfred Lyttelton. Among the women were Lady Ribblesdale, her sister Margot Tennant (afterwards Mrs. Asquith), Lady Elcho, Lady Desborough, and Lady Horner. Week-end parties at which the ' Souls ' assembled were given at Panshanger, Ashridge, Wilton, and Taplow. Among the hostesses on these occasions were Lady Cowper, Lady Brownlow, and Lady Pembroke, older but attractive women, who were gratefully but irreverently called the 'Aunts' of the 'Souls.' One or two outside men were welcomed and were frequently guests on these occasions. Among them were John Morley, Sir Alfred Lyall, Asquith, and myself. We were not 'Souls,' but they liked our company and we liked theirs because of its brilliance.

I was myself always something of a rebel, and I did not stick to any one social group. I became acquainted with some of the racing set, and although I knew nothing about horses or racing, was a good deal invited to their week-end gatherings and to their dinners. Between those and the corresponding gatherings of the 'Souls' there was a little rivalry, and it was not always easy to be loyal to both. However, I had no prejudices. I remember well going on one occasion for a week-end to stay with Lord and Lady Howe (the latter a Churchill and a sister of Lady Tweedmouth). The typical racing set was at first a little shy of me. But I made myself so sympathetic that nothing would please them but that I should be cordially invited to repeat my visit at a similar party in the following week-end. I said that I was a shy person and would be happier and less solitary if they would include in the invitation some like-minded friend. My hostess said that I might bring any man I pleased, so long as he was not one of the 'Souls.' I named some one whom I did not know, but whom I said I could ask. They recognised the name as that of the Secretary of the stern Anti-Gambling League, which had prosecuted various people for offences against the betting laws, and they demurred. But I pressed my point and made it a condition.   Out of curiosity they assented.

When I got to London I told John Morley that I had found a set as remarkable in a wholly different fashion as the 'Souls.' He was interested, for he knew my hostess of the week-end. I said that I had promised to go back on the next Saturday and that I had been authorised to choose a fellow-guest of a commanding type to be with me. Would he come ? He was amused and said he would. We went accordingly. Lady Howe I told beforehand that my new guest would be, not as the others supposed the Secretary of the Anti-Gambling League, but no less a person than Morley. She kept this to herself. When on our arrival we were shown in there was much curiosity, and it was not for a little time that the company, who did not even know Morley by sight, found out who he was. He made himself highly popular. The next afternoon, as we were all sitting out in the garden, one of the ladies mischievously put a copy of the *Jockey* above Morley's head while another took a snapshot with a camera. I was given a copy of the photograph when developed, and it is included here as part of the narrative. But in a little while Morley led me out of the gate on to the Common, and said, ' This very day twenty-five years ago I took a walk with John Mill on Black-heath Common, and now see into what company you have led me.' Morley, as always, was on this occasion very human, and he admired the skill and consistency with which the entertainment was organised, and the concentration with which Mrs.

HOUSE PARTY AT COUNTESS HOWE'S

Hwfa Williams, General ' Bully ' Oliphant, and other guests of distinction in the racing set entered into the party.

Lady Tweedmouth, though the sister of Lady Howe, did not cultivate the racing set or the ' Souls.' I became great friends with her. She was a woman of remarkable character and insight, and of splendid courage. She died in 1904 of an agonising form of cancer. But although she was told by the doctors of the probable date of the approaching end of her life, she would neither tell her friends nor flinch, but insisted, her agony notwithstanding, on carrying out all her engagements and facing impending death without putting off one. Her husband and I were at first the only people to whom she had confided her terrible secret, and we kept it by her desire faithfully. I gave her Emily Brontë's poems to read, and she found them a source of strength. At last she finished the list of political and other social engagements she had undertaken, and took leave of me for her last journey to her home in Guisachan Forest. ' There,' she said, ' I go to die like a wounded stag.' She never lost courage, and she sent me messages while she was awaiting the end not to grieve for her, for she had no fear of pain or of death. A noble woman who lived her life throughout at a high level !

The ' Souls ' met often. No. 40 Grosvenor Square, the house of Sir Charles Tennant, a well-known millionaire, was a frequent scene of their dinners together. The old gentleman himself cared for none of these things. He liked to have one or two distinguished men from the City to keep him company.

The rest of the party he left to his brilliant daughters, Mrs. Asquith and her sisters, to assemble and to entertain. It was all very well done. One advantage to myself was that, although he was of the opposite party, I very often found there and elsewhere among the ' Souls ' Arthur Balfour, who was Leader of the Commons and virtually Prime Minister so far as social questions were concerned. We came together because the Liberals were not up to the mark about questions of higher education. I was so keen about these that I did not mind accepting the opportunity of throwing myself on Balfour's side in them. My great question was how to extend University Organisation in England. There were some excellent Colleges, but outside Oxford and Cambridge very little of University life.

I approached Balfour about the University of London. It was then a mere Board for examining outside students who got from it external degrees by means of examinations without teaching. Valuable as the work of extending degrees to external students had been in the past, it was no longer sufficient. The system lent itself to the purposes of the crammers, and the school teachers in particular used it for obtaining what were virtually little more than trade-marks. The real purpose of University training, the development of the mind in the atmosphere of the teaching University, where teachers and taught could come into close relation, was lacking.

So strongly was this felt that many of the professors in the London Colleges had set their hearts on the establishment of a second and professorially run University, with no external examinees at all. I knew that the opposition to so far-reaching a measure would be too strong to overcome in the then indifferent state of public opinion. I saw that, as a first step at all events, the only way was to pass an Act enlarging the existing University of London by giving it a powerful teaching side. This might be relied on in the end to absorb the other side by reason of its quality. Of this opinion also was my friend Sidney Webb, who as the successful Chief of the Technical Education Board of the London County Council had great opportunities of studying the practical problem.

But the professors thought otherwise and they insisted on their plan. My difference with them was so serious that I had to resign my position as a member of the Governing Body of the University College of London. They wanted a second and professorial University in addition to or in substitution for the then existing University, and I knew that their ambition must fail.

Sidney Webb and I took counsel together. He was a very practical as well as a very energetic man. We laid siege to the citadel. We went round to person after person who was prominent in the administration of the existing University. Some listened, but others would not do so and even refused to see us. In the end we worked out what was in substance the scheme of the London University Act of 1898. The scheme was far from being an ideal one. It provided by way of compromise for a senate which was too large to be a really efficient supreme governing body for the new composite University, and it had other shortcomings of which we were well aware. But it did set up a teaching University, although Convocation, with its control of the external side, would remain unduly powerful. We saw that the scheme thus fashioned was the utmost we could hope for the time to carry, in the existing state of public opinion about higher education in London.

I went to Balfour as soon as we were ready, and explained what we had done and why we had done it in this form. He was both interested and sympathetic, and, after consideration, said that his Government would take the matter up and introduce a Bill fashioned on our lines, although the Government could not pledge itself to stand or fall by it. The Bill was ultimately, after much consultation with me, introduced to the House of Commons by Sir John Gorst on behalf of the Government. He explained it to the House, and concluded by saying that it was on the whole a Bill which the Government recommended.

There was at once a storm. Sir John Lubbock, the Member for the University, opposed it in the interest of the Convocation by whose members he had been elected. Sir Charles Dilke and others attacked it fiercely on various grounds. For some time in the course of the discussion not a speech was made in its favour, and the prospects of the Bill seemed hopeless. I sprang to my feet when an opportunity at last offered, and I spoke for once like one inspired. I told the House of Commons of the scandal that the metropolis of the Empire should not have a teaching University to which students from distant regions might come as to the centre for them of that Empire. I showed how far we were behind Continental nations, and what a menace this was to our scientific and industrial prospects in days to come. I knew every inch of the ground, and displayed its unsound condition. We were far away from the days in which a step forward had been made by calling into being the Examining Body named London University, a creation which had given degrees by examination to those whom the Church had in the old days shut out from University status. That reform was in its time a most valuable service to the State, but it was a service which had become superseded in the light of new standards in University education which demanded much more. The effect of this speech was great. Joseph Chamberlain took me aside and said that it was almost the only case he had seen of the House being turned round by a single speech. Turned round it was, for the adversaries shrank from pushing their opposition and the second reading of the Bill was carried without a division. The next day Asquith sent me an affectionate letter :—

My dear H.,—Before the impression at all fades I should like to tell you how greatly I rejoiced in the brilliant and conspicuous success of your London University speech last night.

It is the best thing of the kind I have ever heard in the H. of Commons, and in my experience I have never known a case in which a single speech converted hostile and impressed indifferent opinion in the House.

The result must be some compensation to you for months and years of unthankful work, and to me, as you will believe, it had all the pleasure of a personal triumph.— Always affectly. yours,

H. H. A.

The Bill went to a Grand Committee upstairs. Balfour sent for me and said that I must put all else aside and take charge of the Clauses there. He authorised me to ask the judges to give me help by postponing cases on which I was engaged and in which it did not seem essential that I should at once return my briefs. At first we won easily in the Grand Committee, and progress looked as if it would be rapid. But one day T. M. Healy appeared at the head of the group of Irish members who had been included in the Committee and sounded a strong note of opposition. Balfour sent for me and said that he had given time because he was not afraid of the others. But the appearance of the Irish on the Opposition side made a great difference to him. If we were to persist with the Bill I must find means of getting rid of their opposition.

Within twenty minutes I had seen Healy, whom I knew well, and asked him why he was opposing a Bill to which he could have no real objection. His answer was that he had no hostile feeling at all to our London Bill, but that there was a country that had a University question more pressing and scandalous than even that of London. I asked him whether there were any terms on which he would withdraw his opposition to us. He replied that if I would promise to come over to Ireland in the autumn and to undertake the reform of the Irish University System in such a way as to do justice to the Catholics, he would not only cease to oppose but would help. I said that I could do nothing effective without the approval of the Government, but that I would go to consult Balfour at once. I went, and I found the latter not only sympathetic but anxious that I should try my hand at a problem that had baffled Government after Government, and that it was wholly in harmony with Unionist principles to try to solve. Sir Michael Hicks-Beach, the Chancellor of the Exchequer, was sent for to come to Balfour's room. He was not less keen, and he said that if a proper scheme could be agreed on there was £50,000 a year left out of the Irish Church surplus which could be drawn on for it.

With this authority to undertake the negotiations I saw Healy at once and arranged preliminaries with him. I was to study the problem through the recess, and to communicate with Redington, the head of the Education System in Ireland, and Vice-Chancellor of the Royal Irish University as it stood. I was to be sure to get into relations with Chief Baron Palles, who would be consulted by the Catholic Bishops, and with certain others whose parts we discussed. On this side of the Channel I was to put myself in communication with Sir Francis Mowatt, the Permanent Head of the Treasury, as well as with John Morley and others.

All this I did energetically, and, the ground being prepared, went to Dublin early in October 1898. There I entered on a remarkable set of negotiations.

I

The scheme was to fashion two new teaching Universities, one in Dublin and the other in Belfast. The constitutions were to be on the face of them identical, but in the composition of the governing bodies that in Dublin was to be predominantly Catholic while that in Belfast was to be predominantly Protestant. The way had been to some extent paved for such provision as to the constitutions of the governing bodies by certain resolutions passed by the Irish Catholic Bishops at Maynooth on 23rd June 1897, and by a statement on the Irish University question published by the General Assembly of the Presbyterian Church on 29th March 1898.

The resolutions and the statement had both, however, stopped short of any details, and had left the plan vague. As this stage in the history of the Irish University question has never, so far as I know, been made public, and as it is of historical interest, I have preserved for reference the diary of the three weeks of negotiation which I wrote for the information of Mr. Balfour. This diary which was mainly written during my journey and is, so far as I am aware, an exact record, I took with me when, my work being finished, I left Cardinal Logue's residence at Armagh. I travelled straight to Whittingehame and saw Balfour. He asked me, when he had considered the outcome, to go up to London and prepare, with the aid of Sir Courtney Ilbert, who was at that time Chief Government Parliamentary draftsman, the Bill and the two Charters which the plan required. This I did at once. The rest Balfour said that he would himself see to.

The diary tells how Archbishop Walsh arranged that I should make a journey from Dublin to Armagh to interview the Cardinal, who had returned to residence there after the meeting of the Hierarchy of Maynooth had broken up. My journey was to be as far as possible a secret one, for the Archbishop said he was sure that I was being closely observed. The expedition was made without mishap, and I had the interview with the Cardinal, the outcome of which is narrated.

I have told in this diary the details of the journey across country from Dublin to Armagh to carry out the interview with Cardinal Logue. My instructions were—not to give my name to any one on the way, because there were so many people watching, and to change at a small junction and proceed to Armagh by an unusual route. This advice was given to me by the Catholic Archbishop, who said that, although he himself was friendly to my plan, I would find the Cardinal hostile. When I got to Armagh, I was to leave my luggage at the station and to go on foot in the darkness to the Cardinal's residence, *Ara Coeli*. I was to inquire the way from women rather than from men, as they were less likely to identify me. I thought all this somewhat unnecessary, but I did what I was told and reached the villa which served as the Cardinal's palace. I knocked at the door, and have recounted in the diary what happened. I was received by the Cardinal himself, scarlet-clad in full canonicals. After he had talked to me most courteously, saying that he was the friend of my plan, as to which he added that he knew that another

section of the Hierarchy led by some one else was an
unfriendly one, I was able to tell him in reply that
I had the approval of the Archbishop of Dublin to
the plan, expressed on paper. 'Then,' said the
Cardinal, ' I approve it also.'

Feeling that my work was done, I was about to
say ' Good night,' with a view to waiting at the
station to catch the midnight train for Kingston
and take the boat on my journey to Whittingehame
to see Mr. Balfour. But the Cardinal said that,
although the rules of the Church prohibited him,
much to his regret, from entertaining me properly,
still the rules of the Church were not so inhuman as
to force him to send me away hungry. A little
was permitted. He opened a door, and there was a
table with two chairs, and on the table an enormous
dish of oysters flanked by a bottle of champagne
We sat down, and passed a delightful hour. His
reminiscences of his youth and his early training as
a priest in Spain were very interesting, as also his
somewhat caustic comments on events since. In
the end his brougham came and took me to the station
and I proceeded to Whittingehame by the Kingston
boat.

When November came Balfour had the Bill and the
two Charters in his hands. He was keen to get
them through, and I was seeing him constantly over
them in London. At last came the day when
week-end Cabinet was to have them before it
Balfour and I had accepted an invitation to spend
that week-end with the Salisburys at Hatfield. We
fixed on a train, and he said that if I would go to

King's Cross early and get a compartment where we could talk alone he would bring the news of the result. He was very hopeful of it. When I looked out from the door of the railway carriage I saw him descending the steps to the platform looking deeply depressed. He told me that his timorous colleagues had, by a small majority, thrown out his attempt. There was no more to be done at that time. He made a speech a few weeks afterwards in the north of England in which he declared that if the Unionist Party could not deal with the University question in Ireland it would have failed in a vital part of its mission.

Nothing more was done then, but the question remained a pressing one. Ten years later, when I was War Minister in the Campbell-Bannerman Cabinet and Bryce was Irish Secretary, the latter tried his hand at this pressing problem. But whether he had not heard of the negotiations of 1898, or whether he disliked the plan, he took a different course. Along with Sir Antony Macdonell, the Permanent Under-Secretary for Ireland, he devised a scheme for reforming and expanding the University of Dublin so that it might provide for the necessities of the Catholic population. I had not been consulted and knew nothing of this plan, otherwise I should have pronounced it to be hopelessly inadequate. It proved to be so. Neither Trinity College nor the Hierarchy would look at it. Bryce, however, at this time became our Ambassador to Washington, and Birrell succeeded him in the Irish Secretaryship. The latter reported to us who were his colleagues that he found the question of Irish University reform in a hopeless condition. I asked him in the Cabinet whether he had looked at the agreed scheme of 1898. He knew nothing of it, and three days later reported that there were no papers to be found dealing with it. I then produced my own copies of the documents, and on further inquiry the Irish Government discovered that they had copies of their own which they had overlooked. Birrell at once communicated with the Hierarchy and also with the Belfast Assembly. Both replied that they adhered to the agreement come to years earlier. He set to work, and the Bill and Charters, although drawn up ten years previously, required but little change. The Bill was introduced by him in the House of Commons. He insisted on putting my name on the back of it along with his own. The measure passed quite smoothly through Parliament. All I had to do was to make a speech about it in the House. The Irish members who had been cognisant of the old negotiations proposed to give me a dinner in Dublin. But I refused, for I thought that it would not be right. It was Birrell, as Irish Secretary, who had got the matter through at last. The solution he accomplished has worked out admirably, both in Southern Ireland and in Ulster.

This completes in outline the story of the endeavours I made in London and in Ireland in University reform. I must now pass to University reforms relating to England outside the metropolis.

CHAPTER V

PUBLIC LIFE BEFORE OFFICE

(1898–1905)

THE early years of the present century saw much of political controversy. The division of opinion over the policy of the South African War had split the Liberal Party seriously. Campbell-Bannerman, Harcourt, Morley, and Lloyd George, with the majority of the party in the House of Commons, were against the war altogether. On the other side, so far as its prosecution was concerned, were Rosebery (on the whole), Asquith, Grey, and people like myself. We had an extensive backing in the form of a substantial minority of the Liberals in the House.

My own view was quite definite. Whether the dispute with President Kruger could have been avoided I did not, and do not even now, know. I doubt whether Milner, with all his remarkable qualities, was the best man to handle it. On the other side, Kruger was an almost impracticable person to deal with. He could not understand us, and he underrated altogether our latent power of facing difficulties. The Jameson Raid had been a first-rate and culpable blunder. I had little doubt myself of Chamberlain's freedom from complicity in it. A long talk with him alone in his smoking-room at Highbury had satisfied me that, if rather short-sighted as to the bearing of events, he had been at least free from taking any part in originating the raid. Milner, who came on the scene only later on, I knew in these days intimately, and I had kept up an extensive correspondence with him. He was a man of most attractive qualities but was difficult to work with. I came in the end to wish that the negotiations before the war had been in the hands of a man of more diplomatic temperament and of qualities like those of Kitchener.

Anyhow the war came, and with it a new question. If a war is clearly wrong, then it cannot be right to support it even if one's own country is involved. But if a new situation has developed itself, one in which the nation is no longer fighting for what is wrong ; if in course of time issues are raised on which one's own country is in the right, and which have to be fought out by our people for the sake of dear life, then those involved in the struggle ought to be supported, and supported with the full strength of the nation. I thought that the character of the war had been decisively changed by what its progress had brought to the front, and because of the misguided views of Kruger. For us to halt would have been to place ourselves in a position of danger from the rest of the world.

Having come clearly to this conclusion, I began by going down to my constituents at the beginning of actual war and addressing them at a meeting at East Linton. I did not mince matters, and the majority of my people in East Lothian declared themselves decisively as on my side. Asquith and Grey spoke in the same sense to their constituents. Rosebery also spoke, though less plainly.

The split in the House of Commons showed itself most clearly over the question as to the way in which the war should be carried on. The Generals in the field were naturally in favour of energetic action with a single purpose. The Boers were not only very good at certain modes of attack and defence, but they were clever in their tactics. They would concentrate secretly at unexpected points, and become at these points very formidable. Farmhouses in the veldt were favourite places for such concentrations. Our own soldiers were therefore keen about destroying farmhouses instead of leaving them behind when taken intact. It seemed barbarous, but what else could they do if they were to succeed in defeating the enemy? War is essentially a barbarous undertaking, and our people were certainly not more but probably less barbarous than the soldiers of many other nations would have felt bound to be. The question was really a military one. But the news that came home was revolting to a very large section of the supporters of the Liberal Party in the House of Commons. They knew little about what was required if military operations were to be successful, for they had never considered the subject. Moreover, to make things worse, the British Army was inadequately prepared, and when this was discovered it gave rise to angry criticism. There was no General Staff, and there was no Expeditionary Force that was at all adequate or adequately organised. Our

troops were too few, and it was difficult to replace
losses, notwithstanding that the Dominions were
helping to the full extent of what they had ready
to send.

In consequence there was an outburst in the House,
not merely against the policy of the war but against
the soldiers in the field. The Generals were called
' brutes,' and every sort of accusation against the
Army was made. Lloyd George led the attacks
and Campbell-Bannerman lent him a good deal of
countenance.

When motions of condemnation were made our
group either voted against them or moved amend-
ments. It was not that mistakes were not being
made, but that we felt that, when we had got to the
stage which the war had reached, to hamper the
efforts of the Army was to imperil the national life.

The situation was indeed a difficult one. But at
last a point was reached at which peace might
be said to be coming in sight. Rosebery addressed
a great meeting at Chesterfield, the arrangements for
which were made by Sir Robert Perks on behalf of
the Liberal Imperialists. In his speech he suggested
strongly that the circumstances were such that negotiations might be thought of. Lord Roberts had
taken over the command in the field, and was pursuing
a fresh campaign with great energy, assisted in his
work by Lord Kitchener. It was ceasing to be doubtful what the end must be. There was a great response
throughout the country to Rosebery's speech. The
Unionist Government was not indisposed to act, and
it did so. After an interval peace was made, but the

terms for the reconstruction of South Africa seemed to us, although a great advance, too narrow to secure a state of things in which Dutch and British might live happily together. It was not indeed until 1907 that Campbell-Bannerman, who by that time had succeeded to power, was able to offer to South Africa a sufficiently generous Constitution. This he did with full co-operation from all sections of the Liberal Party, and not least from the Liberal Imperialists, with whom the efficacy of self-government was a deep conviction.

But I must now return to the University question. My relations with Balfour over this question had become rather close ever since the London and Irish problems had engaged our efforts. But with these results I could not rest, and I went to him again about what was new. The old-fashioned view was that Oxford and Cambridge could not be reproduced and ought not to be even imitated. Nothing higher than University Colleges, of the type which already to some extent existed, could be fashioned without detriment to the ideal of a University. Matthew Arnold himself had given some countenance to the restriction, and even Liberal thinkers like Bryce had to some extent followed him. The latter had, so far as my recollection serves me, originated the phrase ' Lilliputian Universities.' Durham was pointed to as a restricted institution under clerical influences, and the Victoria University at Manchester was described as being little more than a federal body with functions which did not go beyond examining what were hardly more than external students from a group of Colleges which included the University Colleges at Liverpool and Leeds as well as that in Manchester itself. It was said that any attempt of a more ambitious kind was destined to fail. All these prognostications have now passed into oblivion, but they counted for much in the beginning of the present century.

I was of a different opinion. I had discussed the problem with men like Sir William M'Cormick, afterwards to be the guiding spirit of the Treasury Committee on University Education. There was no such Committee in these days, and there were no State grants for any such purpose. I had convinced myself that a Civic University was a possible institution, and that if called into being it would have a great moulding influence and a high standard under the impulse of the local patriotism of the great cities where it was to be established. I found that Joseph Chamberlain was strongly with me in this view.

But the counter-battery of criticism was strong, and Parliament was quite indifferent from want of authoritative leading. Balfour asked me whether I could suggest a means of ascertaining the truth authoritatively and of overcoming the public apathy. I said that if he would select a very strong Committee of the Privy Council to examine and report on the principle there might result a great instrument which he could use. And I pointed out that occasion had arisen for the appointment of such a Committee. Liverpool, where my friend A. F. Warr, the local M.P., and I had been at work, was ready to petition for a Charter for the establishment of a separate

University of its own for Liverpool. It would raise its own funds, the teachers were ready on the spot, and the only question was whether the Government would be prepared to overrule opposition and grant the Charter if recommended to do so by the Privy Council. Balfour agreed to take this course, and the Government assembled the Committee in December 1902. The petition of Liverpool was referred to it for report. Manchester somewhat half-heartedly supported the prayer of Liverpool, but Leeds strongly opposed it, and was backed by a number of persons who were eminent in the field of higher education in these days. The question was whether Liverpool, Manchester, and Leeds were to have their own Civic Universities, or whether the Victoria University at Manchester was to remain a federal body, with the three local University Colleges under it.

It was settled that the President of the Council, the late Duke of Devonshire, should preside over the Committee of the Privy Council and have four colleagues. These included Lord Rosebery, the ex-Prime Minister, who was not unnaturally much interested on my account. The other members were the late Lord Balfour of Burleigh, the Secretary for Scotland, who knew the system in Scotland, where there were four Universities for the population of four millions, while England had only four for about thirty-five millions ; Lord James of Hereford, a Cabinet Minister ; and Sir Edward Fry, the well-known ex-Lord Justice of Appeal.

The hearing occupied the 17th, 18th, and 19th of December 1902. It was conducted like an appeal to

the Judicial Committee. Eminent counsel appeared
for the parties, and each side called witnesses.
I had told Liverpool that if they desired it I
would assume my wig and gown and lead as their
advocate, but on one condition only, that as the
work would be a labour of love, and from my point
of view a very important one, I would accept no
pecuniary reward.

But just before the case came on I found an
unexpected letter from Lord Salisbury, the Prime
Minister, proposing that I should be a Privy Councillor.
King Edward, who had just succeeded, had specially
asked that Sir Edward Grey and myself should be
added to the Council. I had not been a Minister of
the Crown, but I had come into a good deal of contact
with the King in the course of the negotiations for
the establishment of the Imperial College of Science
and Technology, to which I have already referred.
King Edward had accepted the view that it was the
desire of his father, Prince Albert, that the valuable
site of the great Exhibition should be used in part
for the establishment of some such institution for
higher technical education, for a London ' Charlottenburg ' in fact. He was very helpful and was instru-
mental in procuring for us the grant of the requisite
land from the Exhibition Commissioners.

King Edward, while still Prince of Wales, had also
been keenly interested in the Imperial Institute.
This had got into difficulties, and was lapsing into
insolvency notwithstanding the exertions of its acting
head, the late Lord Herschell. The Prince, who
had heard of the success of my efforts towards the

reform of the University of London, sent for me in 1898 and asked me to get the newly constituted University to consent to have a part of the building of the Imperial Institute at South Kensington for its headquarters. ' You alone,' he said, ' can get over the opposition to a plan which will deliver the Imperial Institute and be good for the University.' I took the matter in hand, and brought the Prince to a meeting with the Senate, and terms were ultimately arranged with the assent of the Treasury.

Lord Knollys, who was then the Prince's Secretary, wrote to me on 8th July 1899 :—

MY DEAR MR. HALDANE,—The Prince of Wales has learned with great pleasure that the Senate of the University of London have accepted the Government proposals regarding the University and the Imperial Institute, and he trusts that all the details connected with the question will now be speedily settled.

His Royal Highness will naturally take a great interest in the future prosperity of the University, and if it is at any time thought he can be of use to it in any way, he hopes that the Governing Body will not hesitate to apply for his assistance.—Believe me, yours very truly,

FRANCIS KNOLLYS.

When the Prince succeeded to the throne he acted up to his promise by promoting in every way he could the interests of the new Imperial College of Science. The result of all this was to bring me much into his society. I saw him very often in the end of the century and the beginning of the next. With the plan for the new College of Science and

Technology in the University there were others who gave help that was indispensable. I had called on Mr. Wernher, of the great firm of Wernher, Beit & Co., whom and his partners I did not know excepting as public-spirited men of German origin and as impressed with the necessity for this country of German scientific training. I found him and Alfred Beit and the other members of his firm at their office. They were highly appreciative, and at once offered £100,000 for the scheme. To this they added later on other very large sums. I lunched at Beit's house in Park Lane to meet Cecil Rhodes, who had heard of the scheme for the reconstruction of London University into an intellectual centre for the students of the Empire. He and I went down to Tring Park to spend a week-end with Rothschild. I had much talk with Rhodes, who assisted in getting his South African friends to help further. He impressed me not as an idealist of the kind to which I had been accustomed to look up most, but as a splendidly energetic man of affairs, with a wide outlook and great capacity for getting things through. Sir Ernest Cassel, a man of the same type, in his turn gave a large contribution, and so did the Rothschilds.

Another who helped in a different way but most materially was the Permanent Head of the Treasury, Francis Mowatt. He was one of the largest-minded officials I ever came across. He negotiated the transfer to the new college of the Government College at South Kensington, and the increase of its already large annual endowment. He was a man who never failed to take the bigger side of things into account, and to look to the future, even when considering questions of economy for the State.

Anyhow I became a Privy Councillor just before the Liverpool case came on for hearing, and this precluded me from appearing as Counsel at the Bar. For although an advocate who is a Privy Councillor may conduct cases before the Judicial Committee, because it is a special Committee from which the general body of Privy Councillors are excluded, he cannot appear before a Committee of the full Council. However, this did not cause any real difficulty, for I said that I would go into the box as the first witness for Liverpool and state its case. I advised that the city should retain as one of its advocates Alfred Lyttelton, who knew little about higher education but was tactful and also well known to the members of the Committee. I also suggested Sidney Webb, who knew the subject thoroughly, and my old friend Kemp, who was one of my ' devils ' at Lincoln's Inn in those days. The arrangement was carried out, and I stated the case for Liverpool as its witness with fulness. Lord Spencer was there in a very critical capacity on behalf of the Victoria University, of which he was Chancellor. Lord Ripon, who was the head of the Leeds College, was also present and opposed Liverpool vehemently. In order to get our views informally the Committee used to have us three to lunch with them at Downing Street while the sittings were taking place. Liverpool had this advantage, that we had worked out and knew our educational case more thoroughly than our opponents had been able to do.

K

At the close of the hearing the Committee of the
Privy Council deliberated.   On 10th February 1903
its Report, having been made, was embodied in an
Order in Council of that date.   It was pronounced
that the case was made out for the grant of Charter
for full University status to Liverpool and Man
chester.   Leeds had not petitioned for such a Charter
but it was made obvious that if she chose to do so
later on she would receive one likewise.   The prin
ciple laid down was a general one and a new one
It was added in the Report that the step of granting
these Charters involved issues of great moment, for
dealing with which preparation should be made
especially in respect to the points upon which, having
regard to the great importance of the matter, and
the effects of the changes proposed on the future o
higher education in the north of England, co-operation
was expedient between Universities of a common type
and with cognate aims.

It has always seemed to me that this decision o
the Government as advised by the Privy Council i
1903 was a step of the first importance in the histor
of higher education.   Little notice was, however
taken of it by the public or by writers about Englis
education.   The thick printed volumes containing
the documents and the evidence repose undisturbe
in the library of the Judicial Office in Downing Stree
None the less the decision gave rise to immediat
results.   Further new Universities were set up wit
all possible speed.   Besides Liverpool, Mancheste
and Leeds, Birmingham, Bristol, and Sheffield r
ceived Charters.   Durham was expanded and trans

formed by the addition of Colleges in Newcastle, so as to become a University of the new type. Later on Reading was to follow, and Wales was to have a wholly reconstituted University system. In Birmingham Chamberlain took the lead at once. He had told me that no other city would be able to found a University before his city, and he worked at the plan for Birmingham with characteristic energy and success. Besides all this, new University Colleges were founded elsewhere in England.

Thus early in the century there were established teaching Universities controlled within the great cities to which they belonged. The civic communities had reached a stage at which they had resolved to be content in higher education with nothing short of what was highest. Bristol, in which I had taken a keen interest, was a case in point. Along with other prominent citizens, the Wills family, who had derived great fortunes from the manufacture of tobacco, endowed the new University with magnificent buildings and gifts of money. In 1912 I was chosen to be Chancellor of that University, an office which I have held for many years, and which has given me the opportunity of watching the stimulating effect of the new and developed University life upon the educational institutions of the city and in places around it. On my installation in October 1912 I delivered to the citizens an address on 'The Civic University,' which was afterwards included in the little volume called *The Conduct of Life*.

The interest in Education as a subject of nearly paramount importance did not stop with the Uni-

versities. In 1902 Balfour introduced his Education
Bill, which got rid of the artificial line of demarcation
drawn between primary and secondary instruction
by the famous ' Cockerton ' Judgment, and sought
to unify the English system of education by sub-
stituting in its control the County and Borough
Councils for the smaller and more restricted School
Boards. As a part of the plan the Bill sought to
raise the efficiency of the Church Schools, many of
which were in a miserable condition, by giving them
aid from the rates as well as from the taxes, and
subjecting them to control in matters educational.
The Nonconformists were much dissatisfied, and the
Liberal Party as a whole opposed the Bill hotly. I
saw that no alternative course was open to the Conservative Government of the day, and I thought that
the importance of developing the national system of
education was so great that the Bill, which contained
conscience clauses, ought to be passed. As the result
I differed from nearly the whole of my party, and
supported it. Sidney Webb, on behalf of Labour,
took the same line. But he was not in the House
of Commons, so I was alone there. Even the
other Liberal Imperialists felt bound to the Nonconformists. However, the Bill was passed by a
sufficient majority, and in the result it has worked well.
None of the dangers apprehended have matured.
I wrote a full account in 1925, in the new supple-
mental volume of the *Encyclopædia Britannica*, of the
advance it made in the national conception of school
education.

The next idea that occurred to me was to try to

develop the work of the Universities by giving to
them freely extra-mural functions. If they could
develop adult educational centres in their own neigh-
bourhoods the influence of the higher teaching of the
University type would be brought to bear in some
measure on our working classes, and new openings
would result for spreading the idea of equality of
educational chance. My friend Albert Mansbridge
had already, following the lead given by Professor
Stuart and others, founded the Workers' Educational
Association. With the activities of this body, and
also of the British Institute of Adult Education, of
which I became President, I was before long to be
closely associated. Further reference to this I post-
pone to the record of later activities in my life.

There were other subjects which invited attention
from our group. It must not be supposed that our
notions of a policy for the Empire were of a flamboyant
kind. We deprecated on the one side the want of
knowledge and interest which were common among
average Liberals. On the other side we were without
faith in any schemes, such as those of Preference,
for holding the Dominions together by written ties.
In the discussion of these subjects Rosebery and
others of us took an active part. In 1900 there came
to London a delegation of Australian statesmen, con-
sisting of men who had been engaged in negotiating
with the Australian States an agreement on the terms
of union in a Commonwealth, and some of whom
were later on to rise to great eminence in the public
life of that Commonwealth. The mission of the
delegates was to get the Imperial Government to

agree to and pass, exactly as it had been prepared in Australia, the Bill that became the Commonwealth Act of 1900.

As I had had much to do with constitutional questions before the Privy Council, the delegates took me to some extent into their confidence and consulted me freely about the steps in their negotiations with Chamberlain as Secretary of State for the Colonies. The only point on which I could not wholly agree with them arose from the importance I attached to preserving a right of appeal on constitutional points to the Judicial Committee of the Privy Council. This I wanted to keep, and in the discussions on the Bill in the House of Commons I spoke fully on the point. But their instructions precluded them from assenting to the suggestion that the clause in the draft Bill which took away, excepting when Australia especially assented to it, the right of appeal to the Privy Council when the point was a constitutional one, should be dropped. Consequently Chamberlain, though at the time I think he agreed with me, considered that he ought not to overrule the desire of the delegates, and the clause remained and became part of the Act. He was probably right.

However, I had opportunities, not only in the Commons but elsewhere, of putting points that arose as we Liberal Imperialists conceived them. In May 1900 I was asked to deliver an address on Federal Constitutions within the Empire, at the Colonial Institute, before the Australian Delegates and the Society of Comparative Legislation. The address was reprinted in 1902 in the volume called *Education and*

Empire, which contains addresses delivered by me not only on this but on other subjects. I pointed out that in the Bill which was presently to become law the new Australian Commonwealth was intended at once to be in no sense a mere delegate or agent of the Imperial Parliament but to have powers of legislation analogous to those of that Parliament itself. In 1926 at the Conference this view was to be whole-heartedly confirmed.

During the years which followed the passing of the Act various developments of the principle were established judicially. It fell to me, as Lord Chancellor in 1915, to deliver the judgment of the Privy Council in the only case in which the High Court of Australia had given special leave for an appeal to London on a constitutional question. We then expounded the novelty and scope of the Act of 1900, and established the view thus contended for.

In years subsequent to the passing of this Act our group was active in expounding the new conception of the nature of the Empire. We were the more disposed to do so because the doctrine of Protection, under the form of Imperial Preference, was beginning to be pushed again into prominence by Chamberlain. He was an admirably energetic and strong Secretary for the Colonies. But by 1903 he had definitely gone back to Protection, while we were strong Free Traders. Asquith and I made speeches not only in Parliament but all over England. Our cardinal point was that what was threatening our industrial position was want of science among our manufacturers. We pointed to case after case, particularly in the industries which required chemistry, where business was being lost to this country by the deficiency of our people in the use of science. In the first of the addresses published in *Education and Empire* I insisted on this to the Liverpool business world in detail, and I delivered many more of such addresses in 1903 and the next three years. Our real danger was not one of German invasion, but one of German permeation of our markets by the employment of scientific knowledge. This was one of the features in the case for the increase we were struggling for in the number of the teaching Universities of Great Britain. Some of these addresses were reprinted in a book on *Army Reform* and other subjects some years later on. The campaign in which we were engaged against the policy of Protection which was concentrating on itself public attention was our opportunity for pressing the counter-case for science and organisation.

In 1902-4 I delivered the Gifford Lectures at the University of St. Andrews, which were afterwards published under the title *The Pathway to Reality*. I had kept up my philosophical investigations, and had worked as hard as I dared in this region. But I had also travelled over the country making the Free Trade speeches to which I have referred, and I was in addition earning nearly £15,000 a year by briefs at the Bar at this time. So I was kept pretty closely occupied. My only recreation was dining out in London, and in the recesses spent at Cloan, somewhat broken into as these recesses were by public engagements.

CLOAN

However, the life at Cloan during the autumns of this period was one of real change in occupation. Many visitors came to us, University professors, politicians, men of letters. As a family we were all busy, and much reading occupied our spare time. My mother was the dominating influence. She had grown in outlook as well as in spiritual insight, and had become something of the splendid personality that was to last until her hundredth year was attained. My brother John was developing his distinctive views in physiology, and was even then working at his researches into the phenomena of Respiration. My brother William was rapidly making his mark in his business as a Writer to the Signet and as a manager and owner of agricultural land. My sister had translated and published the three volumes of Hegel's *History of Philosophy*, and had written a Life of James Frederick Ferrier, the Scottish philosopher. The household was both a lively and a serious one, for visitors came in succession, each keenly occupied with some special subject. We did not go much about, because these things kept us pretty closely at home. Cloan became, what it has since been, a place of assembly where there was no lack of congenial occupation of various kinds. My mother surveyed and was interested in it all, and there was no tendency to restraint. Professor Hume Brown, who was regularly with us through the autumns, was in himself a guarantee for continuity in habit of mind.

Besides the Greys and the Asquiths, a certain number of London friends came to visit us, but not as many as a few years later, when the affairs of the

War Office were to constitute Cloan, during the
recess, a centre of attraction of a definite kind.

In 1905 the Liberals of the University of Edinburgh
nominated me as their candidate for the position of
Lord Rector. The University had been Conservative,
and for twenty-five years no Liberal had been chosen.
However, in the autumn of 1905 I stood, and turned
out to have a majority of votes. Later on I delivered
a Rectorial Address, afterwards published as *The
Dedicated Life*. Ever since that time I have avoided
being again a candidate for the office of Lord Rector
in other Universities, notwithstanding tempting offers.
I had said all that I wanted to say in the Edinburgh
Rectorial Address, and my work lay for the future
more in the direction of organisation than of preaching
to the students. The Chancellorship of Bristol has
not been any real diversion from this resolution.

It was about the same period that my friendship
with Bernard Bosanquet became an intimate one.
When I had told Principal Donaldson at St. Andrews,
who offered to me informally but pressingly the
Chair of Moral Philosophy at the University there
after I had delivered the first series of my Gifford
Lectures, that I could not accept, I suggested to him
Bosanquet as the best scholar to be approached.
This was done, and Bosanquet not only accepted the
Chair, but put his very best into the work. His was
a very spiritual nature. He was not a Christian in
any ordinary sense, but so sympathetic and understanding was he about the efforts of the theological
professors to uplift the students that some of them
declared, when he gave up the Chair after four years

of work in it, that he had done more to promote
Christianity than any man who had taught at St.
Andrews, his critical attitude towards orthodoxy
notwithstanding. I saw much of him and of his
wife, not only at St. Andrews and Cloan but in
London. During my busiest times I used to go down
to Oxshott in Surrey, where they had settled for a
secluded country life, and spend the Saturday or
Sunday afternoon in philosophical talk. His Gifford
Lectures are not written in an easy style, but they
appear to me to contain one of the best and truest
analyses in recent times of the character of Experience
and of Reality. For Bosanquet metaphysics was
never more than an instrument. He had great command of the earlier philosophical literature, from the
time of the Greeks down to that of Oxford in the
great period in which he was at that University.
But the passion for truth prevented him from ever
coming under the exclusive domination of any single
set of ideas.

I saw also a great deal of my two friends at Mells.
Lady Horner was a keen critic of my ideas, philosophical and political, and I gained much from her
searching injunctions not to lose sight of what literature and art had to tell on these subjects. It was
very often possible for me to go down to Mells for
the week-end when they were not in London, and
here I met all sorts of people, grave and gay.

Meantime the Liberal Party was slowly emerging
from the stagnation which had followed the ' Khaki '
Election at which it had been defeated after the
South African War for a second time. The new

ideas of our group were beginning to penetrate.
The country was obviously tending to decide against
Protection, and the position of the Unionist Party
was made more difficult by the decision and energy
which Chamberlain was throwing into the Protectionist cause as contrasted with the half-heartedness of
the support which Balfour, the leader of the party,
was giving to it.   It was becoming plain that although
the Unionists still had a large majority in the House
of Commons it was a majority that was so divided
that it was rapidly becoming a stale and inert one,
and was unlikely to be renewed.   The English people
were not yet converted to the Home Rule policy of
Gladstone, the popularity of which had never recovered from the shock of the Parnell divorce case
It was becoming obvious that while Liberalism would
retain Home Rule as its remedy for Irish difficulties
it would not be able to come in at the impending
election with a Home Rule Bill for its main proposal
as formerly.   New ideas on other subjects became
imperative.   For all that had been said against us
as rebels, it was to our group of young men that the
constituencies began to look.   Rosebery was, how
ever, no longer regarded as a reliable prophet for
Liberalism.   He had, apparently deliberately, re
jected the call that came to him after his great speech
at Chesterfield.   Morley was looked on as a man of
fine personality, but he was too much associated
with the Irish question to the exclusion of other
to be the leader that was looked for.   Campbell
Bannerman had been accepted, and he was genial
and popular and respected for the courage with which

he had resisted the policy of the Government in
South Africa.   But he was not identified in the public
mind with any fresh ideas, for indeed he had none.
What was wanted was not the recrudescence of the
old Liberal Party, but a body of men with life and
energy and a new outlook on the problems of the
State.   At these problems some of us had been working diligently, and we had been proclaiming our
faith unceasingly as it grew in us.   The result was
that those who had originally formed the Liberal
League, as a body apart from the ordinary and more
hackneyed political organisation of our party, had
become very influential by 1905, more influential
than could be taken in by any merely superficial
survey.   I do not say that a Liberal Government
could not have been formed without us, but I do
say that it would have been a much less strong
Government, and one that would have been less likely
to be able to cope for a sufficiently long time with
the Protectionist attack, and with the new political
difficulties that were in that year ominously raising
their heads.

Asquith, Grey, and I took counsel together.   What
we believed to be best was that Campbell-Bannerman,
while remaining leader of a party with which he was
very popular, should, if sent for to be Prime Minister,
take a peerage and occupy that office with his seat
in Parliament in the House of Lords.   In that case
Asquith, as Chancellor of the Exchequer, would lead
the party in the Commons.   For the rest we did not
care.   Grey was the natural Foreign Secretary, and
both Asquith and Grey felt that I ought to be Lord

Chancellor. Indeed this was what the Law Lords and the legal public seemed to expect, and Sir Robert Reid, who as ex-Attorney-General and my senior had the better title, had told me that he was not desirous of any judicial position.

But it was not to be. Why things turned out quite otherwise and I was called upon to go to the War Office will appear from what I now write.

Asquith, Grey, and I were thoroughly aware that the Liberal Party, although better off than that of the Unionists, was in a profoundly unsatisfactory condition. We had only one great asset, and that was our Free Trade creed. Home Rule was not a practical possibility for the moment. On education and other subjects the party was devoid of any large ideas. Yet while it was probably about to be returned to power, Campbell-Bannerman being as popular as he was, we thought that he was ill qualified to find for the great progressive force the new basis which it required, and we knew that it was upon this among other things that energetic opponents like Chamberlain were counting. Morley was not really fitted to help; Rosebery had put himself out of court; and the other leaders of the party outside of that section of it that followed our group were hopelessly lacking.

We resolved to take some step. Here Asquith and I were more practical than Grey, who hated having to make any move. I went to Asquith at a country house he and his wife had taken at Glen of Rothes in the north-east of Scotland. Grey had a fishing at Relugas, only about fifteen miles off. After con-

sultation, Asquith and I decided to go over to confer
with Grey. This was at the beginning of September
1905. We talked the situation over with him. It
was decided that it was of great importance that
the King, who would soon have to summon a new
Prime Minister, should be cognisant of the situation.
Asquith thought that, as I had been much in contact
with the King over London University, I would be
a natural channel of communication. Grey did not
dissent, but he thought that Asquith should also see
Campbell-Bannerman as early as possible and tell
him our difficulties. What we agreed on was as
stated above, that if Campbell-Bannerman became
Prime Minister he should take a peerage, and that
Asquith should lead in the Commons as Chancellor
of the Exchequer. Unless our scheme were in substance carried out we resolved that we could not join
Campbell-Bannerman's Government. What we thus
resolved on we used afterwards at times to speak of
among ourselves as ' the Relugas Compact.'

But to place this on a sure foundation it was felt
that we needed the sympathy and possible co-operation of King Edward, and it fell to me to try
to obtain this. When I returned to Cloan I wrote
to Lord Knollys at Balmoral a long letter dated
12th September. From the copy which I have kept
of this letter I see that, after referring to an informal
conversation I had had with Knollys in the previous
July, I told him exactly what had passed at Relugas.
Grey was much interested in his work as the then
Chairman of the North-Eastern Railway, and Asquith
and I had large practices at the Bar. But these

things were nothing to us. If Rosebery ' had been coming to his right place at the head of affairs we could have gone anywhere with the confidence that the tone could be set. But it seems now as if this were not to be, and we have to do the only thing we can do, which is to think out and follow a plan of concerted action.' The only thing that made us pause over our decision was whether it could in any way embarrass the King. It had not struck me that this would be so, if we took ' care to act with the utmost gentleness and consideration in making any intimation to Sir H. C.-B.' Although we hoped to have a considerable following there were others adverse to us who would presently put pressure on him, and it was necessary that, unless there were considerations which we had not seen, we should act quickly. That was why I was writing to him as I had done.

Lord Knollys replied on 16th September that he would show my confidential letter to the King on his arrival at Balmoral. Speaking for himself, he agreed with our views. But he suggested as a middle course that Sir H. C.-B. might at first be Prime Minister in the Commons, and that we should join on the understanding that in six months or within twelve he should go to the Lords. I wrote to him in reply that the difficulty was that, judging by the light of analogous situations in the past, it was within the first six months that divisions over policy were likely to arise in a decisive form. On 25th September he replied that on consideration he agreed with the view expressed in my letter to him, and that we ought to inform Campbell-Bannerman early of it. On King Edward's arrival at Balmoral he showed him the correspondence. The King approved of our ideas, and I was presently sent for to visit him at Balmoral.

I had, of course, sent Knollys's letters to Asquith, for communication to Grey, as they reached me. On 27th September Asquith wrote to me: 'I sent on the correspondence to E. G. and now return Knollys's letter. We went carefully over the whole ground on Sunday. He was a little doubtful of the expediency of approaching the Throne at this stage, but took no exception to what you had written. He was strong for my proposing a visit to C.-B.— not primarily or even necessarily for discussing the personal question—but to prevent in advance any suggestion that in our autumn speeches we were pursuing a hostile or quasi-independent line. He thinks (and I agree) that this may ease the ultimate situation. E. G. was quite clear as to the general position.'

On 5th October I arrived from Cloan at Balmoral in the evening and sat next to the King at dinner. He said that he had read the correspondence with Knollys with much interest. He (the King) had seen Campbell-Bannerman at Marienbad, and he was in his talk far better than in his speeches. I remained at Balmoral for three days, and at the end the King sent for me into his private room. He wholly approved of our ideas, and was favourable to what we suggested. I left the Castle with the feeling that there was no more for me to do, and that the next step must be taken by Asquith when he saw C.-B.

In the end, and after a great deal of negotiation, a new Government was formed when Balfour resigned. C.-B. was at the head of it and I became, not Lord Chancellor, but Minister for War. That I should occupy this post, if not Chancellor, was the wish of King Edward himself, and I have reason to think that he suggested it to C.-B. But the story of these negotiations belongs to the next section. All I have to do in concluding this section is to refer to some miscellaneous matters belonging to the story of the early years of the century.

My diary of this and other periods is largely contained in the confidential letters I sent to my mother. I wrote to her every day, from 1877 down to her death. She preserved these letters with affectionate care, and I have now gone through them.

From 1897 onwards my life was a very full one indeed. Had I not been of strong constitution and physically as well as mentally active, I must have broken down under the strain. As it was, I had little or no illness during this period.

I took no outdoor exercise when in London. My only recreation was to dine out when I was not engaged for meetings. Dine out I did copiously. Sir John (as he had become) and Lady Horner were my constant hosts. I was also very intimate with the Rothschild family. At Tring Park I had a room which was always reserved for me, and I paid week-end visits to Lord and Lady Rothschild with great regularity. With them both I was very intimate. Towards the very end of his life, in 1915, I was in temporary charge of the Foreign Office while my colleague, Grey, was on holiday. It was ascertained there that a steamer had started from South America, and that, although neutral, there was reason to suppose that she contained supplies intended for the Germans. There was no material to act on, and the only way was to resort to private influence. I motored to Lord Rothschild's house in Piccadilly and found him lying down and obviously very ill. But he stretched out his hand before I could speak, and said, 'Haldane, I do not know what you are come for except to see me, but I have said to myself that if Haldane asks me to write a cheque for him for £25,000 and to ask no questions, I will do it on the spot.' I told him that it was not for a cheque, but only to get a ship stopped that I was come. He sent a message to stop the ship at once. I knew his brothers and the other members of the Rothschild family also very well, and used to stay at their houses and dine with them much. My friendship extended to the Paris branch of the family, and to Princess Wagram and Baroness James de Rothschild, Lady Rothschild's sisters. Every year I used to go over to the Château Gros Bois near Paris to spend a week-end before Christmas with Prince and Princess Wagram. Christmas Day was always spent at Mells, and on Christmas night I travelled down to Cloan to my mother, since New Year's Day was in Scottish fashion that recognised at home.

I dined out a good deal to meet King Edward, who used to ask that I should be included in the list of those whom he was to meet, and I went to the houses in London and the country of many others. Somehow it proved possible by contrivance to dovetail this social activity in with the multitude of the legal and political calls on my time. Looking back from the quiet stage of old age on all this, it is difficult for me to see now how it was managed. But I did not play golf or bridge or tennis, or ride, and so I suppose I found the truth of Goethe's saying that time is infinitely long. If we use it fully most things can be got within its compass.

In addition to the duties and occupations to which I have referred I had others. Early in the time of the South African War I was travelling up to London from Mells one Sunday afternoon. Lord Lansdowne, who was then Secretary of State for War, got into the train at Chippenham. We began to talk, and I said to him, 'What we have been suffering from in the South African War is, among other things, that we have not given proper attention to our explosives. They have been eating out the guns and wearing out our resources.' He was struck, and asked me when we got to London to come to dine with him alone. I went, and he said, 'I have been thinking over this. It is evidently a subject which you have studied, and I want you to take the Chair of an Explosives Committee under the War Office and Admiralty which will look into this question.' So I said to him 'We ought to do what the French have done. They had a Committee, the Chairman of which was their great chemist, Berthelot. You ought to appoint the English Berthelot to be Chairman.' 'Who is he?' said Lansdowne, and I said, 'Lord Rayleigh.' H took the matter up, but insisted that I should go on the Committee. I sat on it, with the late Lord Rayleigh as Chairman; with Sir William Crookes, the great chemist; with Sir W. Roberts-Austen, a distinguished man of science in another department, that of metallurgy; and Sir Andrew Noble, who was a great artillery expert. We considered a good many improvements in propellents, and also in high explosives. This Committee sat mostly at Woolwich on and off for four years, and, although it took up time, I found the knowledge gained of great use when I came to the War Office in the end of 1905.

I also presided over the Committee which was appointed to advise on the reconstruction of the organisation for the collection of the Death Duties. Lord Milner, who was formerly at the head of the Inland Revenue Department, persuaded me to undertake this. We carried the reconstruction through. Our Secretary was a very able young civil servant, Mr. Duncan, who afterwards went out to South Africa and became distinguished in public life there.

In 1900 Milner and Chamberlain pressed me to go out to South Africa and undertake the Chairmanship of a Commission of Inquiry into various important questions of reform there. I saw that it must involve a long spell of work and possibly my withdrawal from political life here. After consideration I said I could not go. Alfred Lyttelton took my place, and he ultimately became Secretary for the Colonies in the Unionist Administration.

I had also, towards the end of the 'nineties, served on the Committee appointed by the Home Office to investigate the organisation of our prisons. As an aid to the discharge of my duties on this Committee I had a warrant which enabled me to go to any prison, at any hour, and call on the Governor to produce any prisoner. During the time of our work Oscar Wilde had been sentenced to a term of imprisonment under circumstances which are well remembered. I used to meet him in the days of his social success, and, although I had not known him well, was haunted by the idea of what this highly sensitive man was probably suffering under ordinary prison treatment. I went to Holloway Gaol, where I knew he was, and asked the Governor to let me see him. The Chaplain was called in, and he said that he was glad I had come, for with Wilde he had wholly failed to make any way. I then saw Wilde himself, alone in a cell. At first he refused to speak. I put my hand on his prison-dress-clad shoulder and said that I used to know him and that I had come to say something about himself. He had not fully used his great literary gift, and the reason was that he had lived a life of pleasure and had not made any great subject his own. Now misfortune might prove a blessing for his career, for he had got a great subject. I would try to get for him books and pen and ink, and in eighteen months he would be free to produce. He burst into tears, and promised to make the attempt. For the books he asked eagerly, saying that they would only give him the *Pilgrim's Progress*, and that this did not satisfy him. He asked for Flaubert's works. But I said that the dedication by that author to his advocate, who had successfully defended Flaubert from a charge of indecent publication, made such a book as *Madame Bovary* unlikely to be sanctioned. He laughed and became cheerful. We hit on St. Augustine's Works and on Mommsen's *History of Rome*. These I got for him, and they accompanied him from prison to prison. I afterwards visited him at Wandsworth Prison, and persuaded the Home Secretary to transfer him to Reading. I saw Lady Cowper, and with her aid his wife and children were looked after. On his release there came to me anonymously a volume, *The Ballad of Reading Gaol*. It was the redemption of his promise to me.

CHAPTER VI

THE LIBERAL GOVERNMENT AND THE ARMY
(1905–1910)

THE first week in December 1905 was a very disagreeable one for Grey and me. Asquith was deeply attached to us and he was the straightest of men. But there were other influences at work, and it was plain that forces were being exerted to place him in the Cabinet, even if Campbell-Bannerman and not he were its head. The Relugas arrangement was consequently in jeopardy. To make things worse, Asquith and his wife proceeded to keep an engagement to stay with the Salisburys at Hatfield, where they were during the week in which Campbell-Bannerman was forming his Government. Asquith came to town indeed during the day, but it was difficult to see him as much as the circumstances required. On 5th December Campbell-Bannerman kissed hands. Grey, adhering to our original attitude, refused to take office unless Asquith led in the Commons. The King had suggested to C.-B. that he should accept a peerage on the ground of his age, and C.-B. had replied that he would in the end have to do this but that he preferred to start in the House of Commons, though it might be only for a short time that he would remain there. Grey remained immovable.

I had a large flat at 3 Whitehall Court at this time, into which I had moved from Members Mansions where I used to live. Grey had come from Fallodon to stay with me. Asquith saw C.-B. again, whose attitude about the Commons was not at first an obstinate one, but he said that he must consult with his wife, who would arrive at his house in Belgrave Square in the evening of Wednesday, 6th. Lady C.-B. was a woman of much character, and her decision was ' no surrender.' C.-B. then saw Asquith and told him that this was his decision also, but that he might say to Grey and myself that we could have (Grey) the Foreign Office and (myself) the Home Office. Notwithstanding that Asquith urged him strenuously that I was the person best fitted for the Woolsack, he was resolved that Sir Robert Reid should be Lord Chancellor. Asquith knew that, so far as I was concerned, I would make no particular difficulty merely on this point. The real difficulty was with Grey. C.-B. had communicated with him and had found him resolute. He was uneasy about his chance of being able to set the tone about Foreign Affairs in the delicate situation on the Continent if C.-B. led the House of Commons. He did not wish to accept office.

On Thursday, 7th December, a letter was brought to me from C.-B. :—

My dear Haldane,—I hope I am not wrong in believing that you would be loth to abandon the road of professional success upon which you have already travelled so far, and I have much pleasure in proposing that you should fill the position of Attorney-General. It is, as you know, an office of the highest importance, having relations with many great Departments where your success would be of the greatest value. It involves what are practically Cabinet responsibilities, though not Cabinet rank, and is of its kind the highest office which it is now in my power to offer. At the same time, if I am under a misapprehension as to your desires, and should you prefer to devote yourself to other administrative work, I shall gladly make to you a proposition of a different nature which would bring you into the Cabinet.—Believe me, yours very truly,

H. CAMPBELL-BANNERMAN.

Now the last thing that was likely to appeal to me was the position of a Law Officer. I had had the best that the Bar itself could give me. But that was not the main reason for rejecting anything short of office in the Cabinet. My whole soul had been for years in the effort to bring about reform in higher education and in other departments of administration. To accept the Attorney-Generalship was to abandon influence which I had possessed even under the outgoing Unionist Government. In truth C.-B. in these days neither much liked nor understood me. Later on I was to find him an admirable Prime Minister to work under, but there was no such prospect when his letter came. Moreover I should not have joined any Government which Grey would not join.

The *Times* had announced that morning that Grey refused to serve as Foreign Secretary. Morley, I gathered, had seen the Editor and told him so the evening before at the Athenæum Club, after Campbell-Bannerman had had an interview with Grey. I do not think Morley minded profoundly. He had always resented the Liberal Imperialist group, notwithstanding his intimacy with its members. But he did not comprehend how deficient the spirit of orthodox Liberalism had become. He was a Victorian and lived in a Victorian tradition. Mr. Gladstone, he thought, would have shown Grey the door, and Campbell-Bannerman should have done the same. Morley was worse than the latter, for he was even more hostile and understood as little the new tendencies in public opinion and the necessity of new ideas and energy in the Administration. I had no wish to abandon my position at the Bar and in the House unless it were to be for some very genuine work. But one consideration weighed with me. If Grey and I stood out, our line of policy would probably not be sufficiently pressed on his colleagues by Asquith, who would be taken, by accepting office without us, to have partially endorsed the ordinary tradition. At all events, if Grey as well as Asquith were in the Cabinet the danger of feebleness in resisting criticism from Chamberlain and others would be materially lessened. For the sake of Free Trade it was therefore highly expedient that the Government should be as strongly as possible permeated with the spirit of Liberal Imperialism.

I did not at once answer the letter the Prime Minister had sent me by messenger. In the course of the Thursday afternoon I had a conversation with Lady Horner which influenced my mind. I shall refer to it presently. I got home to Whitehall Court about six on that afternoon. There I found Grey reposing on the sofa with the air of one who had taken a decision and was done with political troubles. But I put before him the thoughts which were passing through my mind, especially about resisting Protection. Were we not thinking too much of ourselves and too little of the public ? The Relugas basis being gone, we were in a weakened position, but we could still do something real in the way of effort to save the situation. Grey reflected. He said there was much in what I had said, but that he could not come to a final conclusion until he had eaten some food. I proposed that we should go to the Café Royal and order dinner in a private room there. We started off, calling on the way, as arranged, on Arthur Acland, who was too unwell to think of office, but was much interested in inducing Grey to join. Acland spoke to us on the lines on which a good many other people had already spoken. It has been said that he altered Grey's mind, but I do not think the conversation made any real difference to either of us. He and I went on to the Café Royal, and there, before we were through dinner, Grey said to me that he thought that, notwithstanding Asquith was now only in the second position in the Commons, he, Grey, ought to take the Foreign Office. 'But,' he said, 'I will not do so unless you also come into the Cabinet.' I replied that it would be all right, for I could bargain with C.-B., whose letter I showed him, about our coming in together.

As the result I left him at dinner, got into a hansom cab, and drove to C.-B.'s house. I found that he was dining alone with his wife. I said I would wait for him in his study—he came at once. I asked him

whether he still wanted Grey. He said he did
indeed, but that G. was very difficult. I replied
that possibly I might help to bring G. in. I had not
answered his letter to myself, but that I could now
do so. I did not want to be Attorney-General. He
then offered me the Home Office. I said, 'What
about the War Office ? ' ' Nobody,' answered C.-B.,
' will touch it with a pole.' ' Then give it to me. I
will come in as War Secretary if Grey takes the
Foreign Office, and I will ask him to call on you
early to-morrow to tell you his decision, which may,
I think, be favourable.'

As there has been much innocent misrepresentation of what really happened in this week, I think it
worth while to reproduce a Memorandum about its
events which I dictated not very long after to Lady
Horner during a visit to Mells in 1906. For, as will
appear from its terms, it was really she who mainly
influenced me to the reconsideration of the decision
of Grey and myself not to join the new Government.
She had spoken to me with great earnestness when I
called on her, with Campbell-Bannerman's letter
in my pocket, on my way on Thursday, 7th, from
South Kensington to see Grey at Whitehall Court.
What happened appears from the Memorandum.

MEMORANDUM AS TO EVENTS IN DECEMBER 1905

' I want to recall to you in their sequence the events
of the early days of December 1905 while they are
still fresh in my memory. I knew from Arthur
Balfour that he meant to resign, and I asked Edward

Grey to come up at once and work out with me a joint course of action. He came about the last day of November. As you know, he and Asquith and I had decided in the autumn that we would act together and stand out jointly for certain things. We agreed that Sir H. C.-B. ought to go to the Lords as Prime Minister because, especially from the point of view of Foreign Affairs and also of coming rapidly to firm and quick decisions on current business in the House of Commons, we felt that this was very important to the success of a Free Trade Ministry. Looking back, I think that our judgment was right, and that the one thing which has averted the evils which we anticipated, and which up to the present stage have been fewer than we foresaw, has been the unexpected size and power of the Liberal majority in the House of Commons. The second point which we held essential was that the Foreign Office should be in the hands, not of Lord Spencer but of Grey. This became easier to accomplish because of poor Lord Spencer's sudden illness. The third was that the office of Lord Chancellor should receive a larger interpretation than it had in the past in point of influence on colonial and general policy, and also that it should be filled by some one who would genuinely represent Grey's views in the Upper House. He and Asquith expressed their determination that it should be filled by myself. Rosebery appeared to have effaced himself, but we thought that with these points conceded we could usefully enter the Ministry and really add to the foundations on which a Free Trade Ministry could be built. At Asquith's

request I had communicated our agreement to the
King and had been summoned to Balmoral, where
the King had intimated his warm approval of it;
this took place in October 1905. In the end of
November I asked Grey, as I have said, to come
to London and stay with me. We determined that
the policy so laid down was vital and that each of
us three must make it a condition of entering the
Government that these points must be conceded.
We had been in communication with Sir H. C.-B.
through Asquith, who had more or less passed on the
substance of them to him before the actual fall of the
Government. In the end of November the Government went out and Sir H. C.-B. was sent for. Grey
returned to Fallodon, and came up again on the
morning of Monday, December 4th. I think it
was Sunday, 3rd, that Sir H. C.-B. went to the Palace
and received his Commission. So far as I know, the
King said nothing of our communication with him
to Sir H. C.-B. Early in the week it was obvious
that things were not going satisfactorily. Asquith
had done his very best about the Chancellorship,
but to that, standing by itself and apart from the
concession of the other two points, Grey and I
attached but little importance, and it was evident
that Asquith had not been resolute about the solidity
of our position. In the end, and about the middle
of the week, it appeared that he had yielded and
was prepared, in response to Sir H. C.-B.'s appeal,
to enter his Ministry in any event. It was also
evident that the Lord Chancellor would be Sir R.
Reid : it was not certain whether Sir H. C.-B. would

go to the House of Lords or not. Up till Wednesday
night it seemed not improbable that he would yield
on this, but on that evening Lady C.-B. arrived
from Scotland and the next morning he resolutely
refused to go. Asquith was now pledged to enter,
and all he could do was to fight hard for the inclusion
of Grey and myself. It was certain that Sir H. C.-B.
wanted Grey to come to the Foreign Office and was
willing that I should occupy the Home Office. The
Colonial Office was already given to Lord Elgin, to
whom I think he had at first offered the Foreign
Office before his mind turned to Grey; but the
attitude both of Grey and myself was Sir H. C.-B.'s
difficulty. Asquith had gone to stay at Hatfield,
and we were not seeing very much of him. We
both felt that the break-up of the old tripartite
arrangement diminished our powers of usefulness.
We thought that the majority might be a weak and
incohesive one and that it was better that reserves
for the defence of Free Trade should be kept in
hand. Consequently, on Thursday, the 7th, Grey
had definitely refused to enter the Government. I had
definitely decided that under no circumstances would
I enter without him, and up to the afternoon of that
day no direct or definite invitation to enter the
Government had been given to me personally. At
four o'clock that day I was presiding at South
Kensington over a meeting of the Committee on
Technical Education of which I was Chairman, when
two messengers arrived with letters from Sir H. C.-B.
and from Asquith. Sir H. C.-B.'s letter proposed
to me to join his Government. If I did not wish for

the Attorney-Generalship he had other proposals to make involving Cabinet rank. Asquith's letter pressed me to take the War Office. I had once in conversation said to him that that was the only office, apart perhaps from the Colonial Office (with the exception of the Lord Chancellorship), that attracted me. I put the letters in my pocket and presided to the end of the meeting. I regarded the matter as finished. Grey's decision while it stood, and I thought it would and ought to stand, bound me. I had to see him before dinner at Whitehall Court and we were to dine alone together, but I did not anticipate any change on the part of either of us. On my way home I stopped at 9 Buckingham Gate and asked if you were in. Mrs. Crawshay and Mrs. Hope were with you, but they left almost immediately and we went downstairs to the school-room. I then showed you the letters. I told you that in my view the thing was now settled adversely and that it was best so. After a little reflection you made an observation; it was this: "From your own point of view and that of Grey this may be right, but you told the King that you would not leave him in the lurch—besides this you are making a real risk for the Free Trade cause. There may be a very heavy reaction against the weak Government which is going to be formed, in which Free Trade will perish." You added that from the point of view of personal comfort the case was clear enough, but that about the question of duty you were not so clear in your mind. Our talk made a great impression on me. I said to you, "How can one join a Government which is almost bound to be weak

M

and discredited from the beginning?" You answered,
"The better for you to be a member of it—the
worse for the King and the public who cannot escape
from it." I left you and went down to Whitehall
Court. I found Grey lying on a sofa in the library.
I told him of the letters. I said that I was going to
refuse, that I was clear I could not go on in view of
his decision—we must stand and fall together whatever happened. (This was your own view as well as
mine.)

'I said to Grey that as a matter of inclination as well
as the result of his own decision I was going to refuse.
The office for which I seemed to myself to be most
ready was the Chancellorship. Moreover, to take
office at all meant an enormous loss of income. I
was making between £15,000 and £20,000 a year at
the Bar. I said to him that one doubt and one
doubt only had come into my mind. Looked at as
a matter of individual convenience the decision
seemed to me unquestionable : was it quite so clear
from an ethical standpoint that we had quite fully
considered the necessities of the King and the Nation ?
It was now about seven o'clock and we had promised
to call on Acland at about half-past seven. Grey
gave his answer to these fresh points, but he was
obviously troubled, and he said, " Let us walk to
Acland's rooms and consider as we go along." He
added, "You are not as clear as you were that we
are right." I replied that I was as clear as ever from
a personal point. My doubt was whether we had
sufficiently considered the ethical question. I told
him I had come to no conclusion, but that I doubted

whether we had exhausted the question, and whether the only tenable ground from an ethical point of view, viz. the desire to keep a second line of defence for Free Trade, was sufficiently substantial. He turned to me as we walked and said, "You are putting on me a responsibility which I cannot bear—that of making you take a decision the moral correctness of which you doubt." I said to him that was inevitable. There could be no question of either of us entering without the other. He was much troubled : I think he felt that we were acting somewhat selfishly. The tripartite policy had been shattered through no fault of ours, and what right had we to adhere to a line of action which was only a means to an end now gone ? He was very silent. As we entered Acland's door I said to him that my doubts were certainly not less strong than when we had begun to talk. He looked very unhappy. Acland kept us for three-quarters of an hour : he poured into us arguments about destroying the prospects of the Liberal Party, to which we both listened without replying. He could not realise why it was that we were listening in silence, and I think he took it to be wholly the result of his own argument. I believe that he thinks so still, and appearances justified this. Doubtless his moral earnestness helped, but the real determining cause of the change of view, certainly on my part, and I think on Grey's also, was the new light that had come in the previous hour of mental wrestling, and the searchings that arose in my own mind from the talk in the schoolroom at Buckingham Gate. Grey felt the change and I felt it, and the last

time I saw Lady Grey before her death a few
weeks later she said to me that I had saved Edward
from falling into a moral blunder which she herself
had not realised. To go on with the story : Grey
and I went off to the Café Royal, where we ordered
dinner in a private room. When we had finished
some fish we decided that the fact that he had
definitely and finally rejected C.-B.'s offer in a
letter that afternoon could indeed make a change of
attitude disagreeable, but could not alter the moral
obligation. He turned to me and said, " You may
do what you please." I answered that I would go
there and then to Sir H. C.-B. Grey said, " If we
enter it is not for pleasure's sake, and we must take
the most beastly things. I will take the War Office."
I said the public interest demanded that he should
take the Foreign Office, and I would ask for the War
Office. I went to Sir H. C.-B., told him I had come
to answer his letter : that I would take one office—
the War Office—on condition that Grey went to the
Foreign Office. He said Grey had refused in a manner
that left him no hope. I replied that if he was willing
to leave to me the conveying to Grey of a renewed
offer it was within possibility that he might hear by
ten o'clock the next morning from Grey personally
that we had both accepted. He was very easy and
pleasant to deal with, and thoroughly dignified.
I went to Acland's rooms, where Grey presently
joined me, and told him it was settled. I wish to
place on record, in case it is ever of interest in the
future, that I think that, so far as Grey was concerned, the cause of the withdrawal of his refusal was

almost, if not quite wholly, due to what passed between him and me; and last, that my own changed attitude was wholly due to what had passed between you and me previously in the schoolroom at Buckingham Gate.

'The whole week was one of the most miserable I have ever spent in my life. The one illuminating hour in it was that of our talk, and the new light that came. I have never for a moment regretted the consequent decision or the vast change which your influence made in the course of my career.'

Next morning, on Friday, 8th, Grey saw C.-B. and confirmed the arrangement. It was a busy day in Court, and I was arguing an appeal in the Privy Council. The usher touched my elbow while I was addressing the judges, and said that Sir E. Grey wanted to speak with me urgently. I begged the Tribunal for indulgence on special business—Grey took me aside and said, 'It is settled. You are Secretary for War, and I am Foreign Secretary.' I went on with the argument in my appeal, but we had not escaped the notice of vigilant representatives of the Press, who were able to point to an indication that the *Times* had probably been misinformed in its announcement on the previous day of Grey's refusal to join.

Such is the story of these days. C.-B. was a reticent man. He gave his confidences only in fragments, and this habit has misled several people who have written about their relations to him into the belief that he had imparted to them the whole history

of what happened.   The real narrative, while it shows
how C.-B. got us into his Government, also shows that
he accomplished this in large measure, though not
wholly, on our own terms and as a fair bargain.
When we had come together under him he proved
an easy person to transact with.   Myself he did not
like at first, and this was hardly to be wondered at.
Knowing what the War Office was, he was said to have
observed, ' We shall now see how Schopenhauer gets
on in the Kailyard.'   For some months he said
nothing to me, and encouraged me but little in the
Cabinet.   But there came a day when, writing about
something else at the end of a little more than a
year, he said : ' As this is the close of a Parliamentary
Chapter, let me most sincerely and warmly con-
gratulate you upon the great success you have wrought
out of your complicated problem and your worrying
labours over it.   It is a great triumph to have carried
such a large body of opinion with you, and I hope you
will have as much satisfaction when you proceed to
carry out and superintend the details of your *magnum
opus.*'

When one did succeed in securing his confidence
there were few better Chiefs to work for than Sir
H. C.-B.   And he knew the War Office well, though
his studies of military problems had not been profound.

The new Government was quickly formed.   We
went together to the Palace to receive our Seals.   It
was a day of the blackest fog that I remember.   When
the ceremony was over we set off with our Seals to
our respective Offices.   I had a hired brougham, and
Grey and Fowler left in it with me.   We stuck in the

darkness of the Mall.   I got out to see where we were
and could not find the carriage again.   Fowler got back
to the Palace.   Grey, after a long wandering round
and round, eventually reached the Foreign Office.
By trudging through the mud and feeling among the
horses' heads I at last got to the War Office, then in
Pall Mall.   Fortunately I had kept hold of my Seals.
I was a little exhausted when I arrived.   I handed
the Seals to the Permanent Under-Secretary to take
charge of, and asked the tall ex-Guards soldier in
attendance for a glass of water. ' Certainly, sir:
Irish or Scotch ? '

The next day the Generals on the Army Council
came to a first interview with the new Secretary of
State.   After a short talk the leader said to me
that they all felt that, without going into details,
they would like to have some general idea of the
reforms which I thought of proposing to Parliament.
My reply was that I was as a young and blushing
virgin just united to a bronzed warrior, and that it
was not expected by the public that any result of
the union should appear until at least nine months
had passed.   This was reported by the Generals to
the King, who accompanied with mirth his full
approval of the answer.

At this time I knew but little of military affairs,
and of Army organisation I was wholly ignorant.
But from the beginning the work fascinated me.
For I saw that here was an almost virgin field, to be
operated on by applying first principles as soon as
I had discovered them.   The Esher Committee had
evolved a very far-reaching and apparently valuable

scheme for the reorganisation of the Staff of the Army, and this had in part been carried into effect before Balfour left office. The Committee of Imperial Defence, on which Lord Esher was working and of which Lord Sydenham, as he afterwards became, was Secretary, were engaged on it. These two had been members of the Esher Committee, with Sir John (afterwards Lord) Fisher as their colleague. I of course consulted them at once, and asked them whether they could recommend to me for the post of my Military Private Secretary an Army officer who knew the subject thoroughly. They advised me without hesitation to choose Colonel Ellison, as he then was, who had been the Secretary of the Esher Committee, and had proved himself to be all that I was looking for. I appointed him and installed him at my elbow in the War Office. He went down with me to Haddington to impart instruction during the General Election which followed on the dissolution of January 1906, and he went with me to Cloan while I was there. Ellison proved to be all and more than all I had hoped for. He never let me off anything, and, what I liked, used to insist on looking for a clear principle before advising action. He had been trained in part in German military surroundings, and had studied military history and organisation copiously. I came to recognise his hand in much of the Report of the Esher Committee, of which, as I have said, he had been the Secretary.

With Ellison I set to work hard, and we soon hit on fresh ideas. From an early stage I began to

study the great principles on which Continental
military organisations had been founded, as set
forth by Clausewitz, Bronsart von Schellendorff, and
Von der Goltz, with the description of Napoleon's
mind in Yorck von Wartenburg's book, written
from the standpoint of the German General Staff.
From the French point of view I was much influenced
by a volume which is too little known to-day, Colonel
Ardant du Picq on *The Moral Factor in War*. But
these works merely illustrated the necessity of careful
thought before action. This was a lesson which I
had learned early, and to apply it to the new question
of Army reorganisation was a natural step. When
the Army Council asked me one morning again for
some notion of the Army I had in mind, my answer
to them was, ' A Hegelian Army.' The conversation
then fell off.

The state of the Army before the South African
War had been almost inconceivably confused. Not
only was there no General Staff to do the thinking,
but the organisation in time of peace was different
from that required for war, so different that there
was hardly a unit that was capable of taking the
field as it stood. After the Report of the Commission
that followed on the South African War some things
had been done, but, excepting when the Esher
Committee reported, nothing very illuminating from
a military point of view had been brought to light.
The Committee of Imperial Defence, which Balfour
had founded, was the other great asset, but this
Committee had neither the scope nor the organisation
which became characteristic of its later days. The

public was profoundly dissatisfied with the state
of our military forces, and a very large section of the
Liberals, disgusted alike with the War Office and
with war, had pledged itself to proceed to a
tremendous reduction of War Office Estimates. My
friend and colleague as Financial Member, T. R.
Buchanan, M.P., was one of the most loyal of
comrades, but very orthodox as a Liberal. Sir
H. C.-B. had made him Financial Member at the
War Office in order, I think, to make sure that I
should not run wild. The argument used by some
of the average Liberals if I wished to get the support
of the party in the House of Commons was—' Do
not attempt great improvements. The attempt will
fail. But concentrate yourself on reducing the
estimates.' My reply was that economy and efficiency
were not incompatible : that I believed we could
obtain a finely organised Army for less money than
at present, but that a finer Army we must have,
even though it cost more. I went to a meeting in
the City within my first ten days of office, accompanied by Ellison and Lady Horner, and proclaimed
this, adding that the Prime Minister had authorised
me to say that if more money turned out to be
essential we should have it. I was not prepared to
go on with my work on any other footing.

In my financial plans I had the devoted help of
a very remarkable man, Charles Harris, whom I made
the Permanent Head of the Financial Department of
the War Office. Harris had been in the Department
for a great many years. He had a fine intelligence
and was both very ingenious and very industrious.

He was profoundly convinced that there was waste at every turn of the organisation.

Ellison, Harris, and I set to work. The first question was what must be our objective, and what was required for its attainment ? In almost every period the peril to be provided against is different from what it is in another period. Once it had been invasion by the French. Changes in diplomatic relations had made this particular peril for the time an obsolete one. In 1906 there was the possibility, I thought it no more than a chance which was improbable, that the Central Powers might invade and occupy France, in which case, with growing German sea-power, our island security from invasion would be much diminished. The continued occupation by a friendly nation like the French of Dunkirk, Calais, and Boulogne, the vital Northern Channel ports of the Continent, was therefore an objective on which to concentrate. The accomplishment of this implied that we should have an Expeditionary Force sufficient in size and also in rapidity of mobilising power to be able to go to the assistance of the French Army in the event of an attack on the Northern or North-Eastern parts of France. The investigations of the Committee of Imperial Defence had in my view made it clear that our Navy could both prevent Great Britain from being invaded, if the Northern Channel ports were in friendly hands, and also look after any Continental fleet of probable dimensions at sea.

Had we organised the requisite Expeditionary Force ? Clearly we had not. To begin with, hardly

a brigade could have been sent to the Continent
without being recast. As they stood, the brigades
were generally incomplete and in a form that was
convenient in peace time but wholly inadequate
for mobilisation. A careful inquiry made disclosed
that in order to put even 80,000 men on the Continent
preliminary preparations requiring at the very least
two months would be required. But that was far
from all. The Continental Powers fought, not with
brigades, but with great divisions and corps, each
containing two divisions. We had not in 1906 a
single division that was a reality. Moreover the
brigades, such as they were, wholly lacked accessories
without which they could not sustain the strain of
war. Their transport was deficient and so were their
medical organisations. The field artillery consisted
for peace purposes of ninety-nine batteries. But these
batteries were seriously short, not only of men in
the ranks, but of reserves. Only forty-two batteries
could be put in the field, a number which a proper
General Staff would have pronounced to be ludicrously
inadequate for the Expeditionary Force required.

We had therefore to provide for an Expeditionary
Force which we reckoned at six great divisions,
fully equipped, and at least one cavalry division.
We had also to make certain that this force could
be mobilised and sent to the place where it might be
required as rapidly as any German force could be.
The limit of time was worked out at fifteen days.
Of the details of the organisation for this it is not
necessary for me to write, for I have already done
so fully in the chapter on our Military Preparations

written in the book I published in 1920, *Before the War*.
One addition I wish to make. It has been stated
that a certain officer, afterwards distinguished in
work of a very different kind, played a large part
in the fashioning of the Army Reforms of 1906,
1907, and the years immediately subsequent. This
is not the case. This distinguished officer did not
occupy a post of importance at the War Office until
1910. He was on the General Staff side then, but in a
post which had nothing to do with the construction of
the Expeditionary and Territorial Forces. The plans
had been fully thought out before 1907. The men
who co-operated in advising me were Ellison, Harris,
Haig, Ewart, and Nicholson. The great task of
translating these plans into action was the work
not of the General Staff but of the Adjutant-General,
General Douglas, one of the most energetic and single-
minded administrators we have ever had at the
War Office.

But I must allude to something that happened
during the General Election in January 1906. Early
in that month I went from East Lothian to Berwick
to address Grey's constituents with him. I found
that he had ordered a carriage to take us after the
meeting for a long drive and private talk. He told
me that the French were concerned about the possibility of a German movement against them in the
summer. How far were we, if an emergency com-
pelling our intervention should arise, prepared with
plans for it ? Had we compared ideas about preparation with the French Generals ? I said that there
had been before my time some general conversations,

but that the one thing needful, the interchange of scientific General Staff ideas, had not taken place to anything like the extent which modern standards of preparedness required. He asked whether such an interchange could not now take place, as a military precaution committing neither Government to any action, but enabling us to be ready for a serious contingency should it arise. I said that the General Staff at the War Office could easily do this, and that it should be done with a written declaration that the conversations were to be wholly non-committal. We both thought that Campbell-Bannerman should be first consulted, and I undertook to go to London and see him. This I did, and had a full talk with him a few days later. The Prime Minister asked whether it could be made clear that the conversations were purely for military General Staff purposes and were not to prejudice the complete freedom of the two Governments should the situation the French dreaded arise. I undertook to see that this was put in writing. I myself saw Colonel Huguet, the French Military Attaché in London, whom I knew well, and General Grierson, the Director of Military Operations at our War Office, saw representatives of the French General Staff. That the conversations were to leave us wholly free was expressed in a letter which was signed.

This initiated a study of the most probable terrain and an interchange of communications as to the possible available military strength of the French and ourselves. The work was done purely between the officers concerned, who accumulated the military knowledge required, and the Governments at large took no part in it. Of course that there had been these communications gradually became known. The Germans heard of them through their Secret Service Department, and the German Emperor told me that this was the case when I visited him in Berlin in the following September. But I replied that such preliminary knowledge was regarded to-day as essential for any Army that was to be prepared for a possible task, and that his own Great General Staff had been the first to teach the principle to the world. He fully admitted that this was so and said he had no quarrel with us for doing this.

As these preliminary arrangements were initiated while Ministers were away on their Election campaigns, there could be no Cabinet discussions of them. But the Prime Minister, Lord Ripon as leader in the Lords, and Asquith had full knowledge of them. Without the guidance we derived through the conversations we could not have been ready in July 1914.

The Expeditionary Force was shaped to meet the demands so defined. In military organisation the form must always be determined by what is the most likely use to which the Army may have to be put. If, for instance, I had to fashion the form of the British Army to-day, I think I should fashion it differently from what was required in 1906. The centre of danger is, for the time at least, more likely to be in the Near or Far East than in France. Consequently it might be best to split the expeditionary organisation and to keep a division in India, thereby diminishing the military charge for the Indian Army and securing the possible presence at short notice of British troops in the neighbourhood of India and at places like Singapore. At least the question is one which would require consideration.

But with an Expeditionary Force at home which may have to leave the country, a second line is obviously required for expansion as well as for home defence. This requirement was the genesis of the Territorial or Second Line Army. There was nothing approaching to such a second line in existence. The Volunteers, although some of them had been brigaded, had neither a transport nor a medical side. The Militia were neither organised nor equipped. They were really useful only as a body from which drafts might be drawn for the Regular troops. As Lord Lansdowne had said of them, it was the custom to plunder them on one side and to pillage them on the other. The Yeomanry were an excellent peace organisation of a separate kind, still largely run by the country gentlemen. But these heterogeneous corps had histories and traditions and people who had been associated with and were devotedly attached to them. To break with tradition and weld their substance into something quite novel was likely to be a very serious undertaking. It proved to be so. It required a comprehensive statute, and this I set myself to draw. The soldiers could not help me much here, so I employed my old ' devils ' at Lincoln's Inn to aid me in constructing a preliminary draft. One of them, my friend John Kemp, came down to

VIEW FROM LORD HALDANE'S STUDY AT CLOAN

Scotland and spent a recess in working with me at
this draft. We completed it so that all the ground
was covered. I then sent for the Government
draftsman, afterwards Sir F. Liddell, and asked him
to throw it into proper Parliamentary shape. This
he did with admirable skill. It became the comprehensive Territorial and Reserve Forces Bill, under
which, when it became an Act, the Volunteers and
Yeomanry were fashioned into part of a Territorial
second line, and the Militia were made into reserves,
sans phrase, for the regular first line. As to these
last, the Cardwell principle of localisation and of
providing every first battalion of a regiment with
a second battalion which in peace time would feed
it when abroad and on mobilisation would form with
the aid of its reserves a fully ready second battalion
was carried to its logical conclusion by providing a
third battalion at the depôt to maintain both against
wastage in war. The organisation was put by the
Bill on a county basis, and the Territorial side of it
was to be looked after by new County Associations
with the Lord Lieutenants at their head.

The Bill was a large and a formidable one, and I
knew that difficulties would be made about finding
time for it in the House of Commons. I met Balfour
during a week-end at Windsor Castle and asked him
whether he would help me. If he would assent to
what in these days was wholly new, a time-table
which would ensure full opportunity for disposal of
the measure within a reasonable number of days, I
would consult his convenience. He said that as the
Unionist Government had not succeeded in disposing

N

of the Army problem it was only right that we should
have our chance. He knew our difficulties and
he got Lord Lansdowne to agree to give us the like
chance in the Lords. He added naturally that the
Opposition could take no responsibility for our plan
on which Parliament itself must pronounce.

An opportunity for progress now came. One of
my colleagues had undertaken to produce a Bill
for a social reform in which there was much interest
in Liberal circles, and it was announced for introduction on a certain date, and time had been set
apart for it. But unexpected difficulties had arisen.
It could not be ready, and in the middle of the Parliamentary session there would be an interval unfilled.
I modestly explained to my colleagues in the Cabinet
that I had a little Bill which would just fill the time.
When they heard what it was they were rather
dismayed. They had not forgotten the defeat of
the last Liberal Administration on the cordite
question, and some of them even said that all I
wanted could be accomplished without any Bill at
all, quoting Sir C. Dilke to that effect. I dissented.
I said that experience in the debates had made me
attach less value to Dilke's knowledge of military
affairs than they did. Moreover I then disclosed
the time limit on which Balfour and I had come
to a definite agreement. The result was that I was
authorised to fill the unforeseen gap in the programme
of the session with the Territorial and Reserve
Forces Bill. At first a large number of the Liberal
rank and file were suspicious. But when I showed
that I had actually brought down the Army Estimates

from over thirty millions to within twenty-eight (including the whole cost of the new reorganisation), the Bill was allowed to pass. This was in 1907. There was of course fighting, but it was touched in no point that was material.

I had then a new experience. The French thought that we ought to have a large Army, raised compulsorily on a Continental scale, and Clémenceau came over and saw Campbell-Bannerman and Asquith. They decided that I should have a conversation with him and show him the difficulties. This conversation I had with Clémenceau alone at Asquith's house in Cavendish Square.

I told Clémenceau that our position as the island centre of a scattered Empire made our strategical position quite different from that of France. A large Navy was what we required, and with it an Army which that Navy could transport to where it was wanted at the shortest notice. That Army, which must be instantly ready, had to be professional and ought not to be of large dimensions. For our expenditure must be in the first place on our Navy. Whether I convinced him I do not know. I explained all this fully, and the French never raised any question about the doctrine subsequently. There were of course people here who called for a larger Army : men of eminence like Lord Roberts. But I do not think that they had grasped either the importance of the naval doctrine of commanding the sea, or what it implied. Of course I knew, and I told the House of Commons so, that if a great war came we should probably have to resort to compulsory service in order to increase and keep up the Army. But in peace time all that could wisely be done was to perfect the organisation so that it could be used, if the necessity came, for expansion.

Still the pressure on me for a compulsory system during peace continued. I knew that Parliament would not give me the money part, but I was also sure of something else. The General Staff later on, at about 1910, pressed me to let them consider a scheme. I said that I should be glad if they would work out and consider one thoroughly, and that they should have every facility for the task. They did so, and finally reported to me that to raise an Army by compulsory service was impracticable, and especially so because the state of things in Europe was unsettled. It would take several years before a new compulsory system could possibly be got into shape and substituted for the existing system. Meantime our comparatively small professional Army would have melted away under increased difficulties in recruiting for service abroad. We should temporarily become so much feebler that our General Staff thought that, were they in the position of the Great General Staff of Germany, they would strike at once. And there was another difficulty. The officers, who required long training, must join the Army as a profession. We had barely enough of them for the existing force, and it was not apparent that we could get more, certainly not enough to give the new troops the training that would be required. Our General Staff, therefore, rejected their own idea, and I was clear in my mind that they had done so wisely. Invaded we could not be, and our Expeditionary Force of six divisions could be brought to such a degree of perfection as might make it in point of quality the finest Army for its size on the earth. Indeed this was just what one of the most distinguished of the German Generals told a well-known British officer after the War was over that the Expeditionary Force had proved to be.

The true path seemed accordingly clear. French, who was in command at Aldershot and who held this view strongly, set to work to train two divisions up to the requisite standard. I used to spend much time with him, and also with Ian Hamilton, who was in the Southern Command, with Tidworth as his headquarters. With him I often went to stay to watch the growth in the standard of excellence in his organisation. He wrote a short book on Compulsory Service, to which I contributed an introduction, while Lord Roberts wrote a reply in a separate volume. On the whole, the majority of experts seemed to think that we had the best of the argument.

The Territorial Force was meantime making much progress. Not only was it being locally organised all over England and Scotland by Regular officers under the eye of the General Staff, but it was creating new developments of its own. One of the most efficient administrators I had among my colleagues at the War Office was Surgeon-General Sir Alfred Keogh. He had in him the passion for excellence in his medical organisation for the Army, and he induced many local physicians and surgeons to join the Territorial Force and throw their energies into the plans which he had worked out for them. He also organised a number of hospitals which were to spring into activity on mobilisation, and a nursing service to which many capable women devoted themselves. When the War came and the Regular medical and nursing services proved inadequate, these Territorial organisations were diverted to their aid, and made a vast difference. The country owes much to Sir Alfred Keogh for his insight and his devoted labours.

During this period I was constantly engaged in travelling from town to town meeting Territorial officers, addressing meetings, and stimulating recruiting and organisation for the Territorial Force. As in earlier days, I did not mind sleeping in trains.

In the early days of my possession of the Seals a distinguished General, who had a seat on the Army Council, had come to me criticising strongly what I had indicated as the great changes for which I felt compelled to press. I told him that if he felt opposed to them it was wisest that he should resign and leave me to work them out. He did resign on the spot, and I filled his place with Sir William Nicholson, who had earlier dropped out on what I thought was a mistaken view. Nicholson was one of the cleverest men I ever came across, both in quickness of mind and in capacity for expressing it. He became Quartermaster-General, and it was clear that he might become, as he afterwards did, Chief of the General Staff. He was not by nature a soldier in the field. I used to tell him, laughingly, that he was born to be a lawyer, and that if he had gone to the Bar he might have become Lord Chancellor.

But he had a great power of grasping military principles and of applying them.

I also telegraphed to Douglas Haig to come home from India and take a high position on the General Staff. This body, which had hitherto existed only in the War Office, I had developed and established throughout the Army by an Army Order and a Memorandum written by myself personally and published in September 1906. Haig had a first-rate General Staff mind. When he arrived in London he grasped the situation completely and gave invaluable guidance in the fashioning of both the Regular first line and the Territorial second line. When the General Staff was in full operation he and Nicholson set to work to do what I proposed to them. They expanded the organisation so as to make it one not merely for Great Britain but for the Dominions and India. When this scheme was completed, there was held in London in 1909 a Dominion Conference on military affairs. The last Conference had failed so far as these matters were concerned because of the desire of the old War Office to centralise authority. But we were now able to say that the Dominions and India could remain completely autonomous. All we asked of them was that they should organise on our pattern local sections of their own of the General Staff, and should appoint to them officers who had a General Staff training at headquarters and in the Staff College. They could send them away if they pleased. But we were willing to lend them officers and to take and train any officers of their own whom they chose to send to us for the training which we

alone were in a position to offer, and who could return
and take the places of those they had borrowed from
us. Haig worked out the details of the plan, and
Nicholson embodied them in admirable drafts for
the assistance of the Colonial and India Offices. I
could not have had finer help than I got from these
two. When the Conference met, the plan was fully
approved as one that solved all difficulties. Sir
Wilfrid Laurier and General Botha took the unusual
course in such a Conference of moving and seconding
a proposal that the speech in which it had fallen to
me as Secretary of State to explain what was intended
should be printed for circulation through the Empire.
This was done, and the distant parts of the Empire
turned out as the result to have assimilated the new
strategical ideas and to have refashioned their military organisations in accordance with them.

Another officer who gave me great assistance in
General Staff matters was General Spencer Ewart.
He was at first Military Secretary, but I found him
so full of ideas that I transferred him to the General
Staff as Director of Military Operations in succession
to General Grierson when he retired.

By this time, the summer of 1906, I was in full
swing over my work. What I felt the most need of
was further knowledge. Germany had organised a
national Army to as near perfection as possible, and
at a cost proportionately much less than ours. I
felt that I would much like to see the German organisation at work. I had been doing what I could to
improve the feeling of the public here towards
Germany. As a people we did not like the Germans.

We neither knew their history, language, or literature well, nor did even our Foreign Office know them. I had made speeches, some of them possibly indiscreet, pointing this out, and these speeches had been appreciated more in Germany than here. Still I thought it my duty to try my best.

As the result the German Emperor sent me an informal message that he would invite me, as some of my predecessors had been invited, to come to see his annual manœuvres in Germany. I replied informally that I was only a civilian who wore a black coat, and that not even the Imperial Command would induce me to get on the back of the peaceablest horse in the whole Mark of Brandenburg. But I added that if he chose to let me come to look at his wonderful War Office I would gladly come. The Foreign Office here raised no objection, and accordingly I accepted the invitation, which I got extended to Colonel Ellison as my Military Secretary. The German Military Attaché here, Major Ostertag, whom I knew well and had treated as a friend, arranged things along with Count Metternich, and we started. But King Edward was afraid lest I should show to disadvantage in the company of the German officers, and he bade us visit him at Marienbad, where he was staying, on our way to Berlin. We paid our King a three days' visit at Marienbad. I said that I would endeavour to take care of myself, and he made me promise to write for him in my own hand a complete diary of my experiences in Berlin. This I did fully. I believe that part at least of the diary is in the records of the Foreign Office, and that it is intended to print it among the pre-War documents that are coming out. The other part appears to have been lost.

We were due in Berlin on the last day of August 1906, but a hitch occurred. Grey was away from London, and in his absence a telegram came, signed by the Secretary of the Foreign Office, to say that the French Press were uneasy about the visit, and that I ought not to go on with it. The King and Campbell-Bannerman, who was also at Marienbad, concurred in my own view that it was far too late to put off the visit, and that the consequences of doing so might be mischievous. I wrote to Grey that I must go on, but that if, contrary to my impression, the consequences turned out to be evil, I would resign, so that he could say that an erring colleague had expiated his temerity. The idea was that a parade at which I was to be present was to be commemorative of ' Sedan Tag.' I pointed out that this was apparently not so, and that, as the Russian Military Attaché in Berlin was to be present, it could hardly be so. I added that I would call on the French Ambassador to Berlin immediately on my arrival there, and consult him. When I did so, he assured me that in his opinion there was nothing in the apprehension of our Secretary of the Foreign Office, who had attached undue importance to the language of some Parisian journalists.

In the second chapter of *Before the War* I have given a fairly full account of the visit to Berlin, and I will not repeat what is written there of my conversations with the Emperor, Prince Bülow, and Count Tschirsky, the Minister for Foreign Affairs.

The Emperor was most cordial. I went with him
to the parade on the Tempelhofer Field, and there
sat in a carriage from which I watched him review-
ing his troops. He galloped up to me and held a
conversation, I standing in the carriage. 'A splendid
machine I have in this Army, Mr. Haldane, now isn't
it so? And what should I do without it, situated
as I am between the Russians and the French? But
the French are your allies, so I beg pardon.' I
replied that if I were in His Majesty's place I should
feel very comfortable with this machine, and that for
my own part I enjoyed much more being behind it
than I should had I to be in front of it. He laughed,
and spoke of the organisation of his War Office,
which he had arranged that I should inspect along
with Ellison. By this time I knew something about
it, and the Emperor interested me not the less because
he looked as though he had not gone into it very deeply
himself. He spoke of his military tutor, Bronsart
von Schellendorff. I had read the latter's well-
known book through, but I found that the Emperor
had apparently forgotten it. Besides other talks for
which I had the opportunity, there was one with the
younger von Moltke, the Chief of the General Staff,
whom I visited at his request in his building in the
Thiergarten. He spoke with approval of our new
organisation of our Army into great divisions instead
of mere brigades, divisions not too large for the Fleet
to transport rapidly, and wondered why we had not
done it before. Just as the Army was the great
thing with Germany, so the Fleet was with us. He
observed that in his building there were no plans for

the invasion of England. I looked out of the windo
at the Admiralty General Staff building, which wa
in sight, and asked him whether what he had sai
applied to that building also. 'No,' he replied, 'tl
German Admiralty has of course thought out tl
invasion of England, but it would be an uncertai
business and might probably result in great damag
to the commerce of both countries, to the profit
the United States.' I drew the inference in my min
that if the Germans ever tried to get at us it woul
be through France, and with the northern coast
of that country as a base. The idea which I ha
already formed was confirmed, and so was the valu
of an Expeditionary Force kept ready for instar
mobilisation.

I lunched with the Emperor and the Empres
Afterwards he took me into his private room and tol
me that it would be wrong to infer that he had an
critical thought about a British Entente with Franc
On the contrary he believed that such an Entente migl
even facilitate good relations between Germany an
France. He wished for these good relations and wa
taking steps, through men of high position in Franc
to obtain them. He coveted no further inch
French territory. It was Delcassé who had mac
all the trouble. I told the Emperor that if he woul
let me speak my mind freely I would do so. H
assented, and I said that things he had said had cause
uneasiness in England, and that this and not an
desire of forming a tripartite alliance of Franc
Russia, and England against him was the reason
the feeling there had been. As for our Entente

904 with France, we had had difficulties with her
ver Newfoundland and Egypt, and we had made
ith her what was simply a good business arrange-
ent over them ('Gutes Geschäft'). He said he
ad no criticism to make on this, excepting that if
e had explained it to him early there would have
een no misapprehension. Things were better now,
ut we had not always been pleasant to him, *e.g.*
ver Coaling Stations. His Army was for defence,
ot for offence. As to Russia, he had no Himalayas
etween him and Russia, more was the pity. But
hat about our Two-Power Naval standard? I
eplied that this was like his own Army standard, a
art of the 'Wesen' of our nation. It might be rigid
nd awkward, but it expressed a national tradition,
nd a Liberal Government would hold to it as firmly
s a Conservative.

The Emperor was, notwithstanding frank language,
greeable in manner. He was apparently unre-
trained in the facilities he gave us for examination
f his military arrangements. The only stipulation
e made was that we should not ask any questions
elating to confidential matters. This we observed
igorously. The German officers treated us very
vell, and gave us a dinner the night before we left
3erlin for London. The War Minister, the Chief
f the General Staff, and thirty-eight Corps Com-
nanders were present at the dinner, which took place
t the War Office. I was but little impressed with
he appearance of the Commanders. They did not
eem to me to be carrying on the tradition of 1870.

In the course of the journey home Ellison and I

talked much of what we had observed. We agree
that the great lesson lay in the way in which unde
the German system the Army in the field was fre
from the embarrassment of having to look after it
transport and supplies. This last duty was
separately organised one, attended to by the admini
strative side to the exclusion of the General Staf
The latter dealt with command and with strateg
and tactics, while all administrative work was handle
only by the ' Intendantur,' which was the provinc
of the War Office. This was so in the field as wel
as in peace time. Command was separated from
administration at home as well as in the theatre o
war. It was deemed as important to prevent th
General Staff from meddling in administration a
to prevent the administrative organisation from
interfering in affairs which belonged to the Genera
Staff. The two sides of the Army were not, as wit
us, housed in the same building. To put them clos
together would have been, in the German view
dangerous. The General Staff building was conse
quently a mile away from the War Office, in th
Thiergarten, while the latter was in the city, in th
Leipsiger Strasse. But the Great Moltke had no
been content even with this, and had said that th
distance between the two ought to have been tw
miles at least.

We were struck with the orderliness of the arrange
ments to which the separation of functions gave rise
and I did my utmost all the time I was at the Wa
Office in London to carry out an analogous divisior
as closely as could be. I have found that when con

fusion arises in military organisation it is usually because the one department has strayed into the field of the other. Had I continued long enough at the War Office to be able to accomplish it, I meant to have combined the three administrative departments, those of the Adjutant-General, the Quartermaster-General, and the Master-General of the Ordnance, under a single head as in Germany. That would have enabled them the better to hold their own against the tendency of the General Staff to encroach.

My visit to King Edward prior to going to Berlin was a very agreeable one. He lived at the Hotel Weimar. Many people came to see him, and, as I was his Minister, I had to see some of them for him. Among these was Czar Ferdinand of Bulgaria, who arrived to see King Edward. But the latter, as he said openly, thought it best to shut me, as his responsible Minister, up with the Czar in a room where we could talk. The conversation was turned from Balkan affairs on to artillery, of which the Czar had recently bought a good deal, not from Krupps but from the French firm of Schneider. There was much talk about these guns.

During my visit to King Edward I went about with him much in a very informal way. The King's German was remarkably good. I heard him make a speech to a deputation of Germans, and when I asked him when he had found time to put it together his reply was, 'I did not put it together. I simply spoke what came into my head, without thinking about the words.' He had, among other things, an extraordinary command of German slang, which he would use freely when he liked.

When I was with him at Marienbad he proposed to me one day that we should go in plain clothes as though we were Austrians and drive out in a motor into the country, and have coffee somewhere, because he said Austrian coffee was always admirable and you could tell when you had crossed the frontier into Germany because of the badness of the coffee. The first thing he did was to make me buy an Austrian hat, so as to look more like a native, and then, in tweed suits and with only a chauffeur and no footman, and in a very ordinary motor, we drove a long way into the country. As we were passing a little roadside inn with a wooden table in front of it, the King stopped and said, ' Here I will stand treat.' He ordered coffee for two, and then he said, ' Now I am going to pay. I shall take care to give only a small tip to the woman who serves the coffee, in case she suspects who I am.' We then drove on to a place the King was very fond of—a monastery inhabited by the Abbot of Teppel—where we had a large tea, and where the King enjoyed himself with the monks very much, gossiping and making himself agreeable.

He was full of courage. One morning at Marienbad, just before he was about to take the usual walk along the parade among the crowd to get his glass of water at the fountain, the police who were attending him came to say that several well-known anarchists had arrived the night before, and that it was not safe for him to walk out. He turned to

me and said, ' We will take our walk, won't we ? '
and then, meditatively, ' A king, like every one else,
can only die once. Besides which, I do not believe
in these nervous police.' We took the walk, and of
course nothing happened.

He was very particular about clothes, and thought
rather badly of my costume one day afterwards in
England at a party in the open air when I arrived in
a soft hat, not very new it is true, but one which I
liked very much. ' See him,' he said in loud tones
to the ladies around him. ' See him arrive in the
hat he inherited from Goethe.'

At Marienbad he was very happy. He knew a
vast number of people, and he had a personality
which greatly impressed Germans and Austrians.
After his death some of the German newspapers
wrote : ' If only Germany had had that man for
Emperor.' It was a pleasure to the King while at
Marienbad to have Campbell-Bannerman near him,
for the latter also went there every autumn. With
Campbell-Bannerman he got on very well.

CHAPTER VII

THE LIBERAL GOVERNMENT

(1905–1912)

It is now time to turn to the story of the work of the Government, and to see how that work developed after December 1905. It is the more interesting to do so because it was during the years that followed 1905 that a change in the attitude of the British public towards Liberalism began to set in. Conservatism, shattered for the time by the failure of its policy of Protection, passed into an attitude of unwilling acquiescence in great changes. The Death Duties and a graduated Income Tax were accepted by the Unionist Opposition as principles on which there was no going back, and the House of Lords was finally deprived of what had been decisive in its power to throw out Bills. But if Conservatism yielded to prevailing influences, so did Liberalism in another fashion. At the General Election in January 1906 the Liberals had an immense success. They got 379 seats as against 155 Unionist seats. But Labour returned 51 members, a relatively small number but enough to form a permeating influence in Parliament

It is a common delusion to think that a party is to be estimated merely by its numbers. The real question is whether it stands for a permeating power in the country. Its abstract programme is not what is important. What matters is the volume and quality of the spirit which has inspired that programme, however imperfectly. For it may even turn out that the underlying spirit has entered into and moulded the views of those who belong to other parties, Candidates, chameleon-like, take on the colour of their environment.

This was well illustrated early in our career as a new Government. One of the things which democracy had pledged itself to get rid of was the result of the Judgment of the House of Lords in the Taff Vale case. Judge-made law had in that case established the principle that a Trade Union could be sued in tort. For this principle there was much to be said if it had been raised for the first time and as a new one. But it was now enounced contrary to the belief which had been entertained about it widely since the Royal Commission on Trade Unions had considered it many years previously, and by the Trade Unions themselves, as well as by some of the judges. For a Trade Union was not a Corporation, and if it could be sued its benefit funds were at the mercy of those who sued it in respect of what were merely trade disputes. The House of Lords, reversing the Court of Appeal, had decided that the Railway Servants' Union could be sued for a tort, and that the money they had set aside for pensions and benefits could be taken to satisfy a judgment. This decision was so contrary to what a vast number of the working people thought right that its reversal became a cardinal issue in the General Election of 1906. The importance of the question we in the Cabinet knew well. The Attorney-General and the Solicitor-General, Lawson Walton and Robson, had studied it; I had been the leading counsel of the Trade Union in the Taff Vale case, and Asquith had devoted much thought to it. But we considered it too violent a proposition to say that a Trade Union should under no circumstances be capable of being sued in tort. We therefore prepared a Bill which sought to restrict the technical operation of the law of agency, so that a distant Trade Union in a different part of the kingdom which had had nothing whatever to do with the dispute might be able to feel secure about its benefit funds, leaving those who had actually behaved illegally to bear the brunt of having done so. But we had under-estimated the extent to which the Labour spirit had operated on the candidates at the Election. When the House of Commons met, a Bill, of which Keir Hardie was the real protagonist, was introduced, and it became plain, notwithstanding the arguments we brought forward, that it was going to be carried against the Government by a huge majority. It passed indeed easily, for we could not resist the numbers pledged to it, and later on the House of Lords, like the Conservative Party in the Commons, showed that they too dared not try to throw it out. That was how the Trade Disputes Act of 1906 came to be passed. Its success in the face of criticism from both parties established something further. A new spirit was disclosing itself, a spirit that was moving the democracy to go beyond the old-fashioned Liberal tradition, and to show that it would be content with nothing short of a demonstration that the democracy was for the future to have the last word.

It is a mistake to judge the so-called Labour Movement by the detailed programmes which from time to time it puts forward. It is no question of such isolated matters as nationalisation of banks or railways or mines, or even reform of Trade Union law. It is not about details that the people care or are stirred. What they seem to desire is that they should have something approaching to equality of chance in life with those among whom they live. Ours is on the whole a conservative people with no liking for violence. Reforms are allowed to be made gradually and slowly, provided they are made surely. It was the same story with the movement for land nationalisation which was led in the 'eighties by Henry George. The people did not really wish to insist on the nationalisation of all land. What they wanted was that its arbitrary use should be controlled where necessary in the general interest, and much has been accomplished since that agitation which has gone far to supersede it. So it was with the Trade Disputes agitation. It brought with it the beginning of many changes, and he would be a rash man who predicted that even the new Trade Disputes Act of 1927 has arrested the progress of the real Trade Union movement otherwise than temporarily.

In all such matters what really counts is the spirit rather than the letter. We Liberals failed to realise in the beginning of 1906 that the spirit was rapidly changing, and that the outlook of Victorian Liberalism was not sufficient for the progressive movement which had set in early in the twentieth century.

Nor was it a matter merely of measures. Campbell-Bannerman wisely enough brought John Burns into the Cabinet. But he did not realise that even then Burns, who had great oratorical gifts but not much knowledge, was beginning to be out of date with Labour. What was needed was a new and enlightened attitude towards social problems, and this in the main we failed to adopt. Labour was working as a party closely in unison, and was pouring out literature which was widely studied. People like the Sidney Webbs were getting increased attention. Problems like that of the Poor Law were drawing on themselves fresh and earnest concentration. It was plain that Free Trade, although the electors were favourable to the principle, was not in itself enough as a basis on which to hold a great party together. It savoured somewhat of the atmosphere of the old Industrial Revolution period, good in itself as it was. There was evidence of this for those that could read it not only in the attitude of the mass of working men and women, but also in that of the more enlightened and less prejudiced representatives of the Universities. The teaching of men like Thomas Hill Green was penetrating deeply, and that turned on much more than *laissez faire*. There was earnestness about State intervention to be seen everywhere.

Campbell-Bannerman lived apart from all this. He was devoting himself to what was to be his great achievement, the grant of a healing measure of complete self-government to South Africa united on

a generously bestowed foundation. Grey was working devotedly at the difficult problems of the Foreign
Office. Just in his outlook and intensely desirous
of preserving the peace of the world, I think that he
was hampered by want of knowledge of the sources
of German mentality. He knew little of the history
or literature or of the spirit of that difficult mentality.
This would have mattered less had the majority of
the advisers on whom Grey had to rely known more.
But they were mainly anti-German in their tendencies.
No doubt the German Emperor was himself partly
responsible for this, and the apparent determination
of Germany to create a great Fleet helped. But we
Ministers would have been more potent in coping
with the situation had we had wider knowledge about
it, and of the history and tradition that had produced
it. Whether Disraeli knew much of that history
and tradition I do not know—I doubt it. But he
had a keen imagination and something of what has
been called the ' international mind,' and this was
valuable in the crisis with which he had to deal. Grey
was splendidly conscientious and just, but he seemed
to doubt whether the Germans were genuinely good
people, and they of course knew that he doubted it.
Consequently, mainly over trifling events, the situation between the two peoples became a difficult one.
I did what I believed I could to help in his attitude
towards Germany, but Grey was in spirit a pure
Briton and I was a good deal less so, and consequently
I could not prevail with him against the tendencies
of his Ambassadors and of his advisers in London.
Moreover, the Germans were misinterpreting his policy

most unjustly, and were becoming increasingly difficult. The development of events in the Balkans was
also not making things easier for him.

Asquith was doing good work. He had decided,
overruling some of his advisers at the Exchequer,
on a graduation of the income tax and on a better
distribution of the burden of taxation, and this was
being carried out. Lloyd George was very active
at the Board of Trade. For myself, I was working
in every direction at the organisation of the first and
second lines of an Army fashioned on a new pattern
designed to meet the case of a possible emergency.

Looking back, I think I ought to have taken a more
active part in the general business of the Cabinet.
But my hands were quite full with military affairs,
and, while I was ready to suggest fresh ideas, I could
only prevail in counsel when the conditions existed
for which I was best fitted, those of working with two
or three colleagues who knew me. Moreover, the
Cabinet was organised on an old system which I hope
will never be restored. It was a congested body of
about twenty, in which the powerful orator secured
too much attention. The Prime Minister knew too
little of the details of what had to be got through to
be able to apportion the time required for discussion.
Consequently, instead of ruling the Cabinet and regu-
lating the length of the conversations, he left things
much to themselves. We had no Secretary, no
agenda, and no minutes in these days. The evils
prevailed that we described in the Report of the
Reconstruction Committee on the Machinery of
Government, over which it fell to me to preside

afterwards, in 1918. Indeed I got the Government of that day to appoint this Committee because I was keenly conscious of the necessity of bringing these and other evils to light.

The Cabinet of 1906 in the years which immediately followed was like a meeting of delegates. It consisted of a too large body of members, of whom two or three had the gift of engrossing its attention for their own business. The result of this and the want of system which it produced was that business was not always properly discussed, and the general points of view that vitally required clear definition almost never. Churchill was as long-winded as he was persistent, and Crewe also when he intervened did so in long speeches. Lloyd George however was very good. Neither Campbell-Bannerman nor Asquith when he succeeded him sufficiently controlled the discussions, and I think that the procedure was a mischievous one. A small Cabinet of a dozen members or fewer would have done the work much better. Ramsay MacDonald managed the Cabinet to which I belonged in 1924 more effectively. But then he had Sir Maurice Hankey as Secretary, with an agenda paper and carefully drawn minutes in which the decisions were recorded.

In these days we lived as a Government too much from hand to mouth, dependent for our achievements on the initiative not of the body as a whole but of individual members. There ought to have been much more systematic consultation among members specially interested, and more frequent social intercourse. But these were the days of social functions of a different kind on an extended scale as part of the routine of Government, and the opportunities for conference were consequently deficient. A luncheon party came punctually at 1.30 and made an end of serious discussion. Much good work was done by the individual Ministers in a Government the members of which worked hard. But from imperfect method not nearly enough team work was accomplished.

The result was that although the Government was on balance an energetic and good one, it was not sufficiently representative of the new spirit which it ought to have represented. No such ideal as that of service rendered as the true basis for the distribution of the profits of industry was thought of. We began slowly to lose what we had of the confidence of the men and women who lived by the work of their hands, and this gradually became apparent. What some of us could do we did, but we did not do enough. Had the Conservatives had a leader of genius they could have broken up our following before the War came, but they had no leader who could initiate ideas, or show the nation that the period of the old ' Industrial Revolution ' was a period that did not provide all that was necessary in 1906. They had little to fall back upon excepting the damaged cause of Protection. In the policy of Education they had ceased to make any such progress as they had made in the Education Act of 1902.

Over the reform of Education the Liberals were pretty bad. Crewe and I were anxious to begin the work of founding a national system. But from the first it was clear that the Nonconformist insistence

on getting rid of the Church School system blocked
the way. The Church Schools were indeed very
deficient. But they could not be abolished at once,
and although we were working through first-rate
administrators, such as Sir Robert Morant, we could
not get the public or Parliament to agree on any
plan of reform. The truth was that, despite the
vast importance of the question, too few people were
keenly interested in Education to afford us the
requisite breeze for our sails. I sat on Cabinet
Committees on the subject, and interviewed earnest
men like Dr. Clifford. But their prejudices I could
not break down single-handed, and I had no keen
allies. In this region I failed.

Meantime I was seeing people like the Sidney
Webbs, and was in close consultation with men like
Morant and other officials of the Board of Education.
I was also able to do something for training intelligence
throughout the Army. But stir up my colleagues
to a large policy about Education I could not. Nor
did I succeed, in truth, much better with the Labour
Cabinet when it came into office in 1924.

I now pass from the general affairs of the Campbell-
Bannerman Government to the special matters with
which I was more directly concerned. After I had
been at Berlin in September 1906, King Edward
invited the Emperor William to pay him a State
visit at Windsor. This took place in 1907. I was
of the party through most of it. I had suggested to
our King that as General von Einem, the German
War Minister, had been very attentive to me as the
King's own Minister when I was in Berlin, he should

be included in the invitation. This was done, and there came also von Schoen, the Minister for Foreign Affairs, and other members of the Emperor's Cabinet. Metternich, the Ambassador here, was also present. Prince Bülow did not come. The main subject of interest then was the Baghdad Railway, for which Germany had got the concession from the Turks. We were concerned, for the new line might open up a new and short route for troops advancing towards India. On the other hand, our co-operation was important to Germany, as much capital would have to be raised.

I do not propose to repeat here the full story of the negotiations at Windsor. I was asked to take part in them because I knew personally not only the Emperor but his Ministers. The history of what passed I have given pretty fully in *Before the War*,[1] in the second chapter, where any one who is interested will find it. It appears also in the second volume of Sir Sidney Lee's *Life of King Edward*. What I wanted and what I asked the Emperor to concede over the Baghdad Railway was a ' Gate,' by which as War Minister I meant the control of the lower section, between Baghdad and the Persian Gulf. The Emperor was willing to concede this, and Grey and Lord Hardinge drew up for me a Memorandum to guide me in negotiating terms. The King approved it, and I saw the Emperor and his Ministers, at the request of the former, at one in the morning, after a theatrical performance was concluded. I have told in my book about the keenness of the discussion.

[1] *Before the War*, by Viscount Haldane : Cassell and Co. Ltd. (1920).

The Ministers were divided, and the argument grew so hot that I interrupted it and said to the Emperor that it was not right that a foreigner, who was outside his Cabinet, should remain present. But the Emperor had a keen sense of humour, and besides he wanted to have my support. ' Be a member of my Cabinet for to-night and I will appoint you.' ' With all my heart, sir.' I remained, and the proposal was approved by a narrow majority, and von Schoen went to London next morning to arrange details with the Foreign Office. After some weeks had elapsed it was blocked, I think by Prince Bülow, the Chancellor. I suppose that I am the only Englishman who has ever been a member of the German Cabinet, though it was only for a few hours. It was, however, useful at the moment, and it showed that the Emperor, whatever his deficiencies, had not only courage but, as I have said, a sense of humour.

The reception at Windsor was a magnificent one. The Castle was crowded. I arrived there on the second or third day and remained till the end. It had been arranged that the costume should be English informal Court costume — white waistcoat, black knee-breeches and coat, black silk stockings with pumps. The Berlin tailors had made the other things excellently for the guests, but the Germans' ' pumps ' were not such a success. After dinner on the first night I was there we sat in the smoking-room, a large saloon in which the Ministers were near the Royalties on a raised dais. I was next to General von Einem, and I noticed that he was in

pain. By careful observation I tracked the source
of his expressions of discomfort to his feet, and I saw
that his pumps had been made too tight across the
instep. At last the two Sovereigns quitted us for
the night, but we were to sit on. I turned to the
Prussian War Minister, and said it was the custom
in Windsor Castle when our Royal Masters left us
to kick off our shoes, and I set the example. He
looked gratefully at me, perfectly understanding,
and put off his pumps with an air of relief from
suffering. He must have told the Emperor, for next
morning King Edward said to me, 'A nice character
you are, giving Windsor Castle a reputation for
having strange customs.' I told the King about
von Einem, and that out of mercy I had said it was
the custom here when the King left the smoking-
room to kick off one's pumps. The King laughed.

After the interview with the Emperor and his
Ministers, which I had very late at night, and of
which I have given an account, I had to find my way
from the east end of the Castle, where the Emperor's
suite of rooms was, to the Lancaster Tower, far
away at the other end. The place was almost in
darkness, and I did not know distinctly where the
Lancaster Tower was or how to find it. I groped
my way along the gallery, full of articles of great
value which were supposed to be guarded by watch-
men. I could have slipped away with many valuable
things had I been a skilled thief, and probably
have got out of the Castle with them. At last I
wholly lost my way, and I thought I should fail to
reach my rooms ; however, I discovered a watchman

asleep, and, wakening him up, was guided to the Lancaster Tower.

The Castle was filled with people, some of whom did not speak English. Consequently I had a busy time during this visit. During the day I went to London, and there took the military guests to the War Office and to luncheon at Queen Anne's Gate. They liked to go in my motor, when I was busy at the office, and to visit, not Westminster Abbey or the Tower, but Maples, Harrods, the Stores, and great establishments of that kind, of which they had heard much.

Although the negotiations terminated in no definite result, they assisted in promoting increased ease in relations between the two Foreign Offices concerned, and things went for a time smoothly. Grey kept the French and the Russians informed about all we did, and he was equally candid with the German Ambassador. Indeed up to 1911 all went well. In that year the Emperor came to London to visit King George after the latter's succession to our throne. I had suggested to the King that I should give a luncheon at Queen Anne's Gate to the Generals on the Emperor's Staff. But the Emperor, when he heard of this, intimated that he should like to come to the luncheon himself. I inquired, through the Ambassador, whom he would like to meet, and he replied that he would leave this entirely to me, but that he should wish to meet some of my countrymen whom he might not see otherwise. I acted on my own discretion, and when he came to my little house in Queen Anne's Gate he found a miscellaneous party. Besides Lord Kitchener, Lord Curzon, and Lord Morley, whom he would naturally encounter at the Palace, I had there Ramsay MacDonald as leader of the Labour Party, Spender of the *Westminster Gazette*, Edmund Gosse, Admiral Sir Arthur Wilson, Lord Moulton, and others. The luncheon party went well, and the Emperor let himself go in an agreeable fashion. I think he really enjoyed himself. Only men were present at the luncheon, but my sister and Mrs. Asquith's little boy were in my study, and the Emperor went upstairs and talked to them. He used to chaff me about the small size of 28 Queen Anne's Gate, which he called my ' Dolls' House.'

The Emperor had a great reception in London. But the public enthusiasm was somewhat checked when very shortly afterwards he sent the famous ship *Panther* to Agadir. The French were much alarmed, and the prospect of tranquillity, which had become so promising, was overcast. I doubt much whether Germany meant more than a demonstration, but so potent was the military influence among the Emperor's advisers that it was not possible to be quite sure. By this time I had got the military organisation into order, and, if the country decided on such a step, I was in a position to mobilise the Expeditionary Force and to send it straight off to the Continent. In order to be quite ready I stopped the manoeuvres that were customary at this time of the year, alleging the intense drought which prevailed as a reason. The money so saved was spent in completing mobilisation arrangements.

STUDY AT 28 QUEEN ANNE'S GATE

Photo: C. Vandyk

I was well aware that the Germans would find this out, and I thought it better to be open with them, though no announcement of what was being done had been made at home. I told their Military Attaché, Major Ostertag, that the General Staff were bound to make preparations for eventualities. He reported this to Berlin, and that we could place six infantry divisions and a cavalry division on the Belgian frontier with great speed. I was on excellent terms with him, and he told me afterwards that the Great General Staff attached no importance to his communication to them. They thought our Expeditionary Force so small as to be negligible. They thought the same in August 1914, and did not take any naval steps to prevent its transport over the Channel. In both cases they judged badly, as some of their leaders came afterwards to recognise.

The Agadir crisis passed, although it left some bad feeling behind. But the necessary military preparations, which of course assumed their final and general form in the Committee of Imperial Defence, disclosed an unexpected difficulty. The organisation of the Expeditionary Force entailed the making of arrangements with the Navy for its transport, to the place and in the form decided on, across the Channel. These arrangements we at the War Office believed to have been made definitely, and we had seen to it that they were, so far as paper could record them, in complete form. But in the end of the summer of 1911, when complete mobilisation arrangements were essential for the event of our being called on to act, we received a shock. At a meeting

of the Defence Committee, at which the First Lord
of the Admiralty and the then First Sea Lord,
Sir Arthur Wilson, were present, along with myself
and Sir William Nicholson as Chief of the Imperial
General Staff, it turned out that the Admiralty
were not of one mind with us.   The Prime Minister,
Mr. Asquith, was presiding at this meeting, and
was inquiring into our joint war plans.   Sir Arthur
Wilson unexpectedly said that the plan of the
Admiralty for the event of a war with Germany was
quite different from ours.   They wanted to take
detachments of the Expeditionary Force and to
land them seriatim at points on the Baltic coast
on the northern shores of Prussia.   We of the War
Office at once said that such a plan was from a
military point of view hopeless, because the railway
system which the Great General Staff of Germany
had evolved was such that any division we landed,
even if the Admiralty could have got it to a
point suitable for debarkation, would be promptly
surrounded by five or ten times the number of enemy
troops.   Sir John Fisher appeared to have derived
the idea from the analogy of the Seven Years' War,
more than a hundred and fifty years previously,
and Sir Arthur Wilson, his successor, had apparently
adopted it.   The First Lord backed him up.   I
said at once that the mode of employing troops and
their numbers and places of operation were questions
for the War Office General Staff, and that we had
worked them out with the French.   The results
had been periodically approved in the Committee
of Defence itself.   Sir William Nicholson asked Sir

Arthur whether they had at the Admiralty a map of the German strategical railways. Sir Arthur replied that it was not their business to have such maps. 'I beg your pardon,' said Sir William, 'if you meddle with military problems you are bound not only to have them, but to have studied them.' The discussion became sharp ; I of course agreeing *ex animo* with the utterances of the Chief of the General Staff. He had a rather too sharp tongue, and I remembered that on a previous occasion Sir John Fisher had said to me that he wished that I would enjoin 'Old Nick' not always to stamp his hoof on his (Sir John's) toes.

The Prime Minister was clear that the arrangements made must be carried out in accordance with the plan of the General Staff. But the Admiralty members were evidently not convinced when the meeting came to an end. The difficulty had its origin in the fact that the Navy then possessed nothing like a General Staff. Sir John Fisher had always objected to having one. He thought that if there were such a Staff the war plans of the Admiralty would leak out. He did not realise that in the twentieth century it was impossible to conduct military operations successfully, either on sea or on land, without close preliminary study on an extended scale. The Navy had in consequence nothing analogous to the General Staff of the War Office, and it was not until the incident to which I am now referring was closed that it got one.

Anyhow, after the meeting of the Committee broke up I took the Prime Minister aside, and said that I could not continue to be responsible for military affairs unless he made a sweeping reform at the Admiralty. He and I were both going down to Scotland that night, having seen that the matter in controversy about the transport and employment of the troops was at least provisionally and for the time settled. He asked me to motor over from Cloan to Archerfield in East Lothian, where he would be, to discuss what should be done. Of course I agreed to do this. The Prime Minister said that he would probably have to make up his mind to changes in the office concerned and might send me to the Admiralty to arrange finally the transport across the Channel, and in any event to form a scientific War Staff.

We all hoped at this time that war would be averted. It has been said that all these discussions of possible perils and the preparations made against them went on in the Committee of Imperial Defence without the Cabinet being cognisant of them. The Cabinet was too large a body to go into details, but some of its lay members took a large part in the proceedings of the Committee. I remember that afterwards, when he had left office, Morley said to me that he had not known of these things. I reminded him that he had insisted on being present at all the important meetings of the Committee, and had even presided over Sub-Committees concerned purely with military organisation. He said that he had not known fully of the discussions with the French Generals. I recalled to him meeting after meeting at which he had listened to the detailed explanations given to the full Committee by the Director of Military Operations of the progress of the examination of the question how we could best resist an attack through Belgium, should one come. I told him that I remembered Crewe, Harcourt, Lloyd George, and other members of the Cabinet being present with him. We looked among the Defence Committee papers which he had kept, and there we found one recording proceedings at a comparatively early meeting at which a detailed exposition with maps was set out. Morley had added a note in his own handwriting, raising a personal query whether he ought to have taken part in this, and replying to his own question that the public interest appeared to demand it. He had forgotten the work of the Committee, but in its carefully kept records there must be the accounts of many meetings at which he and the others I have mentioned were present. There may have been members of the Cabinet who neither put questions nor had sufficient interest in the business of military preparation to ask what it was essential to arrange with the French Generals, but it can hardly be said, in the face of the facts, that either Campbell-Bannerman or Asquith concealed anything from colleagues.

The Admiralty had observed the strictest secrecy about their war plans, such as they were, and I doubt whether the leaders had taken even M'Kenna much into their confidence. Anyhow, when I went over to Archerfield I had a very serious question to discuss with the Prime Minister. I had given so much study to General Staff questions that, although far from desirous of passing, even temporarily, from the War Office, which I had got to know well, to the Navy, of which I had had but little experience, I felt that I was almost the only person available who was equipped to cope with the problem of the Naval War Staff. I think that the Prime Minister held much the same view, but we had been careful to say nothing of impending changes.

I drove over to Archerfield as soon as I had got to Cloan. As I entered the approach I saw Winston Churchill standing at the door. I divined that he had heard of possible changes and had come down at once to see the Prime Minister.

It was as I thought. Churchill was importunate about going himself to the Admiralty from the Home Office, where he was. He had told Asquith that the First Lord must be in the Commons. As I was by now in the Lords this looked like a difficulty. But I said the situation was too critical to permit of any such difficulty standing in the way. I had no desire to be First Lord, but if a real Naval War Staff were to be created and the Admiralty were to be convinced of its necessity, that must be done by some one equipped with the knowledge and experience that were essential for fashioning a highly complicated organisation. Now where was he to be found ?

Obviously Churchill had been pressing Asquith hard. I returned to Cloan and came back the next day. Churchill was still there, and the Prime Minister shut me up in a room with him. I took the initiative.

I told him that his imaginative power and vitality
were greater than mine, and that physically he was
better suited to be a War Minister. But at this critical
moment it was not merely a question of such qualities.
The Navy and the public had to be convinced, and
they would be most easily convinced of the necessity
of scientific preparation for naval war by some one
who already had carried out similar preparations with
the only Service in which they had been made or
even thought of. I was satisfied that in all prob-
ability I could accomplish what was wanted within
twelve months, and if he would look after the Army
till the end of that time I would return to it and he
could then take over the Admiralty. There was
nothing in the idea which the Prime Minister had
that the Chancellorship would soon be vacant and
that I might fill the post. The Great Seal might
go anywhere so far as I was concerned at this moment.
It was a question of executing a great plan if the
emergency arose. And I said that, to be frank, I
did not think that Churchill's own type of mind was
best for planning out the solution that was necessary
for the problem which at the moment was confront-
ing us.

However, Churchill would not be moved, and
Asquith yielded to him. At least Churchill did fine
work in strengthening the Fleet up to the high level
in numbers which it reached just before 1914. No
doubt his persuasiveness was of great value in the
House of Commons. I parted from him at Archerfield in a very friendly spirit. For not only did he
agree about the necessity of a scientific War Staff

for the Navy, a Staff which would study battle plans and also the types of ships and guns, but he made me a proposition. If I would withdraw my insistence on going to the Admiralty to fashion the War Staff there on the lines which had been followed in the Army, he declared himself prepared to ask me to come over to the Admiralty and to sit with him and the Admirals and fashion the new Staff with them. With this proposal I closed. It was the best I could get in the circumstances. We sat shortly afterwards at Whitehall for several days and laid down the foundations of the new War Staff. Churchill wanted it to be put directly under himself as First Lord. To this I objected stoutly, saying that it would be inert unless it were under the First Sea Lord. Prince Louis of Battenberg, a well-trained expert, agreed with me, and the Staff was placed directly under the First Sea Lord. A good deal was accomplished, but more had to be done than was done in the three years which elapsed before the War came for getting the new organisation into anything approaching to sufficient condition. I had opportunities then and afterwards of consultation with naval experts of the younger school which satisfied me about this.

A problem which confronted me at the War Office at this time was the commencement of the Air Service. Numbers of inventors came to see me as the then responsible Minister, including the brothers Wright, and I examined many plans and specifications. But I saw that those whom I interviewed were only clever empiricists, and that we were at a profound disadvantage compared with the Germans, who were building up the structure of the Air Service on a foundation of science. I therefore took the matter largely out of the departmental hands of the Master-General of the Ordnance, and going to the Prime Minister, got his authority to add a special section to the National Physical Laboratory at Teddington. There we installed a permanent Scientific Committee, paid for its work, including our best experts, both theoretical and practical. We were so fortunate as to persuade the late Lord Rayleigh, of whom I had seen much as Chairman of the Explosives Committee, to preside. The Committee began from an early stage to furnish us with guidance of great value. Alongside of it the balloon factory at Farnborough was reconstructed, with the best expert on mechanical problems of this kind that we could find, Mr. Mervyn O'Gorman, a well-known engineer, as the head of the factory. Its function was to produce new types of dirigible, both heavier and lighter than air, and for this purpose to use the results of the Teddington Special Committee, of which Mr. O'Gorman was made a member. A little later on the lighter-than-air machines, or Zeppelins, were handed over to the Admiralty. It proceeded to build some, but would not consult the Rayleigh Committee about the mathematical and physical conditions. An order to build a Zeppelin was given by the Director of Naval Ordnance to an eminent firm of constructors, just as he would have placed an order for a ship. The amount of preliminary research which was required was ignored, and the Zeppelin came to an untimely end almost immediately. The aeroplanes, on the other hand, justified the work of Lord Rayleigh and his colleagues, including Mr. O'Gorman. I had myself, however, little to do with the subsequent developments. My successor, Colonel Seely, Mr. Churchill co-operating with him, finally succeeded in bringing into existence a much-expanded Air organisation, to serve both the Army and the Navy. The criticism of our procedure has been that it was too slow, and that it had even taken less account than was essential of the necessity for scientific foundation. On the latter point I think that we have been until quite recent years defective. Now we are doing better in this respect. But formerly the newspapers and the commercial world kept clamouring for action first and reflection afterwards in a way that impeded progress. It is the energy which is directed by close research that in the end gives the most stable and rapid results.

This part of the narrative brings me towards the close of my story of the preparatory work at the War Office. During the first two years of my tenure of its Seals I had been one of the most active of those who took charge of the Defence Committee, and worked through it as a supreme instrument. After Sir Henry Campbell-Bannerman's death in 1908, the new Prime Minister, Asquith, took a great interest in it, and constantly presided in person. When he could not do so he usually requested me to occupy his place. Balfour had founded the Committee with excellent ideas, but we developed it in new directions, setting up systematically a series of Sub-Committees to deal with special problems. I have always thought that this process of devolution might with advantage have been carried still further, and above all, that, except in so far as it was necessary that they should sit on some of these Sub-Committees, civilians should not have been summoned by the Prime Minister, in whose hands the composition of the Committee exclusively rested, to attend on the main Committee in the numbers they actually did. For their presence tended to restrain freedom of utterance on the part of the sailors and soldiers. The meetings indeed at times resembled a congested gathering. Some of the minds in the Cabinet were fired with ambition to sit on what was really only an advisory and expert body, which they took without justification to be an organisation rivalling in authority the Cabinet itself. This was a belief which it was the duty of the Prime Minister, as head of both bodies, to restrain. One consequence of want of control was that the sailors and soldiers, less practised in speech than their civilian colleagues, let their voices be silenced by the politicians. The adjustment of the balance was a delicate business, but it was a feasible one. I always had the hope, before the Great War was on us, that in war time the Committee would become the great General Staff of the Empire, a real War Council taking cognisance of military questions of every kind in the way I have explained in the preface to *Compulsory Service*. But the cumbrous size of the Committee was always a difficulty in the way of this, and during the War its functions were largely taken over by the Cabinet, a thoroughly bad arrangement. These things happened notwithstanding the exertions

of the able Secretaries, Admiral Ottley and, after him
Sir Maurice Hankey. The latter indeed, by the
composition of what was called the 'War Book,' did
as much as could be done by him to check the
tendency which arose partly from the Prime Minister
not having sufficient time to give to this important
work. In these days, although the Prime Minister
presided over the Committee, there was no Chairman
to relieve him of the duty of continuous supervision.
Under Mr. Baldwin's first Administration such an
office was created, and I filled it myself during the
time of the Labour Government. But since then no
appointment to the post has been made. I suppose
that a selection might have given rise to difficulties
and have seemed invidious. Anyhow, it is, I think,
unfortunate that there has not been since my own
time a Chairman of the Committee of Imperial
Defence.

I had been sent to the House of Lords to assist in
the work of leading it in 1911 while the official leader,
Lord Crewe, was in India with the King. I had
already, when Lord Crewe was ill, been informed by
the Prime Minister that I might have to go to the
India Office, and at an earlier period the then Secretary of State for India had spoken to me of the possibility of my going to India as Viceroy. But I had
not wished to leave the War Office before I felt that
I had done all the work I could do there. In 191
I began to feel that the back of the necessary work
had been broken, and to fear that I was becoming
stale. My old friend, Lord Nicholson, had now left
the War Office and had been succeeded as Chief of

the General Staff by another friend, Sir John French. Sir Douglas Haig had gone to the Aldershot Command ; Sir Ian Hamilton and Ellison were appropriated to the duties of the Oversea Inspectorate.   The pressure of work had become so lessened that I had felt justi- fied in going to sit judicially, as much as I could, in the Privy Council and the House of Lords, to relieve the shortage of judges there.   The House of Commons had decided that it was expedient that I should do so, notwithstanding that I was a Minister. Such is our Constitution that this was not wholly anomalous.

Early one morning in the Whitsuntide recess, in June 1912, I received a message from Lord Loreburn, the Lord Chancellor, to say that he was stricken with illness and must resign at once.   He asked me to communicate this to the Sovereign as he was too ill to do so himself.   I saw the King, and the Chief Whip communicated by wireless with Asquith, who was on the Admiralty yacht in the Mediterranean. The reply was : ' Consult Haldane as to who should succeed him at the War Office.'   To fill the Woolsack at once was an urgent matter, for the House of Lords was about to sit and there was now no Chancellor. Nothing official could be done until the Prime Minister returned on the Monday morning, and great secrecy had to be preserved.   However, we arranged pro- visionally that there should be a Council on the Monday afternoon at which the Great Seal could be transferred, and that I should be sworn in by the Master of the Rolls at 10.30 on the Tuesday morning.

met some of the judges at dinner on the Friday

night. Of course I could not tell them about the resignation or of matters which were not then finally settled. They reproached me for never having come to pay my old friends at the Courts a visit. I said that I should not only like to do so, but thought that I might possibly be able to do so on the Tuesday morning. The Great Seal was given to me by the King at six on the Monday afternoon, and next morning I appeared, according to promise, in Court of Appeal No. 1 to pay my visit to the judges, but in a full-bottomed wig and the Chancellor's robes. That night I dined at Lincoln's Inn with my fellow-Benchers. After dinner I slipped away and crossed into New Square, to look at the staircase of No. 5, where my old garret had been. I went up the stair, and on reaching what once was my door heard barristers at work late, just as I myself more than thirty years before used to stay in chambers to work late. I raised my hand to the knocker, intending to ask to see my old room. But I felt shy and returned down the steep stair unobserved.

It was thus that I returned to the service of my old Mistress, the Law.

Before I actually quitted the War Office I had to undertake another enterprise. I was sent to Berlin to engage in conversations with the German Government about their relations with ourselves, and especially as to the effect of any large increase of their Navy which might compel a corresponding increase on our side. Since the sending of the *Panther* to Agadir, and the march of the French Army to Fez, it had looked as though threats were being uttered on

both sides, and on the 21st July 1911 Lloyd George
had made in the City a considered declaration that
we could not disinterest ourselves if a serious dispute
were to arise.   Whether the French or the Germans
were most to blame for the state of tension which
existed, or whether we had become more concerned
than was necessary, will probably remain matter of
controversy between historians.   At all events the
relations between England and Germany were not
improved, and there was talk in the latter country
of an increase in her Fleet.

In January 1912 Sir Ernest Cassel, who was well
known to the Emperor, and who had made informal
suggestions to Bethmann-Hollweg, after consulting
certain of my colleagues here as to easing the tension,
returned to London from Berlin.   Cassel was doing
everything in his power to smooth matters.   He
brought back a message from the Emperor that the
latter was concerned at the state of feeling that had
arisen in both countries, and thought that the most
hopeful way of improving things would be that the
Cabinet of St. James's should exchange views directly
and personally with the Cabinet of Berlin.   Our
Cabinet decided to act on this suggestion.   Its
members considered that as I knew German and was
personally on friendly terms with some of the principal German statesmen, I was the natural person to
send.   Grey came to see me.   'You must go,' he
said.   I suggested that what would carry most weight
would be that he should go himself, accompanied by
me.   But he preferred that I should go alone, and
Asquith and the Cabinet endorsed what he said.

Grey then sent for Goschen, our Ambassador at Berlin, to come to London and discuss the situation with us. Goschen was an excellent man, but had hardly sufficient imagination to be capable of getting on to more than agreeable terms with the Germans.

The story of my visit to Berlin in February 1912 is set out fully in Chapter II. of *Before the War*, which deals with the pre-War diplomacy. My mission was an informal one. I was to discuss freely and to indicate the mind of our Government, but I was not to conclude an agreement or go further than to bring back *ad referendum* to London materials on which to base final decisions. My brother, the physiologist, went with me as private secretary, ostensibly to confer on scientific matters with biologists at the University of the German capital.

The following extract from *Before the War* describes the position as I found it in Berlin :—

' I arrived in the German capital on February 8, 1912, and spent some days in interviews with the Emperor, the Imperial Chancellor, the Naval Minister (Admiral von Tirpitz), and others of the Emperor's Ministry. The narrative of my conversations I have extracted from the records I made after each interview, for the preservation so far as possible of the actual expressions used during it.

' My first interview was one with Herr von Bethmann-Hollweg, the Imperial Chancellor. We met in the British Embassy, and the conversation, which was quite informal was a full and agreeable one. My impression, and I still retain it, was that Bethmann-Hollweg was then as sincerely desirous of avoiding war as I was myself. I told him o certain dangers quite frankly, and he listened and replied with what seemed to me to be a full understanding of our position. I said that the increasing action of Germany in piling up magnificent armaments was, of course, within the unfettered rights of the German people. But the policy had an inevitable consequence in the drawing together of other nations in the interest of their own security. This was what was happening. I told him frankly that we had made naval and military preparations, but only such as defence required, and as would be considered in Germany matter of routine. I went on to observe that our faces were set against aggression by any nation, and I told him, what seemed to relieve his mind, that we had no secret military treaties. But, I added, if France were attacked and an attempt made to occupy her territory, our neutrality must not be reckoned on by Germany. For one thing, it was obvious that our position as an island protected by the sea would be affected seriously if Germany had possession of the Channel ports on the northern shores of France. Again, we were under treaty obligation to come to the aid of Belgium in case of invasion, just as we were bound to defend Portugal and Japan in certain eventualities. In the third place, owing to our dependence on freedom of sea-communications for food and raw materials, we could not sit still if Germany elected to develop her fleet to such an extent as to imperil our naval protection. She might build more ships, but we should in that case lay down two keels for each one she laid down.

' The Chancellor said that he did not take my observations at all in bad part, but I must understand that his admirals and generals were pretty difficult.

' I replied that the difficulty would be felt at least as much with the admirals and generals in my own country.

' The Chancellor, in the course of our talk, proposed a formula of neutrality to which I will refer later on.

' I left the Chancellor with the sense that I had been talking with an honest man struggling somewhat with adversity. However, next day I was summoned to luncheon with the Emperor and Empress at the Schloss and afterward had a long interview, which lasted nearly three hours, with the Emperor and Admiral von Tirpitz in the Emperor's cabinet room. The conversation was mainly in German, and was confined to naval questions. My reception by the Emperor was very agreeable ; that by Tirpitz seemed to me a little strained. The question was, whether Germany must not continue her programme for expanding her fleet. What that programme really amounted to we had not known in London, except that it included an increase in battleships ; but the Emperor handed me at this meeting a confidential copy of the draft of the proposed new Fleet Law, with an intimation that he had no objection to my communicating it privately to my colleagues. I was careful to abstain even from looking at it then, for I saw that, from its complexity and bulk, it would require careful study. So I simply put it in my pocket. But I repeated what I had said to the Chancellor, that the necessity for secure sea-communications rendered it vital for us to be able to protect ourselves on the seas. Germany was quite free to do as she pleased, but so were we, and we should probably lay down two keels for every one which she added to her programme. The initiative in slackening competition was really not with us, but with Germany. Any agreement for settling our differences and introducing a new spirit into the relations of the two nations would be bones without flesh if Germany began by fresh shipbuilding, and so forced us to do twice as much. Indeed, the world would laugh at such an agreement, and our people would think that we had been fooled. I did not myself take that view, because I thought that the mere fact of an agreement was valuable. But the Emperor would see that the public would attach very little importance to his action unless the agreement largely modified what it believed to be his shipbuilding programme.

' We then discussed the proposal of the German Admiralty for the new programme. Admiral von Tirpitz struggled for it. I insisted that fundamental modification was essential if better relations were to ensue. The tone was friendly, but I felt that I was up against the crucial part of my task. The admiral wanted us to enter into some understanding about our own shipbuilding. He thought the Two-Power standard a hard one for Germany, and, indeed, Germany could not make any admission about it.

' I said it was not matter for admission. They were free and so were we, and we must for the sake of our safety remain so. The idea then occurred to us that, as we should never agree about it, we should avoid trying to define a standard proportion in any general agreement that we might come to, and, indeed, say nothing in it about ship-building; but that the Emperor should announce to the German public that the agreement on general questions, if we should have concluded one, had entirely modified his wish for the new Fleet Law, as originally conceived, and that it should be delayed, and future shipbuilding should at least be spread over a longer period.

' The Emperor thought such an agreement would cer-tainly make a great difference, and he informed me that his Chancellor would propose to me a formula as a basis for it. I said that I would see the Chancellor and discuss a possible formula, as well as territorial and other questions with him, and would then return to London and report to the King (from whom I had brought him a special and

friendly message) and to my colleagues the good disposition
I had found, and leave the difficulties about shipbuilding
and indeed all other matters to their judgment. For I
had come to Berlin, not to make an actual agreement,
but only to explore the ground for one with the Emperor
and his ministers. I had been struck with the friendly
disposition in Berlin, and a not less friendly disposition
would be found in London.'

In the interview which took place the Emperor
struck me as desirous of peace, but as not understanding that the best way to promote peace was not
by displaying the sword. In the fashioning of the
sword Tirpitz seemed to me to be encouraging him
powerfully, though I do not think that even he
contemplated war. Bethmann was of a wholly
different temperament, and appeared to me to look
at the situation much as we did in England. But he
was not strong enough to be able to dispel the atmosphere with which the Emperor was surrounded.

Still I was very well received. I think that the
German public as a whole did not desire war at all,
although they had an undue belief in their power as
an armed nation. On a rumour that I was not really
there to negotiate, down fell the price of securities
in Berlin. However, this made no difference. I got
some small modifications agreed to in the *tempo*
of battleship construction, and a little in reduction
of expenditure on both sides. But Tirpitz was
determined in insisting on his policy of building
up the strength of the German Navy, and I had to
be equally decided in my answer that this merely
meant our having to increase ours. We plainly

could not come to an agreement with the naval advisers of the Emperor in their present mood. I think that the Emperor would have been disposed to agree to put a check on the progress of his Fleet Laws, but these advisers would not let him do so, and he was not really powerful enough to overrule them. Bethmann did his best, but his position was not strong enough to enable him to resist, as a Bismarck— in the end a great peace Chancellor—could have done.

I returned to London and reported fully on the situation to the Cabinet. The Emperor had courteously given me an advance copy of his new Fleet Bill. Our Admiralty experts found in it much that was alarming, and we had no alternative but to go on with counter - preparations. These had reached large dimensions by the time the War came about. Since the Liberal Government came in in 1905 the Navy Estimates had gone up from thirty-one millions to over fifty millions. In the light of what happened it was not too great an increase.

Looking back I have often thought that if when the century opened we had understood Germany better we might have succeeded in inducing her and France and Russia to come to a better understanding of each other. But that required that we ourselves should have known more about the Germans. They are a difficult people because the ' abstract mind ' predominates with them. But that very quality makes them exact and reliable in their dealings when an agreement has once been arrived at. One of the uses of the League of Nations is that it enables the various peoples to come into each other's society, and to talk. But before this can be thoroughly done, knowledge is wanted, much more knowledge than is common among us about the nations with whom we have to deal. This is a topic on which I will not enlarge here, for what I had to say on the subject I said in 1911 at Oxford in the address delivered there on Great Britain and Germany, and afterwards published in the volume of addresses known as *Universities and National Life*. The War has taught us a good deal, but the teaching we and other nations require must assume, if it is to be sufficient, more systematic form.

After I returned to London in February 1912, negotiations were continued with Germany; no longer about the Fleet question, for on this her Government seemed immovable, but about other matters. We hoped that, just as we had succeeded in smoothing our relations with France by the settlement of a number of territorial questions, including Newfoundland and Egypt, we might get on to good business relations with Germany. Africa and the Baghdad Railway were subjects for a discussion which proceeded favourably and in a satisfactory spirit. Indeed just before the War a draft agreement about these questions was arrived at.

I took a good deal of part in the German discussions, and drafted certain difficult despatches in reply to some that came from Berlin. There it was evident that the Chancellor was not being left undisturbed, even in his own work when communicating with us. I also used at times to relieve Grey of the charge of the Foreign Office when he wanted a week of rest

from his harassing labours.   Morley or I used to sit
at the Foreign Office when he was absent on these
occasions, though holidays he did not often take.
Early in 1906 he had lost his wife, who died as the
result of an accident.   She was a woman of great
and noble character, and he was for the time utterly
broken down by her loss.   It was only in strenuous
work that he could find distraction from his sorrow.

I also, as I was robust and did not mind extra work,
used at times to take charge of the Home Office
when the Home Secretary was absent.   This was no
sinecure, for difficult questions which required police
and even military intervention occasionally arose
in these times, which unexpectedly were disturbed
by strikes and riots.   But the soldiers and the
police were both splendidly tactful.   It was a pleasure
to me to hear in the evenings that the former, who had
been sent down to disturbed districts to avert menaces
to property and even to life, had been engaged during
the day in playing football with the rioters.

Such was my life in 1912.   When I took over the
Great Seal it changed, though not as much as the
public supposed.   But before I part from this period I
must refer to an event which made a great difference
to me.   King Edward passed away in the summer of
1910.   I was much attached to him, and he admitted
me to much intimacy with him, perhaps to more
than was the case with any other of my colleagues.
I saw him constantly, both formally on business
and in social relations.   He liked to put me in the
list of those whom he wished to meet at dinner and
on his week-end visits.   Over my Army reforms he

had supported me strenuously, and although these were practically complete when he died, I missed much the old relations in the general business of the Government. For he did not mind anything I thought it necessary to say to him, however plainly.

When he died I felt the sense of personal grief, and those who had been near to him knew well that this would be so. Looking back at letters I wrote then, I find this in one of 10th May : ' This morning the Queen Dowager sent for me. She received me alone in the room where he lay as yet uncoffined, and I took a last farewell of my old and dear Master. His expression was just the usual one—but little changed—as I have seen him lying back in life, with his eyes closed.' ' She told me that he was very fond of me.'

Such are the events that really count in one's existence.

CHAPTER VIII

AS LORD CHANCELLOR

(1912–1915)

I HAVE held the Great Seal twice. The first period lasted from the summer of 1912 to a date in the summer of 1915, nearly three years later. The second period, which began early in 1924, was shorter. It endured only for about nine months. It is with the first period that this chapter is mainly concerned.

One of my ambitions in going to the Woolsack was to accomplish what I had for many years seen to be necessary, the strengthening of the Judicial Committee of the Privy Council as the Supreme Tribunal of the Empire outside of Great Britain and, then, of Ireland. For want of judges that Tribunal had been too often allowed to sit with only three members present, to hear appeals from Dominion Courts of five judges. The Dominions had begun to criticise the composition of the neglected Court, and to point out that the available judicial strength was being concentrated in the House of Lords in preference to it.

Another reform to which my mind had become directed was the radical transformation of our English

Land Laws.   Settlement might cease to be objectionable, particularly in the case of small family properties, where it was a convenient mode of protecting widows and children, if, but only if, the tenant for life were, as between himself and the public, put in the position of a fee simple owner who could deal with the land freely.   The settlement would then be reduced to tying up the proceeds of his dealing, by analogy to the principle of Lord Cairns' Settled Land Act.   The plan of the ' curtain,' behind which the equitable transactions of the statutory owner under a settlement would go on could the settlement be protected, leaving the public to deal with the limited owner as if he were the absolute owner, had been more or less worked out by an eminent conveyancer, the late Mr. Wolstenholme.   His chief disciple, Mr., afterwards Sir, Benjamin Cherry, was ready to place his knowledge and experience at my disposal.   The late Sir Philip Gregory, and one or two other conveyancers of the highest standing, were also prepared to come forward.   When the call came to them they rallied, in 1912, to my assistance, and did very fine work. The primary draftsman was Sir Benjamin Cherry. He worked in consultation with the others, and with the Treasury draftsman, and in 1913 and 1914 we produced Bills which I introduced from the Woolsack. The War prevented them from making further progress in the teeth of the atmosphere of suspicion which it engendered.   But in the Bills were the principles and most of the details of the Acts which have since become law.   After the War was over the then Chancellor, Lord Birkenhead, took up the old Bill where I had left it and worked at its improvement. He had my draftsman, Sir Benjamin Cherry, to guide him, and they produced an amended version, with which I was well content. Lord Birkenhead asked me to become Chairman of a Select Committee of the two Houses of Parliament to which it was referred, and I spent three months in 1920 on the work. Finally Lord Birkenhead, who showed much energy over the subject, succeeded in passing it into an Act, a feat which redounded to his credit. Probably only a Conservative Lord Chancellor, with a powerful majority in both Houses, would have been allowed to get the measure through. And even so this reform illustrated the opinion which I have expressed before, that it is only by the co-operation of successive Lord Chancellors that great reforms of the law can be accomplished. For no sooner was the Bill passed than it became evident that to perfect the necessary changes several other Acts would be required. Lord Cave, who had been somewhat critical of the proposed reform, when he succeeded to the Woolsack, took this view, and he introduced the further Bills. His Government went out of office before he could pass them, and it fell to me, when I was Chancellor in the Labour Government in 1924, to take up the problem again. I framed and passed a number of Bills through the Lords, but the Labour Government went out before they could be considered in the Commons. On Lord Cave's return to office he got them passed with further improvements, together with yet another Bill, and the reform of the Land Laws on the lines devised is now an accomplished fact. The edifice will probably in the future require further modification, but as it at present stands it was planned with great care and detail, and we three Lord Chancellors, when engaged in the work, helped each other and acted not on party lines but in close co-operation.

Returning now to the composition of the Judicial Tribunals of the House of Lords and the Privy Council, I managed in 1913, in the face of a good deal of difficulty, to get an Act through which enabled us to add two new paid Law Lords for the service of these Tribunals. Over this and over the appointment of the two very distinguished judges, Lords Dunedin and Sumner, who were chosen to fill the new posts, Asquith as Prime Minister was most helpful. For it requires all the influence of the Prime Minister to get any Bill for an increase in the number of judges through the Commons. There is an old superstition that there are too many judges for the work that has to be done. I do not agree with this superstition, but Ministers have to reckon with it. I was also fortunate enough to be able to secure the help of two other distinguished lawyers, Sir Alfred Cripps and Lord Justice Buckley, for the work. They took peerages as Lord Parmoor and Lord Wrenbury in 1914 and 1915, and although wholly unpaid, worked as hard as though they were in receipt of salaries. Further unpaid assistance of the most valuable kind was after my time rendered by Lord Phillimore, who was made a peer, and a good deal by others.

During my first Chancellorship an unusual number

of King's Bench judgeships became vacant. With Asquith's cordial assent we decided that in filling the vacancies we would appoint only on the footing of high legal and professional qualifications. The vacancies were filled on this basis, and my successors have adhered closely to the same principle. It is a principle of great importance for the administration of justice.

Another problem which engaged my attention from an early stage was how to bring the work of the Lord Chancellor's Office and that of the Home Office into closer relation. The two Ministers are in the main both Ministers of Justice, and their functions overlap, and this would lead to much confusion were it not for frequent communication between the respective Permanent Officials. The causes which lead to the overlapping are described fully in the Report of the Machinery of Government Committee, in a section which I wrote with my own hand. Until the whole subject of Justice, a subject with immense variety, is systematically reviewed and dealt with, I shall not think that the organisation of this Department of the State can be satisfactory. The Lord Chancellor is required as the Chief Adviser of the Government on legal and constitutional questions. To these and to the supervision of the higher judicial functionaries his main energies should be directed. The Home Secretary should deal, as to a great extent he does at present, with those other phases of this great subject which are mainly administrative. The functions of the two Ministers of Justice should be co-ordinated and should not overlap as at present. If the Lord

Chancellor is to be able to do his work properly he must have the requisite time, and this he can have only if he is relieved from the daily duties of a judge who hears cases, duties which occupy him from 10.30 to 4 on most days of the week, and prevent him from watching in detail all the questions which are occupying his colleagues in the Cabinet. He might also be relieved from the duty of acting as Speaker of the House of Lords and still have quite enough to fill his whole time.

Something of all this I set myself to bring about in my second Chancellorship in 1924. I prepared a Bill for a complete change in the organisation of the House of Lords, which would render the changes possible. But public opinion was not ripe for its introduction, and I keep it in reserve. What I was able to do during the two terms of office was to bring about informally considerably closer relations between the two Ministers, and to turn over to the Home Office subjects, such as the general administration of the Lunacy Laws, which belonged more properly to that Office than to my own. The Staff in the Office of the Lord Chancellor was at the same time developed in scope and efficiency.

But as things stood, one of my primary duties was to sit as a judge and to try to keep at a high level the standard of our judgments. In this my colleagues sought to co-operate with me thoroughly. I never considered that I was equipped by nature for the part of a great judge. It was not that I did not know the law. I knew it pretty thoroughly I had had a long experience at the Bar of the most difficult and miscellaneous kinds of work; and memory had preserved the bulk of my knowledge, notwithstanding absence for over six years at the War Office. But the judicial temperament of the highest order is a very rare gift. Lord Lindley possessed it, and so did Lord Bowen. Lord Watson had it in a notable degree. But I recognised short-comings in my own nature which made me despair of rising to their level as regards the detachment with which they approached the cases which came before them. Still, knowledge of the law, and the desire to be absolutely just, go for a good deal, and I had both of these. But I think that a judge, if he is to reach the highest level, must devote himself, not to many subjects as I did, but to passionate absorption in the law, as, for example, did the late Lord Blackburn. Lord Cairns has been almost the only exception to this rule. In our own time such exclusive devotion to the law is more difficult than it used to be. Not only has the field of law become much wider, but that of politics is more exact-ing. Moreover, to-day the path to the highest in the legal hierarchy lies increasingly through political activities. And a seat in the House of Commons, if it is to be obtained and held, demands more time and energy than was the case in older days.

Until the duties of the Lord Chancellor have been redistributed it will remain difficult for him to avoid devoting a great deal of his time to his work as a judge. During my first Chancellorship I was able to do this. I was barely sixty and still full of physical

energy, almost as necessary for a busy Minister as
mental energy. But I had extra duties. I had to
sit regularly on the Committee of Imperial Defence,
and to attend to the work of the War Office in the
House of Lords. I had to finish the work of the
Royal Commission on the University of London, of
which I was Chairman. Besides attendance at Cabinet
Councils, four days a week at least were taken up
with judicial sittings in the Privy Council and in the
House of Lords. These duties were fulfilled somehow,
but there remained the writing of the judgments,
a heavy burden on the Lord Chancellor, who must
always preside. In those stormy times the House
of Lords often sat till very late, and the writing of
judgments was, therefore, a difficult task, if the
level was to be the level which I had set myself to
keep up. Still, by the aid of a strong constitution
this was managed. Certainly pains were not spared,
and I was very keen about the undertaking. Any
one who takes the trouble to look at the judgments
delivered by the President of the Court during this
period of nearly three years in such cases as Sinclair
v. Brougham, Nocton v. Lord Ashburton (in the
House of Lords), the Bonanza Case, and Attorney-
General for Australia v. the Colonial Sugar Company
(in the Privy Council), will appreciate the amount of
time and research such judgments involved. It must
not be forgotten that in preparing his judgments the
Lord Chancellor has no such secretarial assistance
as is enjoyed by the judges of the Supreme Court
of the United States. He has to rely on himself
exclusively.

LORD WATSON
Reproduced from a portrait by Sargent belonging to the Society of Advocates

Lindley, Watson, and Bowen had passed away or retired before I became Chancellor, but Halsbury and Macnaghten remained, and for some time I had them as colleagues. They were splendid colleagues and they helped me much with the vast experience they could bring to bear. Each of them had great grasp of the cases that came before them and were delightful in point of personality and friendliness. Halsbury worked on, notwithstanding increasing age. Towards the close he became rather deaf, and, as he did not mind what he said to me across the House when I was presiding, the proceedings were somewhat illuminated by whispers to me, which, quite unintentionally, his powerful voice made resound through the Chamber. I recall that on one occasion, being dissatisfied with the quality of the observations made by one of our colleagues, Halsbury whispered to me, in a voice that was audible throughout the Chamber, ' Our colleague is not *par negotiis*.' He fought on against old age when there was no compulsion on him to do so, and it was only quite late in his life that he submitted to the doctors and to Lady Halsbury, who told me that it had become dangerous for him to attempt any longer the effort required by judicial work. His was a very remarkable mind, quick and decided. It was impressive to watch the fashion in which at an early stage he could penetrate to the very heart of the facts in a case. If not a great lawyer, like Cairns or Selborne, in his command of the authorities, he was a great judge in his apprehension of the facts in each case as it came before him. With

R

myself he was on affectionate terms even when I
was at the Bar, and he expressed himself as certain
that before long I should succeed him on the Woolsack. Over my politics he shook his head, and
feared that in this respect I was a degenerate
inheritor from my great grand-uncles, Lords Eldon
and Stowell. But he used to say, in letters and
orally, that this did not, in his opinion, apply to
the law.

Another remarkable colleague was Lord Moulton.
In apprehension he had perhaps the most rapid
intelligence with which I ever came in contact.
He was too impulsive to possess the judicial temperament at its highest level, but his was an extraordinary
mind. When the German Emperor came to Queen
Anne's Gate, on the occasion of the luncheon party
which I have already recorded, Moulton was there.
After talking to him, the Emperor said to me, ' But
what is this man ? You say he is a judge, but he
seems to know everything.'

I was thus very fortunate in the colleagues who
surrounded me in the Supreme Tribunals. With
their aid I got through the work, although it often
involved sitting up into the small hours of the
morning to write judgments and to prepare speeches.
For political contests in the Lords were in this period
very keen. The speech, for instance, which it fell
to me to make when we carried the Bill for the
Disestablishment of the Church in Wales cost me a
great deal of time which I could ill spare, but the
material I had was such that our case, as the Hansard
Report and the Report of the speech show, was a

difficult one to resist as presented. Things got so bitter that I was attacked in every possible way. The criticisms on the Army gave me no trouble, but there were other criticisms to meet which involved a good deal of work.

Through my time at the House of Lords I had a source of rest and refreshment with my old friend Edmund Gosse, now passed away, but then still Librarian of the House. He used to come to me much for general talk. His affectionate friendship and that of Muir-Mackenzie, my principal Secretary as Lord Chancellor, were a source of relief in stormy times.

Before going further with this chapter I ought to refer to an event which occurred while I was Lord Chancellor, and which was the first of the kind in the history of the office. In August 1913 I paid a brief visit to the United States and to Canada. President Wilson and some of the leading statesmen and lawyers in the United States on the one hand, and the Governor-General of Canada, the Duke of Connaught, and the Prime Minister, Mr. Borden, had joined in an invitation to me to take the course, novel for a British Custodian of the Great Seal, who has to remain in our country, of crossing the Atlantic and delivering an address to the American and Canadian Bar Associations and the public generally. The place was to be Montreal, and the occasion the impending centenary of the Treaty of Ghent. The two Bar Associations had agreed to meet there to commemorate the occasion. Mr. Kellogg, then President of the American Bar Association, and afterwards to be Ambassador here and Secretary of State at Washington, came personally to London and pressed on me the invitation. The Cabinet here thought that I should manage to go, but that I should restrict my visit to a week-end, and so avoid having to avail myself of formal invitations to visit Washington and Ottawa, which would probably have entailed the spending of much time which could not well be spared in travelling to other places as the alternative to disappointment. This so-called ' lightning visit ' took place, and the details were fully published in the newspapers of the day. On the preparation of the address delivered I spent time. Its subject was the material for conciliation between the three nations. The theme was that we were reaching a stage in which we might well hope that the Ententes between the nations I was addressing, and on the other hand between them and France and Russia, as well as Germany and Austria, might be so directed as to lend themselves to a still further-reaching Entente. In the spirit of this larger understanding we might hope for and find the best in other nations, and so develop a world-wide ' Sittlichkeit ' or sense of good form, as distinguished from mere law or pure ethics, which should provide a firmer basis for International Law and reverence for International Obligations and establish respect for the rights and duties of foreign nations.

All seemed smooth at that time, but I was haunted somehow by an uncomfortable feeling. The Balkan War had disclosed how unstable the international situation really was, and how much vigilance was required. In the Montreal address I quoted to my audience the prayer of Grotius,[1] but added that its accomplishment appeared to be still a long way off, and that, while we must work for that accomplishment with our utmost strength, we could not be certain of a speedy result.

The address was reported in full in the papers here and in the United States and Canada. It attracted a good deal of attention not only in English-speaking countries but on the Continent. It was published under the title *The Higher Nationality*. Bethmann-Hollweg wrote to me that he not only wholly concurred in ideas which he had shared with me at Berlin in February 1912, but that he should, so far as it was within his power, devote his energies to the cause, and was happy in finding in me an openly declared fellow-worker.

The American Reception Committee, with boundless hospitality, insisted on entertaining not only myself but my sister and Sir Kenneth Muir-Mackenzie, the Principal Secretary to the Lord Chancellor, from London until our return. At New York, where we arrived on a Friday afternoon, we had a magnificent reception. The next day we were taken up the Hudson to West Point, where as the ex-Secretary for War I had been asked to inspect the Training School for Officers in the United States Army. We were immediately after that taken charge of by a deputa-

---

[1] 'May God write these lessons—He Who alone can—on the hearts of all those who have the affairs of Christendom in their hands. And may He give to those persons a mind fitted to understand and to respect rights, human and divine, and lead them to recollect always that the ministration committed to them is no less than this, that they are the Governors of Man, a creature most dear to God.'

tion of Canadian Ministers, and after a banquet at
Albany travelled by night to Montreal, where we
spent two days, on the second of which I delivered
my address in the theatre to a vast audience containing Chief Justices and Judges, as well as members
of the two Bars and the general public. The Chief
Justice of the Supreme Court of the United States,
Douglas White, presided. Borden, Taft, Choate,
Lord Strathcona, who, his great age notwithstanding,
had travelled over with us, and other people of
distinction in politics as well as in law, were on the
platform.

Next morning, Tuesday, we started back for New
York. The Chairman, the American Chief Justice,
and I were photographed together in travelling
costume on the track. We reached New York that
night, and started back in the same steamer, the
Lusitania, for England. The Great Seal was in
Commission during my absence. This week-end visit
was the only one which it has been my privilege to
pay to the New World, notwithstanding a multitude of
correspondents whom I have in the United States and
in Canada.

About this time I began to have questions of health
to attend to. During the Lloyd George Budget in
1910 I had taken a considerable part in the House of
Commons. The Death Duty clauses were very intricate, and as I knew the subject I agreed to take
charge of them. This involved all-night sittings on
the top of my daily work at the War Office. As the
result, Nature pulled me up rather suddenly. I had
an attack of iritis in one eye, so serious that the

doctors despaired of saving it. • It did in the end recover, though I can hardly see with it now. I was kept in bed during the latter part of December and through the Christmas holidays. This would not have mattered so much had it not been that the General Election was about to take place. My family were at Cloan with my mother, but Sir John and Lady Horner superintended me in London through a severe illness, and bestowed on me affectionate care. However, early in January I was able to go down to East Lothian and finish an Election campaign which my sister, who had remained in the north for the purpose, conducted on my behalf, with the aid of Asquith and other colleagues and friends, with much vigour. In the capacity of a ' wounded warrior ' I was able to join them towards the end and be elected at Haddington by a good majority.

But the disaster to my eye was not the most serious trouble. While I was ill the doctors in London discovered that over-exertion had brought on an attack of diabetes. As my father had died of this, it was necessary for me to be careful and to adopt the rigid diet which was the only palliative known in those pre-insulin days. I did so, and for long was able to do my work as closely as ever. But not indefinitely. Twice later on an accumulation of sugar in the blood laid me low. On the first occasion I had a rather serious collapse. On the second I was stricken with acute sciatica. On both occasions—they occurred just before the long vacation—I was taken down to Cloan, and there I recovered after a time.

But I should not have been able to count on good

health but for a fortunate circumstance. Banting had discovered insulin before the time of my second attack. Under the advice of the eminent physicians who watched over me, I arranged to have an injection of insulin into my arm every morning, and this has served me, to all appearances, admirably. It has taken the place of the pancreatic secretions of the ' Islands of Langerhans,' and, although probably physically older for my years than I should be, I have been able to keep free from the presence of sugar in perilous quantities in the blood.

In the end, by taking care, I found myself able to get through as much work as before. The volume of this did not diminish. After the passing of the Parliament Act, a Committee of the Cabinet on which I sat had, under the Chairmanship of Lord Ripon, examined the question of how we could best give effect to the reform of the House of Lords, to which we had pledged ourselves in the preamble to the Act. Differences of opinion arose over the suggestion of a directly elected Senate as a substitute for the existing House of Lords. Only vigorous young men with large funds behind them could have undertaken the requisite candidatures, and the result might have been to throw the authority of the House of Commons into confusion. We did not want to have to choose between being compelled to confine ourselves to young and wealthy candidates as one alternative, or the development of a magnified caucus system as the other. The majority of us came to think that the preamble to the Parliament Act could therefore best be satisfied by constituting something resembling choice by electoral colleges made up of the directly elected members of the House of Commons. But this plan would obviously give rise to much controversy, and would be far from satisfactory to those ardent opponents who desired to strengthen the powers of the Upper Chamber. The result was a paralysing perplexity, such as was to arise years later when the Conservative Party endeavoured to take the matter in hand. But this did not mitigate the attacks which were made on us in the Lords for our delay in fulfilling our pledge. Naturally a full share of the business of dealing with these attacks fell on the Lord Chancellor.

There was another question, too, which was hardly less formidable. In 1914 there had been a threat that, as the Home Rule Bill was being pressed through Parliament, Ulster would resist it by force. If troops were employed, even for the purpose of preserving law and order there while the Bill was passing, it was said that the troops and their officers would be urged to refuse to allow themselves to be employed for the purpose. In the debates on this subject I was compelled to intervene in my capacity of representing the Army as ex-Secretary of State for War. The burden of these days was almost overwhelming. I had to be at the House of Lords soon after ten in the morning for the judicial work, and to sit hearing appeals until nearly four in the afternoon. Then, after twenty minutes with my Secretaries devoted to the general work of the Chancellor, I had to resume as Speaker of the House. The sitting might be short, but more often than not it was very long, lasting sometimes till midnight. I had to find somehow time to look into candidatures for the Chancellor's livings, and to fill up twice as many livings as the two Archbishops together had in their gift. I had also to look after the magistrates, not only in England but in Scotland, many of the lunatics, the administration of all the judicial offices in England, including the County Courts, together with a multitude of small matters. There was not much chance in these stormy days of getting out of town for week-ends. The Liberal Party in the House of Lords was very small, and my presence was required constantly. On Wednesdays, when there was not a Cabinet, I felt bound to attend to what was a labour of love as well as of duty, the sittings of the Committee of Imperial Defence, which generally took place on that day, being one free from judicial business.

When in the spring of 1914 the passions of those who were opposing Home Rule had reached their height, an unfortunate incident occurred at the Curragh. The Commander-in-Chief in Ireland had given some orders which appeared not to have been tactfully worded, and which at all events were misapprehended. A number of gallant officers got into their heads that they were to be ordered to lead troops to shoot down their fellow-Unionists in Ulster. It was in vain that the Government protested that nothing of the kind was intended. The feeling was too violent. I made a speech in the House in which I pointed out that it would be the duty of any Government to protect life and property if there were unfortunately a rising in Ulster, and that we were bound to use troops for the purpose if the police force was not sufficient. I added that while this was so we had no thought of coercing public opinion or of doing more than guard against actual violence. In the sentence which followed I added that we had no intention of giving orders to the troops to intervene, meaning, of course, so long as riots and attacks on barracks, which had been threatened but had not taken place so far, did not occur. This sentence was wrenched from its context and used broadcast as a pledge given by the Lord Chancellor that in no circumstances would the Government use troops in Ulster. When the Hansard rough proof came round the day after the speech for correction, I wished to make it plain that the sentence in question must not be taken apart from its context. The well-understood rule was that members were at liberty to correct expressions which did not convey accurately the sense in which words had been actually used, but that they should not alter the sense of the speech itself. It did not cross my mind that any one could suppose that I was altering the meaning of what had been said. Read with the context the sentence even as it stood was plain enough. It was only when divorced from its context that a wider interpretation, which might have precluded us from doing a simple duty, could be put on it. I therefore inserted the word ' immediate ' before ' intention ' to get rid of any ambiguity. I had, however, better not have done so, for I was at once, in these days of violent controversy, attacked in the House. Outside, I need hardly say, I was accused of falsification and fraud. The Prime Minister himself was called to his face, at the same time, a liar by the Leader of the Opposition in the Commons. Such was the spirit of those days.

The Curragh incident led to an unfortunate attempt on the part of the War Office to reassure the soldiers. Language was used which appeared insufficient for what insistence on military discipline called for. The Cabinet could not endorse it, and in the end Colonel Seely, Sir John French, and General Ewart resigned, the two latter being respectively Chief of the General Staff and Adjutant-General. I did my utmost with the two Generals, who were my intimate friends, to avert their resignations, which were due to a misapprehension on their part about our instructions. But they felt that they had committed themselves to promises and must go. The Prime Minister assumed temporarily the Seals of the War Office. I gave him all the help I could, but I was so busy otherwise that I could not take over what he really needed there. He made two appointments against my advice. One was that of the new Chief of the General Staff. He chose General Douglas, who had been one of the best Adjutant-Generals we ever had. But he had never been trained in General Staff work, and he had not natural aptitude for it. I felt that he was the wrong person to be there if war broke out. And so it proved, for he showed himself unable to get hold of Lord Kitchener's mind when the latter became Secretary for War soon afterwards. But he would have probably proved to be just the Adjutant-General we wanted if he had been persuaded to go back to his old post. The other appointment to which I took some exception was that of Sir Henry Sclater to be Adjutant-General. He had done excellent service in India, but the whole of his experience in Adjutant-General's work had been in that country, and of the new organisation of the Army and the War Office he had little knowledge. These appointments caused me a good deal of concern, which the subsequent course of events seemed to justify.

The Irish situation was becoming very serious. The Ulster Unionists had bought rifles in Hamburg, and there was reason to think that the German Government had stopped the traffic in the Kiel Canal in order to let the *Fanny*, the steamer which carried them, get round Denmark into the North Sea and so escape the vigilance of the British Navy. Indeed, the Germans appeared to be taking an uncomfortably vivid interest in the troubles of the British Army in Ireland, and in the prospect of our military forces continuing in an embarrassed condition. In France, too, the Army was disturbed, owing to mismanagement as regarded stores, and the circumstance that the new system of extended service with the Colours had not become operative. Such was the state of things immediately before the outbreak of the War. But a great deal had been accomplished, and in time. A few days after the War broke out the Prime Minister came to Queen Anne's Gate to see me, and to say something that was unusual for a man of his reserve : ' If the country is prepared for this war, it is to you more than to any other person that it owes it.'

War became certain in the end of July 1914. Just before this calamity Grey had come to stay with me at 28 Queen Anne's Gate. A few days previously Herr Ballin had visited London and had dined with my sister and myself. We had invited Grey and Lord Morley to meet him, for we knew how desirous he was of helping to preserve peace. At that moment I think that he must have been apprehensive that war would break out, although we ourselves were then hopeful that it might still be avoided; for after dinner he spoke to Grey and myself separately about the position of Great Britain, and our relations with Germany. We both told him that so far these were quite good, but that their maintenance was dependent on Germany not attacking France. In such a case Germany could not reckon on our neutrality.

Just before England declared war on Germany on 4th August, Ballin sent me by messenger a letter recalling the dinner and his pleasure at being present, and expressing the hope, based on what he imagined we had said, that if Germany did not try to ' swallow up ' France, England would be neutral. I did not answer this letter, which arrived only the day before war broke out. The only material point about it was that Ballin had represented Grey and myself as having used the words ' swallow up,' whereas we had really said ' attack ' when we defined the condition. The letter did not appear to me to be of importance. But the *Times* somehow discovered that Herr Ballin had sent a letter to me through a messenger. The circumstance was at once made public, and I was questioned about it in the House of Lords. I replied that it was a private letter from Herr Ballin, whom I knew well, thanking me for hospitality, and that it contained no information that could be useful to the public. I therefore refused to read it aloud. For in the first place it would not have been right, particularly for the Head of the Law, who might be expected to set an example in observing it, to publish a private letter without the sender's consent, when the letter had been written in time of peace. Apart from this, I did not want Grey, who had been Ballin's fellow-guest at the dinner, to be dragged into the attack which had begun to be made on myself. Grey and Crewe, who was leading the House, and to both of whom I showed the letter, agreed that there was no reason why it should be made public. This was the incident of the Ballin letter, which was made one of the first grounds of attack on me. I wanted to keep Grey out of the matter, otherwise I think that, notwithstanding that I was Lord Chancellor, the least evil would have been to have disregarded Ballin's legal right and published the letter. It was harmless and a little foolish.

Ballin is now no more, and there is now no substantial reason why I should not publish the letter, which gave rise to so searching a curiosity that £200 was offered at the time for a copy of it. So here it is :—

HAMBURG, 1st *August* 1914.

DEAR LORD HALDANE,—Hardly a week has elapsed since I had the honour and pleasure of spending an extremely interesting evening with you. The atmosphere which then surrounded us was so pure and beneficial, that it was even not disturbed by the serious political conversation that we carried on after dinner.

Meanwhile, with a rapidity which almost outdoes human thought the situation of the world has been completely altered.   One still fails to believe that only because Austria, compelled by a provocation of many years' duration, was obliged to undertake a kind of punitive expedition against Servia, Russia and Germany and perhaps also France and Italy and I must even say England, are to be drawn into a war, in which properly speaking none of these countries can gain anything, but that values would be destroyed to an extent that the human brain cannot yet estimate.

Now one puts here the question : Will England really enter upon this war ?   Last week you gave me in your clear manner the impression that England would only be induced to make a martial intervention if Germany were to swallow up France, in other words, if the balance of power were to be greatly altered by German annexation of French territory.

In view of the critical situation I am far from wishing you to write me about the situation. But what affects me particularly is the news which is disseminated in London from Paris, that Germany wishes to carry on this war, as a kind of preventive war against Russia and France, in other words, therefore, that this period appears to Germany to be particularly favourable for such a war and that she is therefore, precipitating this war without a proper serious cause.   I hope that you and Sir Edward Grey do not attach any importance to this calumniatory assertion.   You know our Emperor personally and are aware that he has made it the task of his life to preserve peace for Germany.   Indeed, I can assure you that it was his most sincere wish to close his life with the fame that, during his reign he had succeeded in carrying out this high purpose of keeping peace. The idea that the German Emperor could let himself draw into the undertaking of a preventive war is for those who know him altogether absurd. And as I know the high esteem and friendship you feel for our Reichskanzler Herr von Bethmann-Hollweg I am sure you agree with me that he is equally incapable of such unscrupulousness.

At any rate, I wished to say this to you and I still hope that it will be possible for England to preserve a friendly neutrality in return for certain guarantees and I equally hope that at the last hour it will still be possible to find a peaceful way out of this terrible chaos.

I beg you, dear Lord Haldane, to accept my heartiest wishes and regards, and remain,—Yours very sincerely,

(Signed) BALLIN.

I shall return at the end of the chapter to the personal attack of which this letter was the prelude.

As I have said, when the War broke out Grey was staying with me. During the week before 4th August, when the British Ambassador to Berlin was recalled, he had passed a time of deep distress. Under my roof he was sparing no effort to avoid the catastrophe. I was helping him with such counsel as I could give, but he was splendidly self-reliant. Telegrams and despatches were coming in at all hours of the night. In order that he might get sleep, I had a servant sitting up with instructions to bring them to my bedroom and waken me so that I might open the boxes with my Cabinet key and decide whether it was necessary to break in upon Grey's rest. During that week he rose to a great height, and the speech he made in the House of

s

Commons before the Declaration of War showed that he had put his whole mind and soul into the discharge of the duty that he conceived to be his.

On Sunday, 2nd August, it was evident to him and to me that the country would almost certainly be unable to keep out of the War. We had arrived at this conclusion on somewhat different grounds. He felt what we owed to France, and that our national interest was bound up with her preservation. I thought, from my study of the German General Staff, that once the German war party had got into the saddle and the sword had been drawn from the scabbard, it would be a war not merely for the overthrow of France and Russia, but for the domination of the world. I knew that if we kept out and allowed Germany to get possession, even for a time, of the north-eastern shores of France, our turn would come later, and that we should be in the greatest peril, our Navy notwithstanding, and that we might go down, without a friend in the world, under a tremendous combination against us. It was clearly wisest to take a great decision, and to throw ourselves without delay into a struggle from which, if the first attack on France could be checked, I believed that the Allied Powers, with their great potential resources, would in the end emerge victorious. My reliance was on sea-power, and on the ultimate weapon of blockade.

Having come to the same conclusion on grounds which did not really differ from mine, Grey and I were immediately reminded of the necessity of prompt action. For a box was brought in, while we were dining together, with a telegram to the effect that the German Army was about to invade Belgium. I had always thought that this would be their mode of attack on France. I knew that this plan had been worked out by von Schlieffen when Chief of the German General Staff, with only this difference, that he proposed to march through part of Holland also, a plan which according to our secret information had been abandoned so far as Holland was concerned. Grey asked me what my prescription was. My answer was ' Immediate Mobilisation.' He said that his view was the same. We decided to go on without delay to see the Prime Minister.

We found him with some company, and took him into another room. As far as I can recollect, the only other Minister who was present and came with us into the private room was Crewe. We expressed our view as to the gravity of the risk and as to what was the first step to take. Asquith agreed to it at once. A carefully worded communication showing that we understood the necessity of speedy decision was sent on the spot to the French Ambassador. I said to the Prime Minister, who was then holding the Seals of the War Office, that as on the next day, Monday, he would be occupied overwhelmingly with Cabinets and communications to Parliament, he had better write a letter entrusting to me the business of going over to the War Office and in his name mobilising my old organisation. He agreed, and at eleven the next morning I returned to my old room and summoned the Army Council. Their breath was somewhat taken away when I told them that I had come with authority to direct immediate mobilisation of the Expeditionary and Territorial Forces, and also of the Special Reserve and the Officers' Training Corps, and that the telegrams, which were all prepared and in store, must be sent out at once, and without stopping to consult either the Finance Department of the War Office or the Treasury. It was a matter of life and death. It was all done without a hitch. The public wondered why they could get no trains to certain of our southern ports. The reason was that the Railway Managers had become Colonels in charge of the railways and were busily engaged that afternoon in arranging for the transport of the Expeditionary Force to Newhaven and Southampton. The formal order for mobilisation was not issued until the next day, but for this we deemed it unnecessary to wait. I told the Generals that the question whether the Expeditionary Force would actually be despatched from our shores, and the question of how many divisions, were questions which would not be decided until the issue of peace or war had been disposed of by the Cabinet, the Sovereign, and Parliament, but that they must be ready, with the aid of the Transport Department of the Admiralty, to send the entire force at once if necessary to a place of concentration which had been arranged several years previously, opposite to the Gap of Chimay on the Belgian frontier of France.

The whole of the necessary arrangements had been worked out in full detail in the interval that had elapsed since 1906. Field-Marshal Sir John French had long ago been designated as Commander-in-

Chief of the British Army. He was admirably qualified for the duty, for he was a real soldier of the modern type. Moreover, he had frequently visited France since 1906, and had studied the terrain. The Staffs had been allotted and the whole of the railway arrangements had been made. These I had myself, when at the War Office several years before, taken out of the hands of the Quartermaster-General and the Engineers and put into the hands of a War Committee of Railway Managers, who were to work in co-operation with the Quartermaster-General's department. They did their duty admirably, and the plan worked without a hitch. It was one of the most striking illustrations of the way in which it has proved possible to bring civilian elements to play a part in military organisation, and to call a nation to arms under a voluntary system.

The mobilisation arrangements were completed. I need hardly say that there was never the slightest foundation for the suggestion presently to be launched, that I had wished to delay the sending of the Expeditionary Force. I had desired to send off all the six divisions from the outset. Careful consultation with the Admiralty had made it plain that they could guarantee that there would be no practical possibility of serious invasion, and after the War was over I ascertained that the Germans had never thought seriously of attempting it.

In the afternoon of Monday (the 3rd) the Prime Minister had asked me to summon a War Council, and to select those who should attend. Among others I summoned Lord Roberts and Lord

Kitchener, who happened to be in London. This Council proved a little timid about invasion, and did not like the idea of all the six divisions leaving the country, but it decided that four should go at once and that a fifth should follow. Sir John French and I wished all the six to start, but we were in a minority. There was available, as we pointed out, a seventh, the sections of which would have to be brought in part from Egypt.

It has been alleged by those who misinterpreted the little that appeared in the newspapers about my activities on the Monday that I wished to return to the War Office and to conduct the War. This is quite untrue. Rightly or wrongly, I took the view that it would be better, having regard to the military organisation of the Allies with whom we should be co-operating, for a great soldier to be at the head of our own military organisation, and I thought that Lord Kitchener was the obvious man. No one else had so great a hold on the imagination of the public. The Prime Minister took the same view, and so did Churchill, but the Foreign Office was unwilling that he should be moved from his post as Consul-General in Egypt. In that country trouble was then apprehended. This difficulty was got over. It was the sole cause of the delay of a few hours in the appointment of Lord Kitchener to the War Office. But I took care meantime to have him in constant attendance at the War Councils which were taking place, and I saw him very often both then and after his appointment.

However, I was unable to prevail on him to adopt,

or even to make much real use of, the Territorial organisation I had provided. And he practically dispensed with the services of the General Staff by letting it dwindle, and by appointing to it some not very suitable men who had no grip of the nature of its work. Kitchener was a man with great power of personality. He had the idea, which had been familiar to him in practice in the East, that the conduct of war was the job of the man at the head. He knew nothing of the modern science of military organisation which had been evolved in Europe. Consequently he was difficult to move. He would not raise troops through the medium of the County Associations, on whom, under the existing arrangements, the duty of recruiting and supplying the troops raised would have devolved automatically. He insisted on raising, not Territorial line after Territorial line, each of which would have stepped into the place of the one in front as it moved away, but new ' Kitchener ' Armies through the medium of the Adjutant-General's Department of the War Office. The result was the confusion which arises from sudden departure from settled principles. Our Army in France was, however, mainly provided for. It was well equipped, and it had its own Headquarters General Staff. But in London there was no General Staff worth the name ; none, for example, that could exercise a guiding and restraining influence when the Dardanelles Expedition was projected.

But Kitchener and I remained on good terms. We used to dine with each other alone and have much talk. Still, move his mind on to modern lines

I could not.　Nevertheless he was a great man and a great moral asset to the nation.

At the time when War and Peace seemed in the balance, there were further difficulties.　The Cabinet which was held on the forenoon of Monday, 3rd August, disclosed a sharp division of opinion.　Morley and Burns were altogether opposed to our entering the War.　The latter took the line that war was something which he could not bring himself to have anything to do with.　Morley shared this feeling, but held in addition that Grey ought not to have let the situation arise.　First he blamed not only Grey but Asquith and myself.　Why he should have reproached me I never quite knew. I used to ask him whether there were no circumstances in which it was the duty of a great nation to fight. He did not dispute that there might be such circumstances.　Nor did he say that we should not be in great peril if the northern ports of France were seized by Germany.　But I think he had in his mind throughout the General Staff conversations which began in 1906, notwithstanding that he had himself, as I have already said, discussed them without dissent at meetings of the Committee of Imperial Defence.　That the War could have been prevented I used to agree with him, but to add that the blame for its not having been prevented dated back to the days long before Grey's time, when we paid too little attention to what was going on even then on the Continent.　Morley's attitude, like that of Burns, was at least based on a principle.　But principle was less easy to discover in the attitude of some of the other dissentients. Lloyd George, Harcourt, Simon, and Beauchamp at first professed to be irreconcilable. When, however, Belgium was invaded by Germany they withdrew opposition, on the ground that duty arising out of our Treaty obligation came in. Indeed, this view was endorsed by the House of Commons and unmistakably by the bulk of public opinion. The result was that in a few days Asquith, who managed the crisis with much skill, had got his Cabinet completely round to his own view. Churchill was concentrating the Fleet boldly and earned well-deserved approval for the energy he showed. He was much with Kitchener. The last-named had been made Secretary for War on the Tuesday night. It fell to me to sound him from Asquith on the subject, and the main conduct of operations at once fell into his hands, aided by Churchill and superintended by Asquith.

My own part from this stage became less and less. I had taken a more optimistic view than Grey of the way things were likely to go. After the battle of the Marne I thought that the Germans must in the end be beaten. This was because the time gained gave the requisite chance for the operation of sea-power. I also laid stress on the Russian ability for endurance. Here I was much too sanguine, but I also saw that the higher leadership in Germany was defective. Its Army was magnificent, and its Navy was very formidable ; but it gradually appeared that neither of these was being used with the certainty in scientific plan and the unshakable decision which characterised the military spirit of 1870. The position of the Emperor, too, was one of uncertainty. Whatever he was otherwise, he did not stand before the world as a Great War Lord. Altogether it appeared to me that, in the end, for a prolonged struggle a democracy was better suited to hold out than an autocracy.

I must now refer to the attacks made on me during the period from the Ballin letter onward. They were mainly made in newspapers, and outside Parliament, but their volume was such that they affected, at least in some considerable degree, public opinion, although they infuriated attached and loyal friends. My motives and the nature of my efforts when I went to Berlin in February 1912 were grossly misrepresented by some newspapers. The Foreign Office, I think unwisely, was averse to publishing the records of 1912. They have, of course, since been made public, not only by myself and others here but by Tirpitz and Bethmann-Hollweg. We are all in agreement on the substance of what took place in the course of my mission, and I think it unfortunate that it was not made known to the public at the time. But this was not all. Every kind of ridiculous legend about me was circulated. I had a German wife ; I was the illegitimate brother of the Kaiser ; I had been in secret correspondence with the German Government ; I had been aware that they intended war and had withheld my knowledge of this from my colleagues ; I had delayed the mobilisation and despatch of the Expeditionary Force. All these and many other things were circulated. They could only have been effectively disposed of by the publication of documents, and to this the Foreign Office was at that time averse. The result was what might have been expected. The Harmsworth Press systematically attacked me, and other newspapers besides. Anonymous letters poured in. On one day, in response to an appeal in the *Daily Express*, there arrived at the House of Lords no less than 2600 letters of protest against my supposed disloyalty to the interests of the nation. These letters were sent over to my house in sacks, and I entrusted the opening and disposal of the contents to the kitchenmaid.

There is generally some reason for everything that happens. It was quite true that I had been a pretty close student of German philosophy and literature, and had much admiration for the power of systematic reflection which distinguished the German people. I had, perhaps too often, reminded my fellow-countrymen of our shortcomings in these respects. But I also knew better than most of my fellow-countrymen the weak side of the German character, and the too great dominance in it of the abstract mind. I had gauged fairly accurately the difference between Germany as it was before the War of 1870 and Germany as it was before the War of 1914. I had estimated the decline in the quality of the Great General Staff, and the danger to his people of an uncontrolled mind such as that of the Kaiser. I had always thought that if Great Britain had been less illiterate about the spirit and traditions of the difficult people across the German Ocean, and had begun, say after the Treaty of Berlin, to show that she understood Germany, the Balance of Power difficulty might have been averted. A concert of Great Powers, of Germany, Austria, Great Britain, France, and Russia, might well have been made the ideal object of diplomats, and if it had, we might in the end have had all and more than a League of Nations offers to-day. But for such an ideal policy we and the other nations also were then ill adapted. We were too ignorant of matters which belonged to the spirit even more than to the letter. So were our agents at home and abroad. Great directing minds would have had to work in consultation over a long period. It was too late when the War began to threaten. The policy, too, would have been one demanding great knowledge, on the part of those responsible for it, of the spirit and history of the nations other than their own. I think that I had more of this feeling in me than was good in a Minister looked to to carry out a national policy, in the Army or in anything else, and that this redundance was what prevented me from enjoying the absolute confidence of the public. I do not think that the public was right in any degree in the suspicions in which a part of it indulged. Looking back, I can find nothing but advantage in the extent to which I acquired something of an ' international mind.' There came to me more knowledge than I could otherwise have acquired, and also more courage. For the sources of strength in foreign opponents presented to me little mystery. I never saw why we could not organise as perfect a General Staff as the Germans or the French, or why we could not have the best system of education in the world. I always thought our own people were at least as capable as those of any other nation. But I liked to study what other nations had accomplished and to appreciate sympathetically the reasons why they had accomplished it. I am not sure that this spirit, good as it is for tolerance, is equally good as a training ground for getting the confidence of the British public. I had gone to Germany too often, and had read her literature too much, not to give ground to narrow-minded people to say that Germany was my ' spiritual home.'

Anyhow, in August 1914 a formidable section of the public here had turned against me. I did not think that this was good for the Government, and in the autumn of 1914 I felt bound to go to the Prime Minister and to say that, as the attacks on me must obviously affect the general position, it would probably be better that I should not remain in office. He laughed at the idea of this, but I took a more serious view of it. If my full story could have been made public I think that the attacks would have been destroyed. But both Asquith and Grey were averse to making public the details of previous negotiations with Germany while the War was going on. I had therefore to remain unshielded, and I had no illusion as to what in the end the result was likely to be. The public aspect of these attacks demanded consideration. In my own view, as things stood, my work, such as it was, had been finished, and I felt that I was no longer contributing strength to the Government. As time went on, and the storm raised against me increased, I saw that the Prime Minister was not likely to be able to form a Coalition Ministry if I remained as Lord Chancellor, and I wrote to him saying so. Nor did I greatly care. Strategical questions had passed into other hands, and I was no longer really needed. I should not have been happy if I had remained even technically responsible for things that took a dubious course when I had no longer power to keep them right. The result was that when Asquith came to the conclusion that he must reconstruct his Government on a Coalition basis, he sent round a circular letter asking us all to resign. I made no difficulty. I think that the Prime Minister was naturally concerned as to the necessity for this, for he and I were very old and intimate friends. So was I concerned, but mostly on his account, for I saw the first signs appearing of the movement to displace him likewise, and I was not sure that he would not have done better if he had displayed more of an iron hand in maintaining his position and that of his colleagues.

Shortly afterwards, when I made a speech to my keen supporters at the National Liberal Club, a farewell speech which was fully published, Asquith wrote an admirable letter which was read out on the occasion. He did more, for without my knowledge he and the King arranged that I should have the Order of Merit. I had not thought of such a thing, and I was a little doubtful about accepting it. It seemed to me then that this Order of Merit was not meant for just such a case as mine, a case which had been made the occasion of violent controversy. However, the Sovereign and the Prime Minister had come to their conclusion without consulting me, and I let the matter go.

I have now nearly completed what I wish to set down about this stage in my personal history. I was never depressed by even the most violent abuse. I knew very well that the reorganisation of the Army was likely to turn out to have been thoroughly made, and on lines which would fit it for its task. I knew, too, that, small as the Army was, the plan of its organisation was one that would lend help to an indefinite expansion if such expansion proved necessary. I knew, too, that the strategical principles which had been adopted since 1911 by the Admiralty in harmony with those of the Army would enable the two great Services to work together for victory. I was well content to endure, for if the Army came home victorious I believed that it would return with witnesses in my defence whose testimony would be irresistible. So it proved in the end.

But before the War ended in our victory I had, of course, a disagreeable time. I was threatened with assault in the street, and I was on occasions in some danger of being shot at. But on the other hand I had a multitude of loyal and devoted friends whose hopes had through years rested on my efforts. Officially I had little overt support that was of any value, and the refusal to publish my diplomatic documents left me under suspicion. But my special adherents, in the Army and outside it, were firm as rocks. After the victory in France came and the British troops had returned to London, with the victorious Commander-in-Chief, Douglas Haig, riding with the King at their head, all London was in a state of rejoicing. I was left alone, solitary in my study at Queen Anne's

Gate. It was after dark that evening when my servant came upstairs to me and said that there was an officer who wanted to see me, but who would not give his name. My servant was careful in these days, for strange people had tried to get into the house to have sight of me, and he had been warned from Scotland Yard to be cautious about letting unknown people enter. However, I told him to show to my room the officer, whoever he was, who had called. The door was opened, and who should enter but a friend who was indeed intimately known to me, Field-Marshal Douglas Haig, come from a triumphant ride with his Sovereign along the Mall. ' I am not going to remain,' he exclaimed ; ' my purpose is to leave with you a book in which I have written something.' With that he insisted on going away. The book was a volume containing his Despatches, and on the page at the beginning he had written these affectionate words :—

' To Viscount Haldane of Cloan—the greatest Secretary of State for War England has ever had. In grateful remembrance of his successful efforts in organising the Military Forces for a War on the Continent, notwithstanding much opposition from the Army Council and the half-hearted support of his Parliamentary friends.

' Haig, F.M.'

Note.—I feel that this letter from Field-Marshal Earl Haig which was amongst my brother's papers may fitly be inserted here.—E. S. H.

' General Headquarters,
' Tuesday, 19th Nov. 1918.   ' British Armies in France.

' My dear Lord Haldane,—There has been so much going on here that I have not been able to attend to my private correspondence. I therefore hope that you will forgive me for not writing to thank you sooner for your most kind letter.

MRS. HALDANE OF CLOAN, IN HER NINETY-FIFTH YEAR

' I appreciate very much indeed your kindly remembrance of my work with you at the War Office. For me that time will always stand out in my memory most prominently because the organization of our Army *for war* dates from then. Until you arrived at the War Office no one knew for what purpose our Army existed ! And I feel sure that all the soldiers who in those strenuous years were working at the War Office will bear witness to the all-important service which you then rendered to the British Army in the Empire. You then sowed the seeds which have developed into the tremendous instrument which has vanquished the famous German Army and brought about a victorious peace. And where would we be to-day without the Imperial General Staff which was your creation and the Field Service Regulations (Part II. Organization) which you forced through in spite of opposition from Army Council and Treasury ?

' I and many soldiers with me, are greatly distressed at the ungenerous treatment which you have received during the critical phase in our country's history : and I hope the day is not far distant when the invaluable services which you have rendered to our Empire may be adequately recognized.

' With heartfelt admiration for the way in which you have done your duty and ignored all the spiteful criticisms of the Press which has attacked you, and again many thanks for your very welcome congratulations on what the British Army has done.—Believe me, Yours very truly,

'   D. HAIG.'

T

CHAPTER IX

OUT OF OFFICE

(1915–1923)

WHEN the Coalition Government was formed by Asquith as its Prime Minister, I found myself without any of my old duties. I had therefore to consider how best to employ my time. As ex-Lord Chancellor I had a pension of £5000 a year. To this no legal obligation is attached. But I had always taken the view strongly that the ex-Lord Chancellors who received this pension were under a binding moral obligation to work as hard as they could in the Supreme Tribunals, which were, indeed, insufficiently manned unless the retired Chiefs could be counted upon. The senior ex-Lord Chancellor, moreover, presides in the absence of the Lord Chancellor himself, and as I was the senior ex-Lord Chancellor it was plain that when the Lord Chancellor was himself presiding in one of the two Tribunals it would fall regularly to me to preside in the other. To work in these great Courts I therefore made up my mind as my first duty.

I had a little leisure at first. My old friend French, Field-Marshal in command of the British Forces in France, pressed me to come to stay with him and see something of the work of the divisions which we had spent so much time in preparing. I went to him at

St. Omer, then his headquarters. On the evening of my arrival we were bombed by German aeroplanes, but these were driven off. The next day I motored to the Commands of some of my old acquaintances among the Generals of the British divisions. But I felt that I should be failing in following the example of Goethe if I did not manage to get under fire. French kindly arranged with our Allies to provide for this. I motored a long way to Notre Dame de Lorette, where the Germans were actually attacking. The French Command arranged that I should keep as much as possible out of sight, but should be brought on to the ground that was being shelled, and I had the experience of Goethe in seeing and hearing the shells bursting round me. No doubt the French officers took care that I should not be conducted into a spot where these were falling too thickly.

My visit was interesting, and the Field-Marshal pressed me to come back to St. Omer in October. This I did, entrusted by Kitchener with the task of finding out how it was that there had been friction over the leading of two of the Kitchener divisions. This task I accomplished, and did something to smooth matters down. I witnessed part of the battle of Loos, particularly the artillery duel.

But desultory expeditions were not enough to fill my time. There was in addition the duty of taking part in the political business of the House of Lords. In order to do this effectively, for a peer who had no official position, a basis was requisite. He ought to be associated in the public mind with some special subject. Now, my special subject had been throughout Higher Education. Accordingly, I naturally asked myself how I could best be of use to the public in this region. Elementary and Secondary Education were by this time being closely looked after by others. The Civic Universities had been established. But there remained one great portion of the field of higher education which waited to be developed. The higher education was then confined mainly within the walls of the Universities. Since 1915 there have been striking increases in the work which has been done in the direction of extending this field. But in 1915 there was almost everything to be done. Public interest in the subject had not then been fully aroused.

The first thing was to look out for men with whom to work. In Parliament there were unfortunately very few who cared for the subject. But outside Parliament there were a fair number. One of the first to co-operate with me was my old associate, Albert Mansbridge. He had been the inspiring spirit of the Workers' Educational Association, which had done and was doing a great deal for the cause of Adult Education. Then there was Harold Laski, a highly gifted writer and publicist. R. J. Tawney was another, conspicuous for the services he had already rendered to the cause, and for the high level to which he had sought to raise the teaching given. There were also prominent men at the Universities, old and new, who were ready to throw themselves into the work. Both at Oxford and Cambridge there were a number who were already making a start.

I visited the Universities in England and in Scotland one after another, and took counsel with this potential body of sympathisers. The leading men in the Universities were apparently prepared to recognise that they could throw their energies definitely into the service of the community much more than under the then existing circumstances. Many of those with whom I was afterwards to work came to Queen Anne's Gate, and we gradually worked out into clearness both our purpose and the method of promoting it.

The purpose was this. The work of the Universities for the State had become more definitely recognised since the War, and their Colleges were at last in receipt of substantial Treasury grants apportioned by the Treasury Committee, of which Sir William M'Cormick was Chairman. The level of the higher education given in the Universities was good, and, through the use of Chairs and equipment, promised to become still better. In Scotland there was also very substantial assistance given by the Carnegie Trust for the aid of the Scottish Universities by a body of Trustees, of which I was myself a member.

But the bulk of the work done by the Universities was confined to the education of the undergraduate and other students within their walls. The question was how best to stimulate public opinion in favour of an extension on a wide scale of their extra-mural work. If a sufficiency of industrial workers could be got together in industrial centres in the evenings, after the day's work was done, to take courses of systematic teaching, then the Universities might well allocate highly qualified tutors who would devote themselves to this kind of instruction, while reserving the rest of the day for their own studies and researches. If funds could be found to establish these posts, the positions would not be unattractive to public-spirited University graduates with the proper tutorial qualifications. Moreover, we knew that the Board of Education was beginning to look with favour on this addition to the national system of education, and to help as far as its limited resources would permit. It was hoped, too, that the Local Educational Authorities would by degrees come in and support the scheme.

Indeed, that scheme was already in operation in certain places, such as Stoke-on-Trent, and the real point was whether it was not capable of extensive development to many other centres. This turned largely on how the working-classes in regions where nothing of the kind already existed would receive the idea. To determine this, we decided that we must start a campaign. I undertook to go to speak at meetings in various parts of England and Scotland. Such meetings were easily arranged, and I engaged myself to travel down to a large number of places, to as many in fact as my strength and my judicial duties permitted. My colleagues did the same, but necessarily less extensively, for they were all busy men. The activity recalled the campaign which had to be undertaken when the Territorial Force was originally being raised. In a single year I found that I was able to address between fifty and sixty meetings in different places.

Our common principle was one of faith in the

effect of higher education on democracy. We did not indeed think that such education was everything. There were other phases of mental activity, such as religion and the love of the beautiful, which were not less important. But we thought that people whose minds were freed from the fetters of ignorance would develop these other phases more readily. We also thought that the student would feel that he had been assisted towards equality with his fellow-citizens, not absolute equality—for nature and circumstances would preclude that—but in the sense of having something more like even chances with his fellow-creatures. The Universities were under existing circumstances too frequently preserves for the sons and daughters of the rich. Our plans, if they could be carried into effect, would at least diminish for a large number the exclusion from the chance of self-development.

I went to many centres, such as Birmingham, Bristol, Southampton, Leicester, Nottingham, York, Durham, Liverpool, Manchester, Leeds, Sheffield, Glasgow, Edinburgh, Dundee, and Aberdeen, to urge on the academic-minded and on the public the claims of possible extra-mural students. The places which were perhaps most striking in their responses were towns in which there was no academic centre, such as Warrington and Lancaster. There the working-class people were emphatic, the women often more than the men, in their desire for better chances of mental emancipation for their children than they themselves had had. The toil of journeys was at times a little severe. The meetings had mostly to

be fixed for Wednesdays and Saturdays, when the
Courts in London were not sitting and I could
travel back through the night to duty the next
morning. If the places were close at hand, as in the
case of the outlying suburbs of London, it was of
course easy to take the meetings. But the response
was almost uniformly everywhere encouraging. And
Mansbridge, Tawney, Laski, and others who were
engaged in the same task, had similar experiences.
There were men, too, such as A. L. Smith, the then
Master of Balliol, and certain distinguished academic
figures in Cambridge, who were working more or
less independently of us, but on similar lines, and
just as hard. As the movement grew it attracted
attention, and the Board of Education began to
appoint Committees, such as the notable one presided over by the Master of Balliol, to report on the
subject.

So much for the plan. As to the means of giving
effect to it we had of course to create some kind of
organisation. The Workers' Educational Association
was not only in existence, but in full activity. We
aimed at in no way trenching on the province it had
established for itself. We were careful to remain
on cordial terms with it, and to assist it in raising
funds. But what we saw to be desirable was a
body which should take little part in direct local
administration, but should work out standards and
forms of organisation on something like a General
Staff principle. With a view to this we got together
the British Institute of Adult Education. Mansbridge
was forming, in harmony with our own effort in Great

Britain, his World Organisation to preach our common doctrine abroad, in America, in Czecho-Slovakia, and other distant places to which he travelled personally. The British Institute group was quite distinct. Its energies were directed to work at home. Among its active members were Laski, young members of the House of Commons like Oliver Stanley and Loder, well-known zealous workers such as G. D. H. Cole and Sir Percy Jackson, active sympathisers like the Archbishop of York, Mrs. Barbara Wootton, and B. A. Yeaxlee. Figures well known in the educational world such as Salter Davies, Sir Henry and Miss Hadow, and Professor Peers of Nottingham University College, threw their energies into the work of the British Institute. We had, too, as its Secretary, an active and able man, T. H. Searls.

At first the Institute was much hampered in its work for want of even the little money that was necessary. This we had to raise by subscriptions, and these were not easy to obtain. But we had some strokes of good fortune. One morning I was alone at his house with the late Sir Ernest Cassel, a man of both great wealth and much intelligence about the necessities of the British nation. I thought that he looked ill. He surprised me quite unexpectedly by saying that he wanted to spend a million on bettering the condition of the poor. I replied that his million, if applied thus at large, would do little more good than if he were to throw a drop of water into a bucket. But if he would spend it on a definite object, such as the higher education of the working-classes, he might do much with it. For a minute he reflected characteristically, and then said that he would spend half of the million on the higher education of the democracy, and another half on founding an hospital where its members might get the advantage of treatment for incipient mental affliction. But, he added, if he gave the former half million in the way suggested, would I undertake the Chairmanship of a body of expert trustees who would lay it out for him? I said I would, and he chose the trustees in the course of our conversation. They included Lord Balfour, Lord Oxford, Mr. Herbert Fisher, Mr. Sidney Webb, Sir George Murray, Miss Philippa Fawcett, and others. Not long afterwards Cassel passed away from sudden heart failure. I had little doubt that his doctor had already warned him that his life would be short when I saw him, but he was a large-minded and courageous man with much self-control. He was able, before he died, to take an active part in the early work of the Trust when constituted. One of the things we did was to make rather a liberal grant for the purposes of the British Institute of Adult Education, and to distribute annual grants from the income of the Trust funds for the purposes of the Adult Education Movement.

We were also helped by the establishment of the requisite central libraries for the students through the action of the Carnegie United Kingdom Trust, which included my sister, and which gave liberally for this purpose.

By slow degrees the activities of the Institute

became in these ways placed on a stable basis. We were by no means the only body working in this region. But we had so many keen minds throwing themselves into our work that I think that we made a substantial difference to the level at which extra-mural teaching by collegiate institutions was given.

The British Institute laid great stress on periodical conferences at which those directly interested could meet and exchange views in consultation. These conferences took place mainly at University head-quarters. The chief meetings were held in September, when those attending could be accommodated for two or three days in College buildings and could talk together. We intended to go the round of all the Universities, and once we met in Manchester. But we found that our working-class supporters had a genuine preference for assembling in the old and beautiful surroundings of Oxford and Cambridge. The annual meetings at least came to be held there, mainly at Balliol and at Trinity, Cambridge. There were also summer schools for our students there and elsewhere.

I was the active President of the British Institute of Adult Education for some years. After that, when I found myself physically less able to travel about, I became Honorary President, Mr. Justice Sankey taking my place as active Head. In 1926 I delivered my last address to an annual conference which took place at Trinity College, Cambridge, in September of that year. Of this meeting I will venture to give some account here. It fell to me to define our purpose and describe the steps that had been taken

towards its accomplishment. I told the gathering
of the unmistakable desire shown by large numbers
of men and women who had never had a chance of
education of a University type that their children
might have some chance of it. It had become plain
that there was much potential public opinion behind
the movement, and that it was highly desirable to
endeavour to organise and concentrate that opinion.
Our purpose had been to act as intermediaries in
bringing together those who were interested in adult
education ; to lay before them the results of the
consideration given to the subject by persons who
had had experience of it ; and to do what we could
to stimulate interest with a common plan in view.
What was wanted was that the movement should
always be one of high quality, and for this the personalities of the tutors and the teachers were of great
importance. I then pointed out that since 1920,
when the Institute came formally into existence,
there had emerged a new feature which was very
prominent in that conference. A large number of
representatives of Local Authorities were now present
and were joining in our work. The local organisations were being more and more permeated by the
influence of the Universities, and were tending, each
of them, to become influenced by the particular
University with which they were connected by their
own choice. The only difficulty had emerged at a
private conference I had had in London with a number
of the Vice-Chancellors of the different Universities.
These had told me that there was no want of possible
tutors and teachers of high quality, but there was a

serious lack of financial power to develop and equip their teaching opportunities. The Universities were indeed giving what they could spare, but more was requisite. We must look to the all-potent force of public opinion, and to some increase of Treasury grants, to aid the efforts of the Universities themselves and of private persons. It was conventionality in public opinion that was holding us back, and this we must endeavour to get rid of. It was all to our good that the Trade Unions were becoming interested in the general subject. They were beginning to realise the truth of what was stated by Spinoza in the fourth part of his *Ethics*, the part which deals with human bondage : ' Since there is no single thing we know which is more excellent than a man who is guided by reason, it follows that there is nothing by which a person can better show how much skill and talent he possesses than by so educating men that at last they will live under the direct authority of reason.' Spinoza implied that higher education meant the getting rid of conventional obstacles so as to enable mankind to see things as they really were.

Education and learning, the address went on to say, were no mere means to an end. They were not there to create a class-consciousness, or even merely to get rid of class-consciousness. They were there to teach people that to all men and women the State should give the right to get such instruction as would free them from the depressing effect of circumstances for which they were not responsible, and which was preventing them from individually having a real chance in life.

At this conference, after dwelling on the advances that had been made in primary and secondary education since 1870, despite shortage in means, we turned the discussion to the growing tendency of such education to lead beyond itself to a yet larger outlook, which could develop into what Spinoza called 'the intellectual love of God,' a love that is not anthropomorphic, but finds God present everywhere, and present in the human soul. Some of us said that the last thing this meant was that there was any conflict implied in this doctrine between science and religion, or between education and religion. The indications were that as conventional ideas were being progressively got rid of, the narrow views which saw conflict threatening were tending to disappear. One man will excel in art, another in music, a third in history, a fourth in economics, a fifth in philosophy, a sixth in science, and so on. But these represent only the best ways in which to take the individual if you want to make the most of his individual possibilities. Knowledge is of many kinds, and what we have to do is to bring together what is inherent in knowledge and the unity of its grasp. That was why the best sermons of our time were telling us to search for God within rather than without ourselves. It was upon adult education, based on this principle, that we should rely as a foundation on which we could appeal to men and women, irrespective of their creeds or position in society, to seek to develop this quality that was latent within them.

Many others spoke at this series of meetings: Tawney, Bishop Gore, some of the Directors of Educa-

tional Studies in various Universities, and the representatives of Local Authorities and of Trade Unions.
I have given this account of the conference because
in its tone and direction it was typical of what our
movement had come to be.

The British Institute also brought out a *Handbook
and Directory of Adult Education*, and founded a carefully edited *Journal of Adult Education*, with articles
written by experts engaged in the work. In this
journal attention is drawn to the widespread growth
of interest in full-time courses extending over more
than a single year.

I may observe here that one of the remarkable
centres of development has been the University College
at Nottingham. The College has, by 1927, the year
in which I write this, created a Professorship of Adult
Education, with a permanent staff of twelve full-time
teachers. These work with the local institutes and
other organisations. In his account of what has
taken place, Professor Peers, the leading spirit in this
sort of work at the College, says that ' already in the
larger places, like Nottingham, Leicester, and Derby,
numbers of classes in different subjects are going on
side by side in connection with the same organisation,
and in the villages educational activities are being
brought together in clubs and institutes, where they
are related to the social activities of the community
generally. These developments, and experiments
which are being made in other parts of the country,
suggest that, in all the more important places, and
indeed in many smaller places, there will be some
community centre which will be the home of intel-

lectual interest, and, linked with the University, will form part of a greater and nobler University in the future.'

Nottingham has been wonderful in the efforts of its citizens to develop education of the University type. One day, just as I was going there from London to lay the foundation stone of the new University College buildings, a letter was brought to me from one of the great banks in London. It contained a draft accepted by the Bank of England for £100,000. It was delivered to me on behalf of an anonymous donor who desired that it should be added to the sum which was being raised in Nottingham for the buildings of what it was hoped would prove to be in the end not merely those of a University College but of a full University. I found later that the donor was a well-known former citizen of the town, who has given yet more for the promotion of higher education there.

Such munificence is not unique. A well-known manufacturer in Hull has recently given £300,000 for the foundation of a University College, and great gifts have in very recent times been made elsewhere. There are idealists in the cause of education, and the way to move them is not to beg of them in the abstract, but to inspire them through the spectacle of the work actually done.

I have now written enough here about the movement to show what its character was. It was already in existence when we began, but its administration was imperfect and it needed systematic form which we tried to give to it. At the best it has got only a little way, and the ground which remains uncovered is vast. But a beginning in the further work requisite has been made, and there is every prospect that this work will go on. For the public have become interested as they were not before, and the Government and the Local Education Authorities are displaying activities which are freshly born. The public opinion that can remove all difficulties is disclosing itself as now nascent, and I have the hope that a new and highly real side is being added to the educational organisation of the country. I am now too old to move about in the service of the cause as I once could, but my interest and pleasure in its progress remain of the keenest.

I must pass on to other matters which belong to this period. The House of Lords is not an arena of the same importance as the House of Commons. But it lends itself more readily to affording opportunities of discussion on topics of general importance. After 1915 I was able to organise there some extensive debates on education, which fill columns of the paper of the official reports but attracted less attention than they might have from the newspapers. Apart from these general debates we had a full discussion of the Education Bill of 1918. This enabled me to point out how easily and completely the religious difficulty promised to be solved in Scotland by the new Act of that year. The Government were taking over all the schools, Presbyterian, Roman Catholic, and Episcopalian, and were maintaining them in full efficiency, on the condition that the teachers should all be trained up to the same standard,

U

in the Universities and otherwise. But having obtained this quality in the teachers as the indispensable condition of their recognition, the Government left the denominations free to select for themselves from the body of teachers thus duly qualified, and did not interfere in any way with the religious instruction given. The result, as predicted then and as disclosed by subsequent experience, has been remarkable. The problem of religion in the schools has practically disappeared. I held that it was only want of courage that had prevented the question from being faced in the same way south of the Border. Fanatics there no doubt were, but they were relatively a small number, and the experience of the Scottish system had shown that they had no real backing from public opinion, inasmuch as the public were left free under such a system to choose their own schools for their children. However, this adjuration has so far fallen on ears that appear to be deaf.

There were other subjects with which I was more or less familiar that were discussed in this period in the House of Lords. Matters relating to the Army and matters concerned with Imperial Defence were among them. But in the House of Lords there was always this difficulty, not less under the Coalition than subsequently. The Minister responsible for the Department seldom sat in that House, and the practice was to delegate the duty of replying on the debate to a very junior Minister, unconnected generally with the Department, and usually a Lord-in-Waiting. All that such a representative of the subject had was a brief, from which he read, and of course he had no authority to give any undertaking, however proper, on behalf of the Department for which he was speaking. This rendered the debates somewhat unreal, and the system continues to this day. It is one of the things which prevents the House of Lords from being a Chamber on the same footing as the House of Commons. If attention were bestowed on this point, and if it were practicable to invite responsible Ministers to come simply to make statements even when not members of the House of Lords, matters might be made better. But in considering House of Lords Reform we confine ourselves to discussing organic changes instead of obvious shortcomings such as I am referring to.

During the years between 1915 and 1924 I was conscious of another difficulty. It is impracticable to produce much effect unless one works with a party. In 1918 the Liberal Party went to pieces, and I had to consider whether it was desirable to try to work with it again in the condition into which it had then fallen. Education being my main subject, I had to look at the prospects as regards this, which was now my chief political concern.

But on educational policy the Liberal Party had for long been very defective. In 1902 they had been unduly dominated by pressure from the Nonconformists over elementary and secondary education. In the movement for the establishment of more Universities they had shown no interest. It was the same thing with the development of adult education. This interested individuals away in the country, but the Liberal politicians in Parliament not at all. There was a similar want of interest in problems relating to the Services and to National Defence. I found I had to consider carefully whether I might not find more support for my ideas in the Labour Party which was now growing up. I did not decide hastily. But early in 1922 when Asquith, moved by an obviously growing public opinion, asked me to come to a meeting which he and Grey were going to address on the subject of education, I replied that it was too late. They could not take up this subject effectively without having immersed their minds in it as it was to-day. It was useless to point to vague references made in speeches to the importance of education. What the public would demand was evidence of earnestness of purpose established by actual endeavour in the past. I therefore did not attend the meeting. We had kept the work of the British Institute group free from politics purposely, and until there was the prospect of a Government fitted and eager to take it up it seemed unwise to depart from the principle on which we had been acting.

There seemed to have set in a period of stagnation in the mind of the Liberal Party. It had no definite tasks such as fell to it in 1906, and it appeared to be lacking in fresh ideas. Towards the solution of social problems it was making but little progress. To-day, at the time at which I am writing, things are better. There is energy and evidence of fresh thought. But then the party is shorn of its members, and is attended by other drawbacks. Moreover, the recent ideas of Lloyd George appear to me to be too hastily put together. What had to be considered in 1920 by any one who was looking for colleagues with whom he could carry on such work as he had set his hand to, was whether to reassociate himself with the Liberals was the most promising way of progress towards the realisation of his ideals.

There was a growing Labour organisation to be taken into account. Labour was gaining seats rapidly. Its support came less from its official leaders than from men and women who had before them an ideal with which I was definitely in sympathy, that of equality of chance in life. Its programme at least fitted in with the educational work on which I had been engaged. As regards National Defence and the organisation of the Empire it had given no particular sign, but it was at least no more deficient than was the party of the Liberals. What seemed wisest was accordingly to continue rather aloof from Liberal organisations and to get such a contact with Labour as would enable me to understand it. I began to speak at Labour meetings and to see a good deal of Labour members. With my old friend, Asquith, I had long ceased to have much opportunity for talk about politics. I began to have much more of such talk with Labour—not only inside the House of Commons but outside it in the country districts. The meetings were partly political, but only partly. For educational ideals of equality were in themselves sufficient for close contact with the rank and file.

So things went on, and for the four years before 1924 I found myself more and more driven by conviction in the direction of the Labour Party. With the exception of the Sidney Webbs, and of some of my educational colleagues who reckoned themselves as belonging to Labour, I was not intimate with their prominent men, nor had I joined any organisation. But my hopes were increasing, and I thought that in education at least there was the possibility of real progress.

During this period I had other activities. Besides heavy judicial work on four days a week, I had been asked to continue my connection with the Committee of Imperial Defence. I had served on it so long as a Minister, and had had so much experience of its administration, that it seemed waste to be severed from its work. So I agreed to serve on some of its special Sub-Committees, and over these I used to preside. This I have continued to do, and to this hour I serve in such fashion. It is only so that continuity can be kept up in the interest of the State.

About this time I also took up a rather heavy piece of work. The Churches in Scotland had decided, as the result of the great litigation of 1904 which I have already described and of the Statute which followed it, on a largely conceived measure of union. The Established Church has been enabled by a subsequent Act to enter freely into union with the United Free Church. The resources of both were to be pooled and to become the property of a single Church.

But to give effect to the pooling of the resources involved legislation on an extended scale, and the difficult problem confronted the Government of what

property could be made available, and of what
changes in its tenure would be required for a complete
amalgamation. Questions not only of policy but of
law, involving knowledge of the law of Scotland
relating to the systems of teinds or tithes, arose
sharply. In 1922 the Government invited me to
take the Chair of the Expert Committee which was
to be appointed to investigate the whole question,
and to report in detail on the reforms required. I
accepted, and I had among my colleagues an old
theological friend of my youth, Sir George Adam
Smith, Principal of Aberdeen University. We sat
for over a year, mostly in Edinburgh, where it was
easiest to collect evidence from the officials of the
two Churches concerned. My health was at this time
not at its best, but I was able to get through the work.
Finally we made a unanimous Report, and this was,
without much delay, embodied in a Statute. I saw
much of the Scottish theologians in the course of
the discussion, and addressed them publicly on the
prospects of what would follow on the proposed
union. It did not seem to me so clear as it did to
some of them that the result would all be gain. No
doubt much controversy would disappear. But
controversy had in Scotland been an inspiring force.
It had lifted great leaders to high levels of idealism,
concerned as it was with things of the spirit rather
than of the earth.

At all events the plan we worked out promised to
be a success, and the negotiations for the formal
completion of the union of the two greatest Churches
in Scotland are so far going smoothly as its result.

Later on it fell to me to introduce and carry through the House of Lords the Bill which embodied the substance of our Report. The Labour Government to which I then belonged went out of office before the Bill could be got through the House of Commons, but in the next session it was passed by the Baldwin Government through that House and became law.

I have said enough to show why during the period down to 1923 I was gradually tending towards the party of Labour, being moved by the ideal of more complete and general equality of opportunity with which that party was associated. I had not embraced and never did adopt the details of the changing programmes which were put forward in its name. But to this general attitude there was an exception. I had come to the conclusion that the coal-mining industry was too widespread and of too great public importance to be left to go on unregulated by the State. I had given evidence on this subject before the Commission presided over by Mr. Justice Sankey. My evidence was directed to a single point. The only way to bridge over the gap in spirit which separated the miners from their employers was to bring them nearer to each other by doing what had been done in my time in the Army for the establishment of better personal relations between the soldiers and the officers. We had set ourselves to train the latter, not only in administration and to attend to the education of the soldiers in the units commanded by them, but to feel the responsibility of presenting to these soldiers an example of self-sacrifice. The young officers had as a rule entered into the spirit of this injunction. A good officer sought to make himself the friend of his men, to take all their risks and hardships, and to see that their wants, in the field and in peace time, were attended to before he thought of his own wants. The effect had been admirable, and the characters and discipline of the men had become perceptibly heightened by the example set to them.

I proposed, before the Sankey Commission, to adapt this method, or one analogous, to the mining problem. I expressed no opinion as to whether there was any reform that could be sufficient short of full control of the mining industry by the Government. But I said, founding this on my Army experience, that those who were to direct the miners in their work, if there were to be State regulation, would probably fail in their plans unless they were first given a proper administrative training, such as young officers were now given. The management of men working in coal mines required technical training, no doubt. But it also demanded that the leaders of the men should have been taught the principles of their business, and particularly how to gain and keep the confidence of those whom they directed. The Chairman agreed. In the Report which he finally signed, and which was really his alone, he did not, as is often erroneously represented, advise immediate Nationalisation. This was not to be contemplated until a period of three years had elapsed, and preparation for the expiry of that period was to be made by recruiting, after adequate training, from the Army and the Navy, and from those already in the mines, as managers who had shown aptitude for dealing with the men under them, a corps of competent leaders who had had such training as would fit them to qualify for the posts of managers in the mines.

That seemed to me the best way out of the friction which had arisen. But the Government, after some hesitation, would not adopt the principle of the Sankey Report, and a Bill was introduced and passed which was wholly inconsistent with it. There followed a great strike. I have always thought that the Sankey plan was the only one which was adequate to the crucial situation that had arisen. Mr. Justice Sankey's services and his moderation have never been fully appreciated by the public. In the end the coal owners got their way, and there has been little but trouble since.

No doubt the problem of the coal industry is a very difficult one. It is not certain that the whole of the Sankey scheme could have been carried into effect without modification. But the crisis was so far-reaching, and the small body of coal owners was apparently so little capable of handling it in a way that could promise tranquillity and improvement in their own business, that I felt bound to express my view strongly in the House of Lords after the Report was published and while the new Mining Bill was on its way through. I remain of the opinion that a matter so grave and so deeply affecting the well-being of the community at large ought not to be left in private hands. I have never been able to hope for much from the suggested remedies of the Liberal Party, or even from the Samuel Report.

I still think that something at any rate analogous to the remedy suggested by Sir John Sankey is the least that can be effective.

An idea came to me in this period which for the moment seemed to have a chance of proving practical. The Unionist Government had not in 1919 succeeded in coming to any common mind with Irish Nationalism about an Irish Parliament. The opposition to any form of Home Rule was very strong, and the Irish leader, De Valera, and some of his principal advisers were in prison. The Viceroy, who had been appointed because he was a soldier, was the ex-Commander-in-Chief, my friend Lord French, and he asked me to come to stay with him at the Viceregal Lodge. He was keen, not merely to keep order, but to do constructive work. I said I would gladly come if he would set me to do something useful for him, and I indicated an idea I had framed. It was to begin by Executive instead of Legislative reform. I knew personally some of the most important Nationalist leaders in Dublin, and I was prepared to talk with them if there was any chance of my being able to negotiate ; for I felt instinctively that they were depressed and might be disposed for some settlement. My plan was to suggest that while an Irish legislature with full powers would be in the end indispensable, a Nationalist Executive was not less important. Why should we not take the first step towards Home Rule by transforming in its spirit the Irish Executive ? A Home Rule Parliament would inevitably, if this worked satisfactorily, follow on it. I had just issued the Report of the Machinery of

Government Committee, of which I had been Chairman, and was full of the idea of such an Executive as the first step in a transition stage. If the Government would set up a Committee of Inquiry in Dublin I was prepared, if asked, to preside over it, and I wanted it to include men like De Valera (who would have to be brought out of prison for the purpose) and representatives of Ulster. At least we might report on a way of rendering Irish administration less obnoxious and more authoritative. French was quite well disposed towards the idea. He was indeed at his wit's end as to how to enforce the law. He asked his leading officials to come to the Lodge to discuss matters with me. They were unexpectedly favourable.

I then made visits in the heart of Nationalist Dublin privately. I saw most of those of the best-known Nationalist leaders who were not in prison. I also saw some of the survivors of my old friends with whom I had negotiated the University question twenty years previously. They were friendly, and finally withdrew to discuss the whole matter in secret conclave. The result was that they reported to me that they had decided not to pull the house down on my head if I would set myself to work out the plan for consideration. This was enough, for my best hope was to get them into personal discussion with the British Authorities about the machinery of Irish Government generally, and I thought that the Committee, if set up, could suggest a scheme in a region of the Constitution with which I was in many respects familiar. Of course, Irish

Reform could not stop at an Executive, but to begin at this end would create a *détente*, and enable negotiations to proceed towards full Home Rule step by step.

French, who was in full sympathy, went to London to see Lloyd George. Unfortunately, the latter was in Paris, and instead of following him there he saw the Minister who had been left in charge of Irish matters. This Minister was shocked and turned the idea down. A couple of years later a full Home Rule Constitution had to be granted. It is just possible that if the negotiations which had been carried so far to a point from which progress without friction was at least apparently practicable had been allowed to be continued, the transition might have been more gradual and might have brought northern Ireland into negotiation with the south. I do not know. I am probably of an unduly sanguine temperament, but I have usually found that something results if once people can be got to come into discussion with each other.

Although before the end of 1923 some questions were discussed in the House of Lords, I did not have much further chance at this time of taking a part in public affairs. But in the end of that year the Conservative Government was defeated at a General Election. They were defeated in that they came back with no majority that was independent of Labour and Liberal support. Advocacy of the cause of Protection had contributed materially to this defeat. It became evident that Labour, which had gained largely at the Election although still in a minority in the House of Commons, might not improbably be called on to assume the responsibility of governing. This actually took place. I reserve further reference to what happened for the next chapter.

CHAPTER X

THE LABOUR GOVERNMENT AND AFTER
(1923–1928)

IN the end of 1923 it was evident that Ramsay Mac-
Donald was likely to be sent for to form, if possible,
a Government out of the Labour Party. He was
ready to try, but he knew well that his task would
be a difficult one. He would have at his back only
a rather small minority in the Commons. The Conservatives, who did not see their way to undertaking
office themselves, would no doubt support him. But
for how long and to what extent ?

Then there was another difficulty. At long last a
Labour Government was coming into office, and its
enthusiastic supporters of the advanced wing thought
of a political millennium 'Socialism in our Time.'
They would not take in that it was only on sufferance
that the party would be allowed to pass its measures
through Parliament.

All these difficulties MacDonald, who was under
no illusion, saw clearly. He was desirous of forming
a Cabinet which might do the best that could be done
in an uncertain situation. In the end of December he
wrote to me to know whether I would try to assist
him in forming a Government. He asked me whether

I would be disposed to take an office like that of Education, where a good deal might be accomplished although no large expenditure would be possible. The idea attracted me, but I saw certain difficulties. The principles of reform in primary and secondary education were already pretty clear, and what was needed was just the thing that was difficult, more expenditure. There would be competition for grants for other social purposes, for pensions and economic services. I did not see in the Ministry of Education a chance of getting much of what was required for the higher education of adults, in which I was specially interested. And I thought that if I were in a sufficiently strong position in a Labour Cabinet I might, even although not at the Ministry of Education, be able to press for these things just as well as if I were the Head of an Education Department to which they did not strictly belong.

I therefore replied to MacDonald in the terms of the letter which follows. I quote it fully because it defines my attitude towards Labour, and to its programme. After sending this I wrote an affectionate letter to Asquith, explaining how I found myself compelled to join my fortunes with Labour, a party different from his. He replied, also affectionately, but deprecating the definite step I proposed to take.

Here is the letter I wrote to Ramsay MacDonald on 24th December 1923. I asked him to come to Cloan on his way from Lossiemouth, and to give me orally his reply after consideration :—

28 Queen Anne's Gate,
Westminster,
24th December 1923.

My dear Ramsay MacDonald,—I realise how exceptionally hard at this stage you must be finding an inherently difficult task. Those who believe in the underlying ideal of the Labour Movement cannot but feel an obligation to do their best to be helpful to your purpose.

But the first thing needful is that you should have a chance of succeeding with it. The conditions of success are not obscure to any one with your experience of our miscellaneous and slightly conservatively-minded democracy. I do not think, however, that all your supporters, judging from their speeches, recognise what difficulties confront you.

Labour may be forced by its adversaries into forming a Government within a month from now. With only a minority in Parliament to support it, they calculate on its being discredited within a few weeks later, by inexperience in administration, and also by artificial adverse combinations. Having regard to the numbers against you, I seem to see only one way in which the difficulty can be averted. If the Labour proposals to the country are so well thought out and so reasonable that sufficient fair-minded people are likely to be of opinion that Labour ought to have its chance, all may shape itself well. Labour may then hope to justify its claim. But if the new Government has not commended itself Labour will be out for a long time.

This creates a very delicate situation. As I have said before now I hope to support you, not the less if myself out of office than if I were in it. I am not troubled by capital levy or by any mere ripple on the surface. What counts as the underlying current is a great purpose. It is

x

for the sake of the broad purpose that I should care to be of use in office, as I believe I could be. But to office I have no personal wish to return. I have spent ten years of my life in Cabinets, and pomps and ceremonies and stipends are nothing to me. But I do care for my ideals having a chance, and to secure that chance there are things that have to be seen to. Without security for this it would be hopeless for me to join you.

Defence, to take an example, is a vitally important subject. I do not wish to return to the Army, or to go to the Navy or Air Force. There is something more fundamental, the general policy guided by the Committee of Imperial Defence. We wish to reduce armaments and expenditure. But we cannot get anything accomplished with a diplomacy that is impotent for want of power behind it. I have worked for successive Governments, ever since the War, in trying to improve the existing organisation. It is a very complicated one, depending on supervision under the Prime Minister by a colleague in the Cabinet with time to give to it but without special office, and selected for his knowledge. He has always other duties. But he is supposed to have time, and also to have learned what it takes years to have learned about. At present the organisation is only nascent. It is under Lord Salisbury, who is doing his best. But close handling, by a Minister with sufficient position, would give confidence right through the Services and the country, and strengthen the position of a new Government.

Then there is Education itself. On this I have been concentrated for years past, and there are definite reforms coming into sight without which my life-work would be thrown away. They do not require my presence at the Board of Education, but they do mean a definite Cabinet policy and some, though not a great deal of, money.

There is, besides, Justice. Here reform is called for more urgently than is generally known. What is required is described in the ' Machinery of Government ' Report of the Committee where Morant, Mrs. Webb, and Sir George Murray were my colleagues. They all concurred in the Report, which I, as Chairman, drew myself. It was the outcome of long study and strong conviction. The task is as delicate as it is extensive. In the same connection there arises the question of the Judicial Committee of the Privy Council, over which I have been presiding through nearly the whole of ten years. Certain of the Dominions watch this closely, and their aspirations have to be studied.

These and other points make me feel that I must have close talk with you before answering the practical question of your letter. I do not wish to part with an independent, if outside, position in which I feel that I am of general use, without the prospect of being able to do some good.

If you can come to Cloan, we shall be in a position to consider these things.

It is therefore not practicable that I should respond to your question affirmatively without thought. But I none the less sympathise deeply with you in difficulties which are, I imagine, certainly not less than you have hinted to me.

I should add that I think that the management of the House of Lords will be a very delicate task indeed. It cannot turn a Government out, but it can indirectly create a far-reaching opinion adverse to it. For there are certain men who understand every form of the machinery of the Constitution, and they will not be friendly.

I leave for Cloan, Auchterarder, on Wednesday morning. —Believe me, yours very sincerely,

HALDANE.

The result of the talk we had at Cloan was that I
told him that I was willing to join his Cabinet on
certain conditions. I wished to resume the Lord
Chancellorship and to lead the party in the House
of Lords. I proposed to carry out what I had advo-
cated in the Machinery of Government Report by
divesting myself of the duty of daily judicial sittings.
The time so set free I would use for definite purposes.
First of all, I would take the Chairmanship of the
Committee of Imperial Defence, a new position which
had been created by the outgoing Government, and
would then preside unbrokenly over the meetings of
the Permanent Chiefs of the Staffs of the Navy, Army,
and Air Force. Other time I would allot to the
superintendence of Justice and the reorganisation
of the Magistracy in England and Scotland. For the
appointments of the magistrates and the distribution
of their number were, notwithstanding what had been
done already, still too much in the hands of the Lord
Lieutenants. What was required was sufficient leisure
for the Lord Chancellor, who was really responsible,
to devote to their careful supervision. Then I would
arrange as much co-operation as was practicable
between the Departments of the Lord Chancellor
and the Home Secretary, with a view to making
Justice a single subject distributed between two
Ministers who might act in harmony. There was
also the work of going through all the Government
Bills at an early stage, and of acting generally as
Constitutional Adviser to the Cabinet.

The new work would be heavy and could not be
done unless I could get free of the duty of daily

presiding from 10.30 to 4 over judicial sittings. But this, I said, I could arrange. The outgoing Lord Chancellor, Lord Cave, liked this work. I was on excellent terms with him. He occupied, when in London, a flat in the Victoria Tower of the House of Lords which had been assigned to the Lord Chancellor. He had furnished it, and was not likely to wish to leave it. I proposed to offer it to him, and to continue myself to live at 28 Queen Anne's Gate, if he would undertake what he would have desired to do in any case, to preside for me at the judicial sittings of the House of Lords and Privy Council.

For the rest, as I was contemplating joining a Labour Government, I should not think it right to draw the full salary of £10,000 a year to which the Lord Chancellor was entitled. I should return to the Treasury £4000 a year out of it, and, the unavoidable expenses of the position notwithstanding, manage on the £6000 a year which would remain.

After a prolonged talk at Cloan, MacDonald expressed his concurrence with these proposals, and on these terms I became Lord Chancellor in his Government. All the arrangements were carried out. I used to go to the House of Lords just after ten each morning, and having seen that the judicial business of the day was in progress, spend an hour and a half in starting the day's work as Chancellor with my Secretaries. Sir Claud Schuster, the Permanent Head, was very quick and highly experienced. We got the work launched before twelve, and I then walked over to Whitehall Gardens, where the Staff of the Committee of Imperial Defence were at work. There, after settling the operations for the day with the Secretary, Sir Maurice Hankey, who was also Secretary to the Cabinet, I would often preside over a small meeting of the Chiefs of the Staffs of the three Services. We devoted much time to discussing possible emergencies which might have to be encountered. The Chiefs used to take away and to work out with their own Staffs the details of the counter-plans required. Later on they reported. The maxim I ventured to commend to them was based on old War Office experience, and I offered to have it put up in letters of gold. It was that ' Thinking Costs Nothing.' We accomplished a good deal of defence work of a permanent character in this period.

After a brief interval for luncheon I returned, either to Whitehall Gardens or, more often, to the House of Lords, to finish the business and correspondence of the day. I made a point of seeing each of my various Secretaries, and of consulting with them over the work with which they were entrusted, whether it concerned magistrates, or clergymen, or Home Office communications. At 4.15 I dressed and went fully robed into the House, and then took a good deal of part in the discussions. We introduced a considerable number of Bills, many of them of a not very controversial order. Questions about the policy of the Government were constantly put to me as Leader of the House. But matters relating to Foreign Affairs were by arrangement mainly dealt with by the President of the Council, Lord Parmoor, who was directly interested in the working of the League of Nations. I took charge of a good many important

Bills, such as the Housing Bill, the Scottish Churches Bill, and the Land Law Reform Bills. So matters went on in the House of Lords through the session during which we remained in office.

There were, of course, frequent Cabinet Councils and a few meetings of the full Committee of Imperial Defence. We had, for instance, to consider the project for a Channel Tunnel, as to which we adopted a very conservative view. The Cabinet Councils were usually held at 11.30 in the forenoon, the regular hour, but if the business was such that we had not sufficient time for it at a sitting of two hours, we held further meetings in the evening. These were often fixed for hours to which those of us whose ways were not those of the average working man found awkward, 8.45 p.m. for instance. But no difficulty was ever made ; it was a point of honour to attend punctually, and the meetings were always full.

Ramsay MacDonald managed his Cabinets very well. A man of an attractive manner, he knew how to let a colleague run on without checking the length of his statement prematurely. In this he was aided by the carefully-drawn-up Agenda which the Secretary of the Cabinet, Hankey, had prepared for him. MacDonald had always read his papers and knew the points. Indeed, all the members of the Cabinet worked hard and came prepared. Nor were they lengthy in speech on this account. They made their points briefly and forcibly, trained to do so by Trade Union discipline, and MacDonald was an excellent President. We always got through our business, and he was full of tact in avoiding digressions. We smoked during our sittings, a practice which conduces to calmness. I had always a spare cigar with me for my colleague on my right, Thomas, the Colonial Secretary, a colleague who showed great acumen as well as grasp of public business.

Particularly in the early days of 1924 I was of use in a special way to my colleagues, for I had had experience of the nuances of the Constitution, and of the proper course to be taken by Ministers, in theory servants of the Crown as well as its advisers. Notwithstanding his want of previous training, MacDonald managed our relations with the Sovereign with tact and with a proper sense of responsibility. We were in office for less than a year, and we were not only treated well at the Palace, but on the whole by our opponents, who let us get through our Bills. These were of a comparatively moderate character, as was to be expected in the circumstances. In the House of Lords we were occasionally threatened, but the moderating influence of the Leaders of the Opposition then, Lord Curzon and Lord Salisbury, saved us from being much maltreated.

So things went on until the autumn of 1924, when two events occurred which in the end destroyed us. One was what was known as the Campbell incident, a mistake in procedure over a criminal charge, not in itself of vital importance, but enough to put a weapon into the hands of the adversary with which he could belabour us. The other was more serious. One afternoon in the Lords, Lord Curzon unexpectedly asked me whether the Labour Government had assented to the proposal of a treaty with Russia and of a loan to her. I replied that I knew nothing of any such transaction, nor did any of us Ministers in the Lords. He stated that the evening papers had announced the proposal as a fact. And I could only answer that they were probably wholly misinformed.

But it turned out that the papers were right. The proposition for a treaty had become known in the Commons. There had been no Cabinet Council on the subject, and, at most, only one or two members of the Government had been consulted. It appeared that sudden pressure had been put on the Prime Minister by certain of his supporters in the House of Commons, and that he had assented to the idea of a favourable answer to Russia and to a guarantee of a loan. The awkward thing was the suddenness with which the new departure had been entered on, and the shock which this gave to public opinion. There was a hurriedly assembled Cabinet. We could not go back on what had been done without shaking the Ministry to its foundations. But it was obvious that this decision, together with the other incident of the Campbell case, would put us at a disadvantage in the House of Commons, and not improbably at the General Election which would not be far off.

So it proved. We were in a hopeless minority in the House of Commons, and at the General Election which followed we were roundly defeated. The democracy, which has a curious amount of conservatism in its every section, turned against us.

Looking back on my experience as a Minister in the

Labour Government, my feeling about it is divided.
The Cabinet was a very industrious one, and it
contained some men of first-rate administrative
ability. Ministers like Snowden, Thomas, Wheatley,
and Sidney Webb were as capable in the conduct
of affairs as one could wish to see, and were also
excellent in Council. On the whole, the Government
accomplished its real task, that of bringing the
people to cease to look at public matters from a ' class-
conscious ' standpoint, and of spreading the ideal
of equality of opportunity. Education was much
discussed, and Trevelyan made vigorous efforts,
but the importance of adult education was not
fully taken in, although the principle was accepted.
National Defence was carefully supervised, although
the subject did not come much before the Cabinet.

In Foreign Affairs the prominent figure was
MacDonald himself; he was Foreign Secretary as
well as First Lord of the Treasury. I do not think
that he would have experienced difficulty in continuing the two offices, if he had not felt it his duty to
address a great many meetings and to see a great
many not very important people. I believe that he
could have combined his two functions easily, but
he liked to be the conventional Prime Minister,
and to have something of the pomp and glory of
his position. Unfortunately, too, he had a passion
for spending his week-ends at Chequers, the country
house which Lord Lee of Fareham had established
and endowed as a country house for the Prime
Ministers of England. When this generous gift was
announced in the House of Lords, I rose and shook

my head and prophesied that it would prove a dangerous temptation. Prime Ministers who have sprung from the middle classes and are attracted by the pleasures of a country-house life to which they are not accustomed, are apt to be unduly drawn there. The result is that they lose two days in each week in which they ought to be seeing their colleagues and having at least a few of them for talk on the Saturday and Sunday evenings. It is consequently very difficult for a colleague to see his Chief at the only times when the latter can be readily available. This difficulty has not been confined to the case of Ramsay MacDonald. But with him it proved a damaging obstacle. It was almost impracticable to get hold of him even for a quarter of an hour, and the consequences were at times mischievous.

I recall, for instance, in my own case, a minor but important matter, the plan of the Committee of Civil Research. Experience of the Defence Committee had shown me how valuable it would be for the purposes of the Prime Minister if he had a skeleton body to which he could refer questions of a technical but civil character, as he could refer military questions to the other existing Committee. I raised the point at the Cabinet and offered to work out a plan. The proposal was approved.

I got together the Heads of the Treasury and the high officials of the Defence Committee. We drew up the scheme and embodied it in a Minute which needed only the Prime Minister's initials to give it executive effect. Every detail was complete in it, even the proposed Secretary being named, and there was no fresh expenditure involved. But this sort of reform did not interest the Prime Minister, who had never given his mind to administration. I begged him in vain for a few minutes to be diverted from his other and rather miscellaneous occupations. I could not get this, neither could I or the officials concerned procure his signature. The result was that when we went out of office the scheme remained excellent on paper, but a mere scheme. Needless to say, the officials, who were keenly interested in it, at once recommended it to Mr. Baldwin's Government when it came in, and the Conservative administration secured much applause for something the nature of which they appeared to have barely grasped.

As Foreign Secretary, when left to his own judgment, MacDonald displayed a fine and unusual quality. He had travelled extensively, and had interchanged views with a number of Continental statesmen. The result was apparent in a certain breadth of view which he showed. He had something of the ' international mind ' which enabled him to understand and get the sympathy of foreign Ministers. He had no prejudices for or against them, and I always admired the way in which he surmounted difficulties in negotiation. I think that his staff at the Foreign Office appreciated this pretty fully, however much they may have winced at moments under his unconventional ways. Trained as an administrator he had never been, nor had he been moulded by the influence of those highest forms of education which can sometimes take the place of such training. This prevented him from ever being master of his subjects

at the highest level of excellence. He did not care
for first principles in the way that Peel and Gladstone
did, nor was he, like them, fond of prolonged study
of his topics. But he was as Head of the Government
an attractive figure in personal intercourse, and he
had the gift of ready and picturesque expression, and
a quick mind if not a profound one. He had also
plenty of courage, and was unfailing in courtesy to
his colleagues.

Looking back, I have never ceased to be glad that
I accepted his invitation to serve him in the office I
held, and I think that during his administration the
public got rid of many prejudices, and rose to a fuller
comprehension of the duty of the well-to-do towards
the less fortunate. The change of general attitude
was manifest in small things as much as in great.
Immediately on our taking office, the Government
decided that cabs should be allowed to use the
London parks just as freely as carriages, a trifling
change, but one that showed how the current was
flowing.

MacDonald was a Socialist, but a moderate one.
He did not believe in any sudden revolution, and he
never, so far as I could observe, gave countenance to
any such plan. But he did much to make the ideals
which underlay Socialism understood, and to win
over to his views Liberals and Conservatives alike.
They may repudiate the suggestion that to-day
they have pronounced socialistic leanings. But
the study of the Statute Book and the debates and
public speeches since 1924 suggests another view.
It seems pretty clear that in twenty years' time the

Conservatives will be idealistic in just the same sense as Ramsay MacDonald is to-day.

The Labour Cabinet took up certain matters which have since been dealt with, much more extensively but on similar principles, by the Baldwin Government. One of these matters has been Electrical Organisation. The Labour Ministers realised keenly the necessity for developing production and with it employment. We were satisfied that this country was far behind others in the effort after this development. Nothing but the creation of electrical energy and its distribution throughout the land would bring back production to small centres, as well as increase it in great centres. We thought that the task was so great a one that only the State could carry it out, and that it could be carried out in such a way as to provide a system that would produce by its own earnings the money required for its own expenses. The Cabinet appointed a small Committee to go into the question as thoroughly as possible. Snowden presided, and Sidney Webb and I were among his colleagues. I pressed that we should begin by asking the best electrical experts to come to advise us. This was done. As the result of deliberation we decided on certain principles. Generation, transmission through a ' grid ' system, and local distribution were three subjects which would have to be treated distributively but under the supervision of the State Electricity Commissioners, who were to be given large powers for this purpose.

I had taken a deep interest in the whole subject for more than thirty years, and I knew something of the scientific details. I saw the experts constantly, privately as well as at our Committee. In the end we decided on the broad lines of a scheme which was not very different from that embodied by our successors in the Electricity Bill of 1926. We went out of office before we could lay the scheme in detail before Parliament, but Mr. Baldwin's Government took it up, with the full support of the Labour Party, with whom it had become a part of Labour policy. Wisely the new Cabinet referred the plan for still further consideration to a new Committee, presided over by Lord Weir, a very able and enlightened man of business. With him sat Lord Forres, who had seven years earlier been Chairman of a Board of Trade Committee appointed to consider the Report of the then Coal Conservation Committee. I had been Chairman of the Coal Conservation Committee, having among my colleagues Mr. Smillie, M.P., as representing the miners, and we had been unanimous in recommending a large scheme of electrical development in the interest not only of the public generally but of the coal industry. Lord Forres's Committee had confirmed our view.

Before the introduction of the Government Bill of 1926 Lord Weir's new Committee on Electricity published a valuable Report. It approved the plan suggested originally by the Labour Cabinet Committee but proposed some developments of it, mainly in detail. Mr. Baldwin's Government adopted the scheme in this further form, and introduced a great Electricity Bill in the Commons in the spring of 1926. The Bill was an excellent one. Of course it interfered a good deal with the generation of electricity from stations in the hands of private companies. In consequence it was bitterly opposed in the House, but almost exclusively by Conservative members. Labour supported it stoutly, and it came up to the Lords in an autumn session. Of course I fought for it with all the strength I could command, and so did those of whom I was Leader in the Lords. The Bill passed in the end by a large majority. I think that the Conservative Government, and particularly Sir Douglas Hogg, who piloted it through the House of Commons, deserved much credit for the way in which they took the Bill up and pressed it through despite much opposition from a body of their own followers. It is now part of the law of the land, and I hope to live to see it begin to produce far-reaching effects in the stimulation of our industries, both central and local. It was the work of the Conservative and Labour Parties. The Liberals later on published general arguments in support of the principle, but they came on the field too late to be able to influence the result, and, so far as I read what they have written, I do not think that they can claim credit for having done the hard spade-work required for mastery of the vast technical difficulties. In speaking of Liberals I except, of course, Lord Forres.

The system of generation and distribution which has at last been founded on a very wide basis will indeed take years before it can become fully operative. But it is not wholly disadvantageous that there has been delay. For the plan finally adopted incorporated the results of the growing earlier experience

LORD HALDANE AND PROFESSOR EINSTEIN AT QUEEN ANNE'S GATE IN 1921

of other countries, and we ought to emerge in the forefront so far as proved and adequate organisation is concerned.

There were many things which the Labour Government might have accomplished and placed to its credit had it gauged the mind of the public better. But it introduced a distinct change of attitude towards social requirements, and, although it perished sooner than it need have done, it was, I think, entitled to look back on its period of office as a period in which good and substantial work was accomplished. MacDonald may not have achieved all that he hoped for, but alike on Home and Foreign affairs he left a mark.

When MacDonald went into Opposition in the beginning of 1925 he asked me to lead his party in the House of Lords. I was rather reluctant to continue in any official position, but there were reasons why assistance from me personally was desirable. Although we were the second largest party in Parliament, and consequently clearly entitled to be looked on as the official Opposition in the House of Commons, the position was not quite the same in the House of Lords. For there the Liberals were considerably more numerous. They claimed to be recognised as the official Opposition in the Upper House, and Lord Beauchamp on their behalf strenuously claimed that he and they should occupy the Front Opposition Bench and speak from the box. I challenged their claim vigorously and said that it must be decided on by the House of Lords itself. That meant that Lord Curzon, the new

Leader, and his colleagues would have the responsibility of advising the House as to its decision. They did deliberate, and Lord Beauchamp and I saw the Leader of the House and stated our cases. I was of set purpose brief and restrained. We stood for the Opposition in the Commons, and it was difficult to see how there could be two Oppositions. I would, however, welcome Lord Beauchamp and any of his colleagues who liked to come to sit alongside of us on the Official Bench. Lord Beauchamp took a much more pronounced line. He relied on his numbers, but Lord Curzon pointed out that his Party in the Lords was, to all appearances, hopelessly split, and that while Lord Beauchamp apparently looked to Lloyd George as his Chief, Lord Grey and others took a very different view. In the end, Lord Curzon decided, as I had anticipated that he would, in our favour. There ensued a little soreness on the part of Lord Beauchamp, but this we could not help.

I was, of course, now committed to taking charge of the Opposition in the Upper House as its Leader. We had only about ten members of the Upper House in our ranks, but we made a point of paying close attention to the business and to the Bills, and acted as though we constituted a larger party than we were numerically. Things had on the whole gone smoothly, but not invariably so, and I laid down that we were not in a position to indulge in fireworks, and that, while we sat in the House as staunch adherents of Labour, that fact must not commit us to everything that anybody chose to say in the name of Labour. In particular, while we should endeavour to keep in

agreement with the ex-Prime Minister, we were not
to be bound by the decisions of what was called
the Executive of the Party, a small body which,
following an example that had failed in Australia,
claimed to lay down principles independently of
the responsible leaders in Parliament. We must
also hold ourselves unfettered on questions of Foreign
policy, and as uncommitted to such plans as that of
the Protocol, notwithstanding that they had sometimes the approval of outside Labour Conferences.
The business of the Opposition, as I conceived it,
was to scrutinise closely and to oppose Bills and
Resolutions that seemed from our point of view to
be wrong. On the other hand, we were there as
a party of progress, and accordingly, if the Conservative or any other Government introduced good
Bills or Resolutions, it was our duty to support
them.

This policy we carried out. Naturally, it led at
moments to friction over questions of Home and
Foreign policy. At one stage things got so difficult
that I intimated that I should lay down the Leadership in the Lords if my principle were interfered with.
The fear, I think, of losing the privileged position of
occupying the Front Opposition Bench weighed with
my doubting colleagues, and I was requested by
MacDonald and by them to continue to occupy the
position I filled. That I should have to continue
I rather regretted, for the sittings after four, following
on a long day of judicial work, were heavy for a
person of my years and dubious health. However,
I have continued in a position of political freedom

until 1928, when I am writing this, without having been checked by Nature or by Labour colleagues.

The House of Lords is a highly courteous assembly, and it is easy to conduct business there without much strain. The other House is one where there is a demand for physical energy that is not required in the Lords, and I doubt whether in most cases it is a place suited to members much over sixty. But in times when a Government has a large majority, so that Ministers and others do not require to be always in attendance, matters are no doubt easier. I should not like at my age to be back there. It is a place for younger men, unless a member is exceptionally situated.

The same thing is true of the multitude of Committees and other voluntary organisations with which a man gets associated in the course of a long public life. They draw on his physical energy, if but little on his mental activity. I have, myself, of late years got out of as many as I can. Daily judicial sittings, the political work of the House of Lords, and the occasional public duties from which one cannot escape, are in themselves quite enough to fill life full for an elderly man, so far as external things are concerned. And then there is the leisure required for thought and study. A peaceful home with books all round is what one really needs. Much company and much going out to other people's houses become hindrances instead of helps.

Nevertheless, in this period I saw a great many people, many of them of foreign nationality. Einstein stayed at 28 Queen Anne's Gate when he visited

London. Rathenau, a man of the highest quality as well as of great eminence in his own country and on the Continent generally, used to come to see me at Queen Anne's Gate and to write to me. Von Gwinner, the President of the Deutsche Bank, Professor L. Brentano, and other well-known German writers, turned up in my study in a steady stream. I had fewer Frenchmen and Italians, but still a good many. Of Americans, Canadians, and Australians a large number came. Visitors from India, Hindus and Mohammedans, came in large numbers. Among my friends from the East were well-known metaphysicians, such as Professors Radhakrishnan and Dasgupta. Then there was the British philosophical and scientific world, and certain of the leaders of the clergy—apart from a succession of politicians and lawyers. My sister used to say that I had retired from the business of a ' General Practitioner ' and had become a Consultant. Anyhow, I have through these years had a full and interesting life. I incline to the view that, despite its drawbacks, old age is preferable to youth. Friendships continue in it, but in a form adapted to the years of the friends. Anyhow, speaking for myself, I want nothing further now, either of public recognition or of private relationships. What I possess of the latter, whether with relatives or with friends, are affectionate and sufficing.

Since the War I have kept up my foreign friendships. I have paid two visits to my old University of Göttingen. Some of the professors have also been with me here. In the United States I keep up my relations with such men as Chief Justice Taft, Wendell Holmes, and Brandeis among the judges, and Dean Pound and Frankfurter among the jurists of the Harvard School.

I have also very pleasant relations with representatives of the Churches at home, notwithstanding that my attitude to the Churches is one of detachment. The two Archbishops have come for years past to stay with us in September at Cloan, and so have other friends like the Dean of St. Paul's and some of the Bishops.

Altogether, the autumn of life has been so far a tranquil one. Such is the power of the ' contingent ' in our individual existence that one does not know whether this will continue so. One must rely on the power of self-detachment, and on courage to face whatever may be in store.

CHAPTER XI

LOOKING BACKWARDS

THE chapters now completed record the memories that I wish to preserve. They contain in outline the chief events that belong to the story of my life. There has been a current that can be traced in them.

For a current there has been, though in its flow there have been deviations. Had I been a more potent personality in the sense in which the word is popularly understood ; had I been endowed with certain gifts, physical and social, which I did not possess, I should probably have accomplished much more. I might, for example, have been able to bring the Liberal and Labour Parties into a unison which they ought to have possessed but so far never have. But it was not given to me to gain the confidence of great masses of men and women in the way which this task required, nor did I stir a finger either to accomplish it or to attract the Press. The result has been that a good deal of my work has been little known. The best I can say for myself is that I have not been slack in either thought or action, and that some substantial results have emerged from time to time.

But we ought never to disturb ourselves about the

quantity reputed to have been ours, or about our own
prominence with the public.   Even for those who have
been most fortunate in the eyes of the world accomplishment is only relative.   Nor is there any truth
attained which any one dare look on as final.   For we
are all limited in varying degrees and ways.   We
little know our own limitations.   Our duty is to work
without turning our eyes to the right or to the left
from the ideals which alone can light up our paths.
It is not any finality attained that can ever be ours ;
what is ours can be no more than the best quality
of which we are capable, put into the effort towards
the attainment of what we have set before ourselves.
The effort towards it is one which we daily find ourselves called upon to make anew.   We have to think
of how to live before we can learn how to die.   God
is not outside us, but is within our breasts, ' an
almighty, ever-present Deity.'   This is a principle we
do well to make our own as early as we can in life,
and to keep always before our eyes.

I think I may say that I have had impulses in this
direction throughout my changing circumstances.
The moulding influence on me before I was eighteen
of Hermann Lotze at Göttingen, and the appeal made
to me by the great thinkers of Germany and Britain
that carried that influence on, counted for much from
an early period.   I doubt whether there has been a
day in my life since then when the principle above
mentioned was not to some extent in my mind.   I do
not think that this has made me in the usual sense
a religious man ;   for the influence has been mainly of
a reflective kind, and religion, in the ordinary meaning,

SKETCH OF VISCOUNT HALDANE
Made in the summer of 1928 by Philip de László

is not so much an affair of reflection as of the will and
of the emotions directed to an object apart from the
worshipper.   But in the way in which these things
worked on me they have shaped from within my
habits of thought and my interests, and that
deeply.   Ordinarily religious conviction may subsist
apart from study and from other activities of the
spirit, and that makes it the more easily understood.
But with me this was not so.   Originally under strong
evangelical conviction, I passed from the form of
such conviction before I was eighteen years old.
But after that it penetrated my entire mental
activities in a fashion that was wider, and it trans-
formed the character of my reflection itself.   How
that came about this is not the place to discuss.
The reasons for the result and of its growth have
been already recorded in a succession of books which
I have written, beginning with *The Pathway to Reality*
(the Gifford Lectures which were delivered at St.
Andrews University in 1903-4), and later on in *The
Reign of Relativity* (1921) and subsequent essays.
These works are concerned with what human experience seems ultimately and essentially to imply.   They
describe an outlook to which, after more than half
a century of meditation, I found myself finally compelled.   That outlook is not now likely to change
substantially.

As against it the physicist may think that he can
succeed in resolving the Universe into an assemblage
of point-events, material or mental, with relations
that can be most properly expressed in quantitative
equations.   For some at least of his critics the ques-

tion will at once arise as to how the physicist, for whose reflection such an assemblage is present, is himself to be accounted for along with his reflection. For his mind seems to lie at the very foundation of the experience with which he is concerned, actual or possible.

Meditation in this direction led me away from the facile postulates of scientific method in the Victorian period, here and on the Continent. That method of scientific approach does not appear to have been rendered more easy by the recent revolutions in outlook on it which are arising with much insistence in the physics and biology of the twentieth century.

Still, when one is driven to reflection as entering into all experience, and as constitutive of its foundation, one is left with the sharp question as to what is the nature of such reflection and how is it related to the system of reality ?   What is the nature of mind as more than an individual activity, and how does it enter into our particular personality ?   If we say that mind so greatly conceived is God, then we must revise the metaphors in which religion describes the Creator.   He cannot, so it came to seem to me, merely move a universe from outside it, a phrase which for philosophy and science alike has little meaning.   He cannot fall within experience as a mere object in it, actual or conceivable.   For He is the condition and foundation, apart from which experience in no form has any significance.

No doubt in every popular religion, in those of the West as well as those of India and the East, God is described in terms which to some extent describe Him as a possible object for percipient knowledge. But however much beyond may be pointed to, such descriptions are obviously only metaphorical, and of this art and religion itself in the highest forms are the living witnesses. The metaphors may be symbolic of a deeper-lying reality, but in themselves they are inadequate to such reality. The God of the Psalms and at times the God of the New Testament are alike open to this comment.

But if we turn to the other extreme, the God of theoretical metaphysics, the God of Spinoza and not less of Kant, is defective in another aspect. He is too abstractly conceived to be expressive of the supreme living fact within our souls. The God of metaphysics, if He is to be the ultimate foundation of all that is within us as well as without, ought to be present in our feeling as well as in our logic. From the latter He may get the highest place but no immediate actuality. We may be, if our minds are of a rare order, 'God-intoxicated,' as Spinoza himself was said to be, but the depth of such feeling is not for the ordinary man. That was why Hegel set out, not, as is popularly imagined, from logical forms, but from human experience as the source of his quest after what is ultimately the real. And that is why art and religion are never superseded by metaphysics.

Not the less metaphysics has a function that is essential. It disentangles into principles the implications of experience. There seems to me to be no one final form to be arrived at in this kind of inquiry. From the East to the West, through century after century, the investigations of philosophy have gone on. They have brought much to light in their successive systems without which our view of life would be narrower and poorer to-day. But just as every man selects the form of art and religion that appeals to him most, so it is with philosophy. It has no single form which we can treat as authoritative. What we have to do with philosophy is to study it and to assimilate its history as a sustained criticism displaying a progressive evolution of ideas about what is finally real, and to be content with such sense of harmony in our minds as this study has brought about. The finite and the infinite appear in the end to be no longer independent existences. This we find even in Hindu thought, as we find it in Plato and also among the leaders of modern Western philosophy. The highest comes out as the most real, and it is always the more spiritual that appears as the highest. That is why no doctrine like that of point-events, with quantitative external relations rendered in equations, has ever permanently satisfied reflection.

It has been for this reason that the belief that the more experience is spiritual the more it is real has influenced me through the course of life, during more than fifty years. I have said enough to make it plain that I do not mean that the particular creeds have satisfied me. They have appeared as at best symbolic of what is higher, but not more, and I will add that I think the sense of this has held me back from being looked on as in the ordinary sense a 'religious man.' That description imports as a rule a creed. If not, it means that one has lived the life of a saint. Now, of failure to have lived such a life no man is more conscious than I am. But for me the ultimate test of failure or success has lain in how life appears from the standpoint now stated, a standpoint which has not only influenced conduct, public and private, but has made the events of life happy and easy to live through. One can abstract oneself, with greater or less success, not only from illness and pain and depression, but even from the fear of death. There is little that matters when the principle is grasped and held to, and hesitation and unhappiness become replaced by a life that is tranquil because freed from dependence on casual ups and downs.

As I have said, I do not think that most people would have called a life so moulded a religious one, for, at all events in my earlier days, it was largely concerned with the surrender of self to the ideals of daily life as much as with the infinite basis which life implies. Moreover, it was solitary in the sense that it took me away from the definite creeds of the Churches, and from the religious opinions which were current among those with whom I mixed. These creeds and opinions I have always treated with deep respect, but they have not embodied for me any lasting foundation for faith. They are for me symbolic, but not more, and like all symbols they appear inadequate and often untrue when put forward as expressions of belief. The fuller view of which I have spoken has satisfied me, inasmuch as it has given me a sufficient solution of the problems of existence, and has taught me that it is not on how to die but on how to live that one ought to concentrate. Death is in this view but an event which comes as the necessary outcome of the course of organic life. It belongs to what falls outside the inmost nature of spirit. We do not pass out of an independently subsisting world with it ; that world on the contrary passes from us, and we can contemplate it as so passing, and thereby we are lifted above the event. This does not mean personal or individual continuance, but it does signify that as mind we are more than we take ourselves to be, when immersed in the changing events of life. The finite turns out to be inseparable from the infinite, however little it is possible to form a picture of their oneness in the fashion in which we depict to ourselves external nature. Something like this John Henry Newman seems to have had in his thoughts when, in the earlier though not in the later part of the ' Dream of Gerontius,' he drew his picture of the dying saint.

Such a view is not that current with the majority. They usually seek to express what lies beyond in language that can be no more than symbolic. But the symbolic form is not for many of us tenable, while the idealistic principle which leads up to it is apparently unassailable. At least, speaking for myself, I have found it so far not only sustaining but sufficient to rest upon.

It has often struck me that we of the Western world have contracted our outlook by failure to take in the full significance of the development of reflection on ultimate things in India. There the modes of thought may indeed have been too pictorial to satisfy the requirements of the methods employed in exact science, even in matters speculative. But in the course of her Eastern development that has emerged which has been more than merely pictorial. I have never been in India and am not likely now to go there. But in my later years I have studied her philosophical literature, and I have had many native friends there, some of them men of learning who have been thorough students of our thought as well as their own. There is in Bengal particularly a philosophical outlook which has moulded even Indian political aspirations, among Mohammedans as well as among Hindus. The exponents of this outlook have come to talk with me in London and in Scotland for years past. We seem hardly to realise how much of a suggestive spirit of their own they have to bring to us, a spirit which may not always assume a very practical form, but yet is one that ought to be taken into account at every turn by those responsible for seeking practical reforms in the system of Indian government. For want of knowledge has brought in its train want of sympathy. Without such sympathy we may well continue to succeed in ' policing ' India, but it is difficult for us to gain the confidence of the Indian people. The finest level of Indian mind is not really difficult to understand, however difficult it may be to interpret the practical aspirations of the people out there. For it is the soul of that people that is the key to their outlook. The preliminary study that is desirable for the would-be Indian reformer is neglected excepting by a very few, and is neglected mainly because of the difference in spirit between the East and the West.

It would be out of place here to follow out further the kind of idealism that has throughout had hold of me. It is enough to say that its essence led me to the belief in the possibility of finding rational principles underlying all forms of experience, and to a strong sense of the endeavour to find such principles as a first duty in every department of public life. That is the faith that prevailed with me when at the Bar, when later on I undertook the reform of the Army, when I was Lord Chancellor, and when I sat on the Committee of Imperial Defence. It prevails with me to-day not less than in earlier days, and it helps in the endeavour to bring together the apparently diverging views of those with whom one has to deal. That has seemed to me throughout to be as true of the Army and of the administrative services as it has seemed in the case of judicial duties.

I am now, when writing this, in my seventy-second year. Life will close before long, but I do not think that my outlook will alter before the world passes from me. That world in the case of each of us has been made what it is largely by the reflection which has been directed to it, and the question is whether the basis of that reflection has been true.

No one who has set before himself seriously the task of discovering the truth about the meaning of life dare feel confident that he has been wholly right in his result. Where Plato and Aristotle and Kant were not sure of their knowledge how dare we be ? But then we are not living in the world to discover final truth. There is no such truth. What we find is always developing itself and assuming fuller forms. But we can discriminate quality in what we find before us. Our criticism of life, if not our constructive doctrine, becomes more firm as we gain in knowledge and in the interpretation of experience that knowledge brings. Of knowledge we can at best master only a fragment. But if that fragment has been reached by endeavour that is sufficiently passionate, the struggle towards it yields a sense of quality, of quality in the very effort made, which stands for us as being what we care for beyond everything else, as being for us truth, whatever else may not be certainly truth. And so life is not lived in vain though in the ends attained it may seem to have failed.

I have no sense of success on any very large scale in things achieved. But I have the sense of having worked and of having found happiness in doing so. Better that than more honours and more wealth, and more esteem from men. For the happiness gained has a character in it of which nothing beyond can take the place. So far as external circumstances are concerned, I would not if I could take the chance of living life over again. A distinguished living statesman and man of the world once asked me whether, even with the aid of such knowledge as experience had brought, I would like to try to begin life anew. My answer was in the negative. ' For,' I added, ' we are apt greatly to underrate the part which accident and good luck has really played in the shaping of our careers and in giving us such successes as we have had.' His rejoinder was to the same effect as my answer to his question. 'I would not,' he said, ' myself try again, for I do not feel sure that good fortune, irrational as it has been, would attend me in the same way.' The contingent plays a large part even in the best ordered lives, and we do well to ask of philosophy to teach us how to make ourselves detached from the circumstances it brings, whether happy or otherwise. The best that ordinary mortals can hope for is the result which will probably come from sustained work directed by as full reflection as is possible. This result may be affected adversely by circumstances, by illness, by misfortune, or by death. But if we have striven to think and to do work based on thought, then we have at least the sense of having striven with such faculties as we have possessed devoted to the striving. And that is in itself a course of happiness, going beyond the possession of any definite gain. It was this that Faust discovered at the end of a life spent mistakenly, nearly up to its close, in the pursuit of his individual pleasure. He found at last that it was in work done, not for himself, but for others, that the satisfying quality of which he had been in search lay. Then, for the first time, and in a different sense from that which was intended by the words when used in his covenant with Mephistopheles, he found that he could say to the moment, ' Stay, thou art fair.' His soul was saved from the clutches of the fiend who, despite the warning given to him by the Deity at the beginning, had misunderstood man in his higher development, and had underrated what was required to give him happiness.

So it may turn out in some degree with each of us, whatever our circumstances and our capacities. This creed is one which fits into what is highest in the various forms of religion. It is open to all of us—provided we keep ourselves humble in mind and avoid self-seeking and vanity.

WORKS OF VISCOUNT HALDANE

ESSAYS IN PHILOSOPHICAL CRITICISM (with Professor Seth). 1883. Longmans, Green & Co. Ltd.

Translation of Schopenhauer's WORLD AS WILL AND IDEA (with Mr. Kemp). 3 vols. 1883. Trübner & Co.

LIFE OF ADAM SMITH. 1887. Walter Scott.

EDUCATION AND EMPIRE. 1902. John Murray.

THE PATHWAY TO REALITY. 2 vols. 1903. John Murray.

THE CONDUCT OF LIFE. 1904. John Murray.

ARMY REFORM AND OTHER ADDRESSES. 1907. T. Fisher Unwin Ltd.

UNIVERSITIES AND NATIONAL LIFE. 1912. John Murray.

HIGHER NATIONALITY. 1913. John Murray.

BEFORE THE WAR. 1920. Cassell & Co. Ltd.

THE REIGN OF RELATIVITY. 1921. John Murray.

THE PHILOSOPHY OF HUMANISM. 1922. John Murray.

HUMAN EXPERIENCE. 1926. John Murray.

AFFIRMATION. 1928. Ernest Benn Ltd.

SELECTED ESSAYS AND ADDRESSES. 1928. John Murray.

INDEX OF PERSONS AND SUBJECTS